BETJEMAN'S
ENGLAND

BETJEMAN'S ENGLAND

JOHN BETJEMAN

Edited and introduced by
STEPHEN GAMES

JOHN MURRAY

First published in Great Britain in 2009 by John Murray (Publishers)
An Hachette UK Company

2

Preface, Introduction and Selection © Stephen Games 2009
Text © The Estate of John Betjeman 2009

The right of the author has been asserted in accordance with the Copyright, Designs and Patents Act 1988.

The editor and publisher would like to acknowledge with thanks the following for allowing the usage of copyright material:

Extracts from 'Forefathers' and 'A Pastoral' by Edmund Blunden (© 1922, 1925) are reproduced by permission of PFD (www.pfd.co.uk) on behalf of the Estate of Edmund Blunden.

'One Night of Tempest' by R. S. Thomas, *Collected Later Poems 1988-2000* (Bloodaxe Books, 2004) is reproduced with kind permission of the publisher on behalf of the Estate of R. S. Thomas.

A CIP catalogue record for this title is available from the British Library

ISBN 978-1-84854-091-0

Typeset in Monotype Bembo by Servis Filmsetting Ltd, Stockport, Cheshire

Printed and bound by Clays Ltd, St Ives plc

John Murray policy is to use
and made from wood grown
processes are expected to cor
origin.

John Murray (Publishers)
338 Euston Road
London NW1 3BH

www.johnmurray.co.uk

To Jori, Nina, Sarah, Melina and Cosima

Contents

CONTENTS

CORNWALL

DERBYSHIRE

DEVON

DORSET

ESSEX

GLOUCESTERSHIRE

HAMPSHIRE

KENT

CONTENTS

SOMERSET

WILTSHIRE

YORKSHIRE

PERIPHERY

Preface

Betjeman's England is constructed around some sixty television programmes that deal directly with the architecture and topography
of England. Betjeman made many more films than are contained
here – notably his series *The Englishman's Home* (1957) and his *ABC
of Churches* (1960–67) of which, apart from the first episodes of each,
only fragments have survived. He also made films in which others
participated, notably a series called *Pride of Place* (1966–7), which he
co-presented with Arthur Negus. But in terms of the films that he
hosted alone, *Betjeman's England* comes close to offering a reliably
thorough guide.

As always, editorial choices have had to shape the selection and
treatment. For example, the script has survived of Betjeman's film
about St Brelade's, Jersey – Church J in his *ABC of Churches* – but a
letter has also survived that he wrote to his producer, Ken Savidge,
that covers all the ground in the film and much more. Given the
attraction of showing how Betjeman visualised a film in advance, it
seemed more revealing to publish the letter rather than the script.
In the same way, I have included a letter to Peter Hunt, another
producer, suggesting a treatment for a film about Canterbury
Cathedral but I have not provided a transcript of the quite different
film that was eventually made (in which Betjeman was pleased to
narrate a poem by a Canterbury choirboy that ran, 'If I happen to
trap / My toe in a tap / Or to step in a large bowl of trifle, / I wear
a top hat, / Sit down on a mat / And shoot at my aunt with a rifle').
On the other hand, two alternatives proposals have been included
for a short fund-raising film about Winchester Cathedral precisely
because they show different approaches. These might be seen, I
accept, as arbitrary decisions.

Film commentaries don't necessarily read well on the page, because they are written to support images. In the pages that follow Betjeman invites us some sixty times to look at something: an instruction the reader clearly cannot follow. Nevertheless, I was very rarely tempted to rewrite his words, because his request often proves to be redundant. When he says, for example, 'notice the headstones in the churchyard, all of different shapes', we understand this simply as 'the headstones in the churchyard are all of different shapes' and accept the information without difficulty. Rarely does it jar that the words are secondary to the missing images – and this comes as a happy surprise. In the few cases of difficulty, however, notes on what the camera is seeing have been added to the text in square brackets or, in the case of verse, in footnotes.

The layout of the commentaries has, however, been revised to conform to a standard book format rather than the two-column format of the original film scripts in which shooting directions appear on the left and speech on the right. This raises legitimate questions about presentation, especially where Betjeman alternates between prose and poetic forms of narration. These questions were aired in the Introduction to *Tennis Whites and Teacakes* (John Murray, 2007) but, to recap, when Betjeman was writing to an already edited film, the production secretaries tended to type his words as short lines to match the action. When these lines are now transferred to the wider one-column format of a book, must they still be reproduced as short lines? And must long sentences that happen to sound like sequences of blank verse (unrhymed iambic pentameter) always be treated as lines of blank verse? The approach taken by *Tennis Whites and Teacakes* was to try to reveal whether Betjeman's television writing was essentially prose or essentially poetry. Where the narrative adopted a regular metre, rhyming or not, it was set as verse; otherwise it was set as prose. This seemed to make sense and made plain for the first time just how much Betjeman's speech patterns tended towards the poetic. But its irregularity on the page meant that his narrative flow was constantly being interrupted as words bounced back and forth between formats, sometimes leaving single lines or pairs of lines hanging awkwardly in the air. Edward Mirzoeff, the producer of Betjeman's

Bird's Eye View programmes (1969–71) and 'Metro-land' (1973), objected, in addition, that printing the words in a new setting meant they no longer always followed the pacing of his films. On the other hand, the scripts are not properly punctuated. In the end, a decision has to be taken on whether Betjeman's commentaries must always correspond to the original layout or whether they can be presented in a new way for readers who don't know the films. Mirzoeff says that he has always felt, with Betjeman, that the scripts could not be published separately from the images and should therefore not be published at all: that they are, and must remain, television – a dual medium of sound and vision. *Betjeman's England* takes a different view and shows that, freed from their original formatting and the need to defer to the films that gave rise to them, the texts work remarkably well as pieces of independent writing. The commentaries to the films, mostly published now for the first time, have been set out in such a way as to make the experience of reading them as easy as possible and to give a sense of their own autonomy. (As for the three films that appeared in *Tennis Whites and Teacakes* and that have been reprised here, they are given even more of a prose form than hitherto.) No doubt future editors will take a different view again. On other questions of style, readers are invited to consult the prefaces to *Tennis Whites and Teacakes* and the first of the collections of Betjeman's prose that I edited, *Trains and Buttered Toast* (John Murray, 2006).

Even more than before, tracking down John Betjeman's television scripts has given rise to a huge research effort and, as in the past, I am indebted to the Special Collections Department at the McPherson Library of the University of Victoria in British Columbia, where Betjeman's archive resides, and in particular to John Frederick, who dug out material and answered my queries with extraordinary efficiency; to Jeff Walden of the BBC Written Archives Centre in Caversham, Berkshire, who steered me round the BBC's elephantine collections and helped me with many enquiries; and to the staff at the British Library at King's Cross and the Newspaper Reading Rooms in Colindale. I was also helped by the staff of the British Film Institute, among whom were Kathleen Dickson, Natasha Fairbairn and Ros Cranston.

Personal memories and memorabilia were furnished to me with great generosity by: Betjeman's producers (in order of their film-making) Ken Russell, Ken Savidge, Jonathan Stedall and Edward Mirzoeff; by Shirley Charters (then Cobham), one-time production assistant to Peter Woosnam-Mills, who also put me in touch with John Legard and with Steven Foxon; by Michael Woosnam-Mills in Bordeaux; and by members of Malcolm Freegard's family (his wife Molly, daughter Alison Tyabji and eldest son Jonathan), colleague David Cleveland and personal assistant June Lewis. (I am greatly obliged too to the photographer Nick Lloyd for putting me in touch with Ken Savidge, to Joyce Arram for putting me in touch with Shirley Charters, and to Antony Woosnam-Mills for putting me in touch with Michael Woosnam-Mills.) This book could not have appeared with as much fullness of detail had it not been for their extraordinary contributions, Ken Savidge even doing a drawing for me of what a 1960s mobile studio would have looked like. I only wish that I could have incorporated more of what they talked to me about.

John Heald of the John Betjeman Society was, as ever, encouraging and I drew heavily on his *Sir John Betjeman Checklist* (The Betjeman Society, 2005), co-compiled by Peter Gammond, and on William S. Peterson's invaluable *John Betjeman: A Bibliography* (Clarendon Press, 2006). I thank both for their kind advice on specific points. Bevis Hillier's three-volume biography of Betjeman was a constant source of reference, as was Candida Lycett Green's two-volume collection of Betjeman's *Letters* (Methuen, 1994–5) and her anthology of his prose, *Coming Home* (Methuen, 1997). It was enjoyable to be in contact about questions of mutual interest with Kevin Gardner, in Texas, who rediscovered Betjeman's *Poems in the Porch*, now published by Continuum (2008).

Other individuals who helped me include Stuart Montgomery of the Test Card Circle; Alison Hobson of the Fairford History Society; Richard Thomson at Milton Abbey; Andrew Webster, consultant to the Chapter of Canterbury; the Revd Mark Bond, rector of St Brelade's Church, and the Revd Martyn Shea, of St Mark's Church, St Helier, both in Jersey; Helen Turner and Ian Kemp in north Cornwall about the Pentire estate; Steve

Hartgroves of the Historic Environment Service of Cornwall County Council; Basil Abbot, David Summers, Maggie Swayze and Tony Billett about Diss; the Revd Alison Kennedy of St Paul's, Vauxhall; David Johnston of Savills in Sevenoaks on Mereworth; Nicola Dyer, custodian of Chastleton House; Anne Richman of the Chelmsford Travel and Visitor Information Centre and Helen O'Sullivan of the Maldon Tourist Office about Creeksea; Tim Dwyer and Abegail Morley on Benenden; Lorraine Dobb at Hardwick Hall; Emily Blanshard, Jancis Williams, Georgina Mead and Dudley Dodd on Stourhead; Catherine Dunhill at the Westcountry Studies Library for information on Woolbrook Cottage; Isabel Sedgwick at the National Trust, Wicken Fen; Ros Abrams; Erika Abel, UK Media Relations at Shell; John Legard, for background information about the British Transport Film Unit; John A. Sass about the filming of windmills; Tom Styche; Scott Anthony; Rachel Richards in Northlew; Binny Baker of the Yorkshire Film Archive; Catrin Jenkins of the National Library of Wales; Emma Cocroft and Emma Hyde of the North West Film Archive; Louis H. Cohen of the Nederlandse Kring voor Joodse Genealogie; Frank Delaney; Catherine Percival; Jane Findlay of the London Transport Museum; Jill Barlow and Sue Baxter of Cheltenham College; James Dyson; Katherine Mager of the East Anglian Film Archive; Michael Marshman of the Wiltshire & Swindon History Centre; Mike Brewis at South West Film & Television Archive; David Parsons at Northern Region Film & Television Archive; Richard Shenton at the Media Archive for Central England; and Louise Watson at the BFI and Michael Brooke of Screenonline.

As far as the production of this book is concerned, my thanks go to the executors of the Betjeman estate for approving the use of the material and specifically to Candida Lycett Green, Betjeman's daughter, and Clare Alexander of Aitken Alexander, who acts for the estate; to Roland Philipps at John Murray for seeing the value of a book of Betjeman's television programmes; to my editor, Bernard Dive, for bringing a refreshing quality of intelligence to its compilation; and to my proof-reader, Nick de Somogyi. Thanks are also due to Florin Vascu and his team for building me a bedroom I can

xv

at last retire to happily; to Sophie Georgette, for mostly staying in her cot uncomplainingly at night and thereby giving me more time to write; and to my darling wife, Bea, for keeping our ship on an even keel.

For ease of reference, the films that follow have been set out in four sections according to whether they deal with England as a whole, English regions, specific places, or areas beyond the English borders. An appendix on p. 293 charts the chronology of when the programmes were made.

Finally, as before, every effort has been made to clear permissions. If a quotation is found for which permission has not been granted, please contact the publisher about taking the necessary remedial steps.

Stephen Games
Muswell Hill, 2008

Introduction

John Betjeman was one of England's best-loved television person-
alities, a man whose comforting voice and crumpled appearance
made him as much a public institution as the monuments he helped
to preserve. He was not obviously a heroic figure: more than anything he represented human foible and it is perhaps because of that,
and his emotional honesty about the things that pleased and pained
him, that the public warmed to him as their ambassador against the
dark forces of bureaucracy and philistinism.

Betjeman's heyday on television ran from the second half of the
1950s to the early 1970s. That means that his original core audience – those who remember him from first time round – is now
shrinking fast. For younger people, his memory is kept alive mostly
by his poetry so that perceptions of him are also shrinking fast.
Admittedly he always insisted that he was above all else a poet but
because of his frequent appearances in the press as a campaigner for
architectural conservation and because of his broadcasts on radio
and television, he was equally likely to be thought of as an activist
and 'telly star', to use his own words. If we are to understand him
today – even if we wish only to understand his poetry – we have to
construct a truer picture of him, and that means taking into account
his other activities. His work on behalf of old buildings has been
dealt with elsewhere but there has been very little effort to look
closely at his creative work outside poetry and to assess its value in
relation to his achievement as a whole.

The aim of *Betjeman's England* is to correct that imbalance. This
fourth collection of Betjeman's prose writings contains some sixty
television programmes that Betjeman wrote and presented. Except
in a handful of cases, the scripts have never been seen before by the

public. Following the publication of *Trains and Buttered Toast*★ and *Sweet Songs of Zion*,† which first made available the best of his BBC radio work, and of *Coming Home*‡ and *Tennis Whites and Teacakes*,§ which included examples of his occasional writing and journalism, the availability of his TV scripts should act against any future tendency to focus on him only as a poet who did his best work as a young man and then went into decline.

The story of how Betjeman became a television performer and writer follows on from the story, already told in *Trains and Buttered Toast*, of his rise as a radio broadcaster in the 1940s and '50s. As a young man newly down from Oxford in the late 1920s, Betjeman was keen to work in the exciting new medium of radio but was not taken seriously by the majority of those of his contemporaries who had already got BBC jobs. Between 1932 and the outbreak of war, he was only commissioned a handful of times by Broadcasting House in London, invariably as a comic turn, albeit a knowledgeable one. His proposals for serious talks – about architecture and conservation – were treated with bewilderment, as was he. At a time when historic buildings and traditional landscapes were being decimated by a massive and popular building boom, his concerns were not thought important enough to warrant much public attention. His own personality – that of a rebel and joker – may even have damaged the case he most wanted to make.

Not until he moved out of London to Uffington (then in Berkshire, now Oxfordshire) in 1934 and made himself known to the BBC's new Western Region studios in Bristol did his fortunes change. In Bristol he found an older, slower city which seemed to offer him a perfect base from which to attack the metropolis he felt had rejected him (even though he had formerly aspired to be one

---

★ *Trains and Buttered Toast* by John Betjeman, ed. Stephen Games (John Murray, 2006).

† *Sweet Songs of Zion* by John Betjeman, ed. Stephen Games (Hodder & Stoughton, 2007).

‡ *Coming Home: An Anthology of Betjeman's Prose, 1920–1977* by John Betjeman, ed. Candida Lycett Green (Methuen, 1997).

§ *Tennis Whites and Teacakes* by John Betjeman, ed. Stephen Games (John Murray, 2007).

of its brightest young things). Crucial to this reinvention of himself
was the BBC Bristol producer James Pennethorne Hughes, who
had been in the year below him at Oxford. Pennethorne Hughes
invited him to make two series of six-part broadcasts in 1937 and
1939, looking at the damage caused by modern town planning to a
number of West of England towns. This established Betjeman as a
serious broadcaster and one whose ideas at last started to commend
him to the BBC back in London.

Around this time, Betjeman was also noticed by the BBC's new
Television Department. Television, at the time, was a lowly outpost
of the Corporation and Betjeman was not alone in thinking little of it.
In May 1937, when a newly appointed producer invited him to come
'and discuss with us the possibilities of this new medium', he wrote
back, after a visit, that he found the BBC's experimental programming
'a little boring'. The producer, Mary Adams, eight years older than
Betjeman, persisted and eventually, with some difficulty, got him to
perform twice in front of a camera over the next couple of years. In
his first appearance, in September 1937, he talked about how to make a
guidebook. In his second, in December 1938, he joined other celebrities in trying to name familiar objects, while blindfold, by touching
them. Betjeman later described these programmes as 'tripe'.*

In spite of Betjeman's dismissal of television, he was very keen
on the ideas of John Grierson, the man usually credited as the
father of documentary film-making in the UK and a profound
influence on television in the 1960s. During his eighteen months as
film critic of the *Evening Standard* in 1934–5, Betjeman had written
enthusiastically about the work of Grierson and the circle of pioneering film-makers Grierson had brought together at the Empire
Marketing Board – Edgar Anstey, Stuart Legg, Paul Rotha, Harry
Watt, Basil Wright, Betjeman's schoolfriend Arthur Elton and
others. On one occasion he had written about how Grierson had
revealed to him the incompetence of most film commentary:

> It occurred to Mr John Grierson, as it has often occurred to me, and
> even more frequently to you, I expect, that there is nothing more

* Unless otherwise indicated, all quotations come from correspondence and other
documents in the BBC's Written Archives Centre.

irritating than the sickening commentaries provided for short films. Let me improvise an example.

> Here is the old-world village of Rime Intrinsica, right in the heart of dear old Dorset. My! It is old-world, isn't it? Look at that funny old farmer! He lives in the funny old house with the roofs nearly on the ground. (*Laughter.*) But then he has a lot to do with the ground, hasn't he? (*More laughter.*) So I suppose it comes quite naturally to him to live in such a place.
>
> What a wonderful old boy! There he goes, driving his old sheep. See, they're trying to get over a stile.
>
> No wonder they look sheepish. (*Laughter.*) There he is, going into the wonderful olde hostelrye where mine host is giving him right good old ale to quaff you! Ho! Ho! (*Music off.*)

Well, we've all had to put up with pretty silly nonsense from lantern lecturers, but nothing quite equal to the stupidity of many commentators whose words accompany much magnificent photography today.

That is the tragedy of it. The photographs are so good and the scenery they depict is so interesting that it is a pity our enjoyment should be ruined by listening to futile jokes and obvious comments.

'This is an old house – do you see how the stones are all crumbling?' 'Of course I do, you fool,' I always want to reply. 'Why bother to tell me what I can see for myself?'

The General Post Office Film Unit [which Grierson had set up in 1933] is among the first to get rid of needless commentary.*

In a later review, he complimented Grierson on '[his] latest experiment . . . to employ a poet to write a poem to a series of shots of collieries, most of them at a standstill'.† He also greeted Grierson's feature-length *BBC – The Voice of Britain* (1935) as 'the most important documentary film yet made in England'.

---

* *Evening Standard.*
† He went on, 'The poet is a tall, thin friend of mine, called Wystan Auden. He produces tall, thin volumes of verse that actually bring him in money. He is one of the few poets to achieve this. The poem for the film is recited on the sound track, and a choir sings specially composed music by Mr Britten, a young composer.'

Coal Face (1935), the collieries film that preceded Grierson's better-known *Night Mail* (1936), combined non-naturalistic words, choral music and coal-mine imagery with natural sounds, dialogue and statistics. The result, as the film historian Ian Aitken has pointed out,* was that a film that was meant to function as government propaganda nonetheless offered up trenchant social criticism, in line with Grierson's own left-wing politics. Betjeman, keen to engage in criticism of his own about planning, could only have been impressed. Although he did not analyse Grierson's work with any sophistication, he must have taken from it high expectations of what film-making was able to do and been that much more disappointed by what the BBC was actually doing.

What he was not interested in, he told Mary Adams, was the type of studio-based programming that she was in charge of and that she was commissioning to fill the BBC's air time. As he told her:

> The value of television seems to me to be its possibility of outside work. I mean, when television cameras can show to millions of people actual scenes of shooting & dying in Spain, then it will become the most valuable propaganda medium in the world. When it can actually drive down the Great Worst Road† picking up the noises & then catch the silence of a cathedral close, it will awaken people to the repulsiveness of their surroundings.

All TV programming shut down at the start of the war. When it started up again in 1946, Adams resumed her attempts to get Betjeman to take part and he continued to resist. Television technology had not moved on in the interim but Betjeman had. In radio, he had gone from being a London comic and a Bristolian sceptic to a wartime morale booster. Between March and November 1940, he had written and presented four talks for Pennethorne Hughes, broadcast nationally, in which he'd talked about love of country and the determination to survive. In each talk he'd found an ingenious way to accommodate his pacifism and his doubts about the war

---

* See Ian Aitken, *Film and Reform: John Grierson and the Documentary Film Movement* (Routledge, 1992).
† Betjeman's habitual name for the Great West Road: the A4.

within a conventionally propagandist government line.* His broadcasts had been halted by a thirty-month secondment to Dublin as British Press Attaché but he successfully picked up where he had left off on his return to England in mid-1943. With his friend the poet Geoffrey Grigson as his producer, he presented more wartime commentaries, mostly on literary subjects, and started giving poetry readings – a confirmation by the BBC that his voice had the necessary quality of comfort and familiarity to be useful to Britain in troubled times.

Betjeman's ability to respond to the national mood was probably sensitised by his appointment, in February 1940, as film officer to the Films Division of the Ministry of Information. He had been given the job by the art historian Kenneth Clark (whom John Reith had put in to sort out administrative conflicts in the Division) on the basis of his quirky mind and his experience at the *Evening Standard*. Betjeman's work involved commissioning short public-information films and checking scripts. He seems to have enjoyed his year there. He came in contact with the leading names in British film-making and had endless opportunities for schoolboy pranks (described at length in his biography).† Clark and the director Sidney Gilliat, who had written the screenplays for *The Lady Vanishes* (1938) and *Jamaica Inn* (1939), agreed that Betjeman was often written off as an unproductive eccentric within the Films Division but that his creativity, open-mindedness and lack of self-importance made him more of an asset than many of his colleagues.

What bothered Gilliat was not Betjeman's silliness – Clark once had to ask Betjeman to remove his bicycle clips from his ears while listening to a briefing – but Betjeman's obvious preference for documentaries over movies, which Gilliat felt acted against

---

* One talk, given in the summer of 1940 when German bombing was at its height and in response to audience demand, began, 'I used to wish I had been born about 120 years ago. I should have liked a childhood in the days of the Prince Regent [but] today I'd rather be alive in the present than at any other time.' A later talk urged listeners to stay cheerful by calling on their favourite memories during the dark hours of winter.

† See *John Betjeman: New Fame, New Love* by Bevis Hillier (John Murray, 2002), Chapter 11.

the interests of film-makers such as himself. Gilliat ascribed this bias to Betjeman's friendship with two important documentarians, the American Robert Flaherty and Arthur Elton, both of whom Grierson had invited to make films for the Empire Marketing Board as early as 1931. This ignores the fact, however, that Betjeman abhorred the 'tastefulness' and commercialism of Hollywood and preferred film-making that had a social purpose. He was, after all, a supporter of the Labour Party and took part in its party-political broadcast of 1962, *Enjoying Life*. In January 1941 he was the only MoI film officer to stand up for the Boulting brothers' film *Dawn Guard* at its preview, when the left-wing thrust of the script had taken other MoI staff by surprise.

Among the short films that Betjeman is credited with commissioning at the Ministry were three Gilliat scripts: *Mr Proudfoot Shows a Light* (1941), about blackout procedures; *From the Four Corners* (1941), a film about the Empire, in which Leslie Howard reminded the British what they were fighting for; and *Partners in Crime* (1942), about avoiding black-market products. He advised John Paddy Carstairs, who had just made *The Saint in London* (1939) and was currently working on an Ealing comedy with George Formby, about the need for a clever fade-out in three films on the dangers of gossip that Carstairs had agreed to write. He encouraged Peter Graham Scott, who went on to make *The Avengers*, *The Prisoner*, *The Troubleshooters* and *The Onedin Line*, to make propaganda films. And, according to a letter he wrote to Grigson at the time,* he scripted at least one MoI film himself.

After Betjeman's wartime experience of film-making at its most ingenious, Adams's post-war attempts to encourage him into programme-making at its most primitive failed to win him over. In one exchange, in May 1949, she offered him a free hand to broadcast as long as he remained in the confines of the Alexandra Palace studio; by return he offered her a location documentary looking into the workings of the Marquess of Bath's 8,000-acre Longleat estate, with its spectacular Elizabethan palace. This led to

---

* John Betjeman, *Letters*, vol.1, ed. by Candida Lycett Green (Methuen, 1994), p. 261.

a discussion with one of her assistants, Andrew Miller Jones,* and a follow-up letter (see p. 250) that prompted Miller Jones to comment, 'John Betjeman you are a philosophical ignoramus,' in reply to a remark that the car-maker Lord Nuffield was a devil and Lord Bath an angel. A month later Miller Jones produced a cut-down programme that Betjeman took no part in, consisting of nothing more than Lord and Lady Bath sitting in the studio and talking about the history of their house.

Adams tried again in June 1951, offering Betjeman a fortnightly slot for three months in which he could ad-lib on something that had excited him during the previous week or so. Excusing himself on the grounds of 'strain, lack of experience and finance', he repeated his wish to get out of the studio, proposing a church tour using a mix of pre-recorded film and live camerawork. Adams was twenty years behind, he felt, and still thinking of TV in terms of radio. 'I was very interested when you said to me that you thought there was far too much talk and not enough silence in television,' he told her. 'A church might enable one to use silence. Who knows, one might almost encourage worship.' Adams still didn't take the point. 'We feel pretty certain here you'd make a success of television if you'd ever settle to it,' she replied. 'Do come – I'm sure it wouldn't be a strain once you'd got into your stride.' Her attitude convinced him that people in television understood less about their medium than he did.

When Betjeman didn't oblige, Adams asked George Barnes to intercede. Barnes had joined the BBC in 1935 as a radio talks producer in London and was made Assistant Director of Talks the following year. In 1940 he had had to support Betjeman and the Corporation after Betjeman had wrongly claimed, in a talk about the poet Sir Henry Newbolt, that a poem of Newbolt's was a lament for a dead son, a claim that the son in question wrote to the BBC to dispute. Barnes went on to befriend Betjeman, who was two years his junior, inviting him to his club in London, to his house in Kent and subsequently to France, where their two families spent their

* Andrew Miller Jones (1910–94) went on to become the first producer of *Panorama*. Betjeman wrongly addressed him in 1949 as 'Mellor-Jones'.

summer holidays together between 1949 and 1952. Barnes thought Betjeman brilliant and undeveloped and became his principal sponsor within the BBC, repeatedly trying to push him into projects that would advance his career, while always failing to observe that these required a level of discipline and intellectual effort that Betjeman found uncongenial as well as imposing on him the moral obligations that went with being – and being seen as – Barnes's protégé.

In July 1946 Barnes became the first head of BBC Radio's newly created intellectuals' network, the Third Programme, and in October 1950 he was switched to the top job in Television: 'D.Tel.B.' (Director of Television Broadcasting). Two months later, Betjeman made a less glamorous switch of his own, from book reviewing for the *Daily Herald*, which he hated, to book reviewing for the *Daily Telegraph*, which he also hated. By the time of Adams's appeal for help, Betjeman had already talked to Barnes about getting out of reviewing and Barnes had offered him alternative work on television, which Betjeman had turned down – as he always did. At Adams's behest, Barnes now sounded Betjeman out about a one-year contract but made the mistake of quoting her and her misapprehensions:

> Mary was right in believing that the best outlet for you in Television programmes at the present time would be a talk not strictly related to a subject but tied to anything which had excited you visually in the previous fortnight, since this method would give you a chance of talking with the illustrations that television can give you about the things you care about.

Neither Barnes nor Adams seemed to have registered that Betjeman had been delivering talks at the rate of one a fortnight on the radio over the previous two years and did not want to duplicate this demanding and, in his view, unremunerative work on TV.

The start of Betjeman's slow breakthrough into television can be dated to 1952. The BBC had asked Marcus Cooper Ltd, a company specialising in films for and about British industry, to make a series about stately homes. Two programmes had been made so far, the first about the much-altered Tudor mansion Cobham Hall, in Kent.

Barnes thought the films 'competent, attractive pieces of work' but they had run into problems with the BBC's American distributors for using a commentator who sounded too English. What was wanted was 'a neutral voice unobjectionable to the American public' that would save the cost of revoicing the soundtrack for the USA. With touching faith, Barnes invited Betjeman to join him at a screening of the films to see if he could have done the commentary any better. Betjeman duly attended but was more interested in the quality of production, as Barnes later reported to Cecil McGivern, his Programmes Controller:

> I was very impressed by Betjeman's criticisms on that score. He showed how much the imagination of an artist can bring to the composition of films of this kind. It may be that that can only be bought with a much higher shooting ratio than you can afford. Nevertheless I hope you will speak to Marcus Cooper about the criticisms [Betjeman] made, mostly those of omission, for example, do not talk about a brick mansion, get the camera right up to the brick and let us see what Tudor brick looks like and how patterns were obtained in it before going back to see the whole front of Cobham Hall. These houses are lived in: the cameras must show that, for example, by the filled ashtray, the crumpled chair, the turned down bed, or less obviously by showing the rooms in the order in which someone living in the house would use the rooms . . . The point, I think, is that this is a competent job of work but he showed how we can improve every time we do a new one.

Barnes's fatherly satisfaction at Betjeman's reactions could only have tried the patience of those of his staff with more experience – and worse provocations followed. Betjeman wrote to Barnes (waggishly signing himself 'Alexander Korda') to say that 'if your executives would like to consider trying me out on a film, I should do my best to find time to devote to one film, and then if that was a success, we might go on with others.' He no longer simply wanted to write a commentary for a film that was already shot, he added some time later: he wanted to advise the director on what to shoot 'and indeed to have myself a share in the direction'. When this breathtaking offer came to nothing, Betjeman agreed that it might be better if he could actually watch the way the BBC handled a film recording

and a live outside broadcast first he wouldn't interfere in any way
– so that he could get a more informed idea how he could improve
on them.

Barnes, ever forgiving, set about satisfying Betjeman's wishes in
early 1953. He called three of his most valuable staff to join him for
lunch: the BBC war correspondent Robert Barr, who'd made the
Corporation's first television documentary in 1946; the drama producer John Elliott, who was currently filming at Corsham outside
Bath; and A. Berkeley Smith, the BBC's Assistant Head of Outside
Broadcasts, who was preparing to transmit a live programme
from Gloucester Cathedral. In due course Barnes announced that
Berkeley Smith and Elliott had both agreed to let Betjeman sit in
on their shoots. For his efforts, he got a letter from Betjeman's then
secretary, Jill Menzies, saying that 'the great man asks me to thank
you' but that he couldn't spend two days in Gloucester, as proposed.
He would drive there in the morning, talk to Berkeley Smith in
the afternoon 'if necessary', and go home again after the rehearsal
in the evening.

The upshot of these visits could not have been anticipated. On
6 March, Betjeman wrote to Barnes that he was unexcited by John
Elliott's work at Corsham ('I have watched films being made before
now . . . All I saw was a dull shot, all carpet, of four ugly students
playing chamber music') but was very taken by Berkeley Smith:

> Your introducing of me to Berkeley Smith is something for which
> I will always be grateful. My dear Commander, he really is a man of
> genius. I watched him that day in Gloucester. Not only was he on
> excellent terms with the huge staff of thirty people, of whom he was
> clearly the respected *commander*, but he has an eye and an ear which
> are a delight. He really loves Gothic architecture and he understands
> ceremony and drama.
>
> There is nothing I could teach him, beyond introducing him to a
> few places which might inspire his eye. But there is a lot that he could
> teach me. Already he has made me interested in television . . . I was
> very impressed by how well he conveyed the spirit and the plan of
> Gloucester Cathedral, and how human and reverent his approach to it
> is. I thought [Richard] Dimbleby's commentary could not have been
> better.

From wanting to be a director, Betjeman now wanted merely to be Berkeley Smith's amanuensis:

> I would dearly like to go to some building in an area from which television can be done, and which I had selected, with him and see how it could be televised . . . If Berkeley Smith can interpret something so complicated as Gloucester Cathedral, how beautifully he could interpret a village church, again using OB cameras, not film, except for a visual introduction. The film part of the Gloucester programme I thought the least effective. [But] what does impress me very much is how good the architectural detail looks on the television screen, carved stone, carved wood and that sort of thing. It is particularly impressive when interspersed with general views, as he intersperses it, and with long, raking views, sweeping round until they centre on a single object.
>
> I will leave it to you, Commander, to see whether you can arrange for Berkeley Smith and me to go somewhere like, let us say, Thaxted, or King's Chapel, or Fairford, and see what we can do with it. Or some unrestored church in a remote village where we can shew the village as well. I would not only like to do churches with him; I am perfectly certain we can do towns and houses.

Barnes received Betjeman's letter while he was away in New York and was delighted. 'Please show this to C.P.Tel. [McGivern],' he told his secretary, Mrs Minerva Corteen, 'and ask him if we can get on with the project outlined. I am very excited indeed about this because Betjeman is one of the most brilliant broadcasters, and is unique in his knowledge and way of conveying knowledge to people. Please let me know what is proposed.' Two weeks later, on 1 April 1953, Barnes received a remarkable memo from Berkeley Smith:

> Mr Betjeman saw two hours of our preliminary research at Gloucester. Previously, at lunch, I had been able to give him an idea of our OB method of working, our physical limitations and how those limitations might be overcome. I pointed out that we are restricted to one thousand feet of camera cable and that, at the moment, we must ensure that any building we cover contains sufficient variety of shot and story to fill our general minimum period of thirty minutes. For this reason the small village Church, however beautiful, is not satisfactory but the Church and surrounding village would provide sufficient material which could then be covered partly by OB and partly by film.

Berkeley Smith explained that the main problems that outside broadcasts then faced were technical but allowed, perhaps a little vaguely, that Betjeman 'could be a great deal of help to us in suggesting methods and treatments'. Penshurst Place, in Kent, which Berkeley Smith had looked at the previous summer and which brought together a church, a house and a village, was one location where he would welcome ideas. It could be broadcast on a summer evening, using OB for panoramas and exteriors and film for interior shots and details, or on a winter evening if it was acceptable to use film shot in daylight. He doubted whether Betjeman could add anything to the filming of 'big churches' such as Winchester, Wells, Norwich and Southwell Minster, which were all planned for the next year, but was open to the idea of summer-evening programmes without film, perhaps at the ruined abbeys of Fountains or Tintern.

Berkeley Smith's memo is the true starting point for Betjeman's film-making, because it is the record of what was effectively a short course on location work. Berkeley Smith had unlocked the secrets of how outside broadcasts and film worked, how they differed and what each medium could and couldn't do. Hearing about mechanical systems — their rootedness in reality and the machine-like complexity of their parts — was exactly what Betjeman enjoyed. The schoolboy in him relished what he called 'the dependable world of technical terms' — a love that grew out of trainspotting, as he acknowledged in his commentary for a film about the running of British Railways' last steam train, in 1968.* (Trainspotters enjoyed not only trains but also the paraphernalia of trains and their special vocabulary, he said: '"flanged wheels on a fixed rail", "blast pipes", "coupled driving wheels" and "the balancing of revolving and reciprocating parts"'.) He was also drawn to the human aspect of film-making: the mutual respect between crew and director, all working in a common cause. This echoes the modern ethos, social realism and political thrust of Grierson and his distrust of artificiality — the artificiality of the studio, which exists in no real place, and the artificiality of film, which consists of edited highlights of pre-recorded sequences that exist in no real time.

* *Railways for Ever*, British Transport Films Unit (1968).

Three weeks later, Barnes pressed Berkeley Smith to meet Betjeman and involve him in a series for the summer of 1954. 'It is very sweet of you to take this trouble,' Betjeman told Barnes on receiving the news 'but I don't think you will get anyone on the television to accept my services.' He was almost right. Barnes's campaigning on Betjeman's behalf led to just three commissions in the next three years.* It was a start, but nothing like what Barnes wanted for Betjeman and nothing like what Betjeman imagined he was worthy of. Nor does it suggest that Barnes's initiatives were being wholly welcomed inside the Television Department.

The struggle Betjeman was having in making headway in film was not matched by his activities in other fields. By the time he was forty-eight, he was an established if quixotic figure in public life: a poet, writer, newspaper columnist, campaigner, architectural critic, book reviewer and radio broadcaster, with a very large following among women (a *Times* columnist of the time described him as the favourite reading of wives under hairdryers). He had already made around two hundred appearances on the wireless, where he was a popular contributor to religious programmes and a favourite contrarian on *Any Questions?* and *The Brains Trust*. Only on television did his way seem blocked. Frustrated by his inability to make films, he agreed in the summer of 1954 to appear in the pilot for a new television panel game, *Where on Earth?*, devised and produced by David Attenborough. The first programme aired on 8 July 1954, to disappointing reviews. The *Daily Mail* headlined its notice, 'Self-conscious travellers in new TV parlour game' and the *News Chronicle* asked, 'What on earth is this?', though the *Daily Express* felt that Betjeman's presence in the programme had given it a fillip. In spite of that, the show disappeared without trace.

During all this time Betjeman's attitude to the BBC had soured over the issue of how much he was paid. Since his first attempt to get

---

* The first, in October 1954, looked at Cardiff Castle and was introduced jointly by Betjeman and the Director of the BBC's Welsh Region, A. Watkin-Jones, who was also a Welsh historian. The second, in April 1955, was a tour of Wells Cathedral. The third, in January 1956, was a film about Osterley Park House, under the title *Robert Adam: Architect to an Age of Elegance*, in which technical problems led to the film unit having to be changed and rehearsal time being lost.

more money out of his radio contracts manager during the war, he had convinced himself that he was being dishonoured by the higher sums being offered to celebrities such as Malcolm Muggeridge and J. B. Priestley. 'His insecurity was amazing,' comments one of his later producers. 'He always used to say that he'd end up in the workhouse. However nice he was to work with there was this petulance that was the other side of him – just like A. J. P. Taylor, who was also obsessed that the BBC was conspiratorially underpaying him.'*

Having always been paid piecemeal rates by the BBC, Betjeman now tried to win an annual contract. (This was an unusual turn of events, because Betjeman had been turning down just such offers from Barnes for more than ten years.) In 1955 it occurred to him that the coming of independent television in September might nudge the Corporation into snapping him up to stop him joining the competition. Armed with this thought, he approached Barnes privately in January and said he'd give up the *Daily Telegraph*, where he was still reviewing as many as a dozen books a week, if the BBC would guarantee him £1,000 a year for two years. Embracing this opportunity of winning Betjeman for the Corporation and giving him the security and status he craved, Barnes took soundings and then offered Betjeman £700 for year-long availability, including taking over a book-review programme that Arthur Marshall presented on Sunday afternoons. Betjeman turned the offer down, furious that anyone should presume to encroach on his Sundays. Another round of memos circulated and Barnes now offered the £1,000 that Betjeman had been asking for and that he understood Betjeman would accept. In April a draft contract was sent for signing but Betjeman stalled, raised more points and then stopped replying to letters. The following year, when Betjeman instructed a literary agent to try again, the moment had passed. 'Betjeman is good value but not such good value as a television performer as we first thought,' one of Barnes's staff reported in a memo. There was general agreement that commercial television was less of a threat than feared and that he'd work for the Corporation whether he was tied to an exclusive contract or not.

* Edward Mirzoeff in conversation with Stephen Games, 2008.

As recounted in *Trains and Buttered Toast*, Betjeman responded by refusing to do any work for the BBC for a while. When he did eventually resume, there was a notable change in the type of work he took on. Instead of serious and arduous radio talks, he became a frequent guest on panel and game shows, which he found more sociable, more popular, better paid and more fun than talks. Asked by the BBC TV producer Nancy Thomas whether he'd like to take over from Dr Glyn Daniel as chair of *Animal, Vegetable, Mineral?* in December 1956, Betjeman replied, 'My dear thing, I should love to. It is money for jam and it is a pleasure.' The attraction of being the chairman, he had told her the previous year, was that it was 'less embarrassing than not knowing the answers'.

Another apparent realignment occurred when Betjeman made a series of television advertisements for Shell-Mex, the petrol company. Betjeman had first got involved with Shell in the early 1930s. Disgruntled with his work conditions as assistant editor at the *Architectural Review*, he had got the firm's publicity manager, Jack Beddington, to sponsor a series of guides to the counties of England that Betjeman would write and edit. The two met again in 1940 when Beddington was brought in to succeed Kenneth Clark as head of the Ministry of Information's Film Division during Betjeman's year there. (Beddington's qualification for the job was that while setting up the Shell guides for Betjeman in 1933 he was also starting Shell's in-house film unit, with Edgar Anstey as the unit's first producer.) Now, in the mid-1950s and with commercial television pending, their paths crossed a third time.

Beddington introduced Betjeman to a small company called Random Film Productions, which specialised in making films about cars and motor racing and already had several contracts with Shell-Mex. Beddington, now an independent advertising impresario, had come up with the idea that Shell should buy three-minute advertising slots in the ITV schedules to show short tourism films that indirectly promoted Shell petrol (and its new additive 'ICA', which its posters claimed 'cuts power loss due to engine deposits'). Betjeman met the head of Random, film director Peter Woosnam-Mills, and together they made half a year's supply of weekly shorts called *Discovering Britain with John Betjeman*, for which Betjeman chose the locations and wrote the commentaries. The twenty-six films went out on Friday evenings, the first – about Avebury – on the second night of ITV's existence: 23 September 1955.

The films are beautiful vignettes of a mostly pre-industrial England and do many of the things that Betjeman had told Barnes that films should do. Close-ups of details are intercut smoothly with long shots, the sequences move naturally at walking or driving pace, and views of machinery in motion – at Stisted Mill and Crofton Pumping Station – have just a flavour of the industrial-filming genre. That said, Gordon Lang's camerawork is conventional, reflecting his past experience with Peter Woosnam-Mills. Shirley Charters, who as Shirley Cobham was Random's production assistant, is adamant that Betjeman had no directorial input into them and was very much Woosnam-Mills's junior partner. Apart from supplying ideas about locations and architectural features and chatting excitedly on reconnaissance missions and during the long car journeys to and from them, his work was limited to sitting at a Moviola viewing machine and writing commentary.* Except in a couple of cases, he did not appear in front of the camera but merely voiced the commentary – in a donnish and sometimes hurried, high-pitched tone, as if speeded up in the editing. (Among his mannerisms, he had a habit of estimating dates rather than declaring them outright – 'Oh, about 1760, I should think' – rather like a wine taster, as if dating was a matter of feeling rather than fact. It was a way of distancing himself from the new breed of architectural historians and showing that his knowledge was not academic and learned but accumulated and instinctual.)

The Shell films ran each week until the spring of 1956 and were the first major piece of filming that Betjeman had been involved with. How he could have been unabashed about promoting cars when the rest of his life was spent attacking them remains a mystery. And yet in July 1955, shortly after the filming began, he wrote to his friend the artist John Piper to say, 'I don't think I've enjoyed

---

* Shirley Charters in conversation with Stephen Games, 2008.

anything so much since our Shell and Murray* guide days.' Barnes, passionately hostile to commercial mass broadcasting, felt betrayed when he discovered what Betjeman had been up to but all the more intent on finding a project that would win him back. Towards the end of the year he agreed to let Betjeman make a teaser for his *Collins Pocket Guide to English Parish Churches*, which was nearing completion after eight years' work. The result was a failure. 'I can see the difficulty of finding a theme for a subject so diverse as this,' said Barnes to the producer John Read when he saw the first cut in February 1956, but 'I felt that the commentary was a little bit didactic.' The project was shelved, though some of the material – about a single church, St Boniface, in Bunbury, Cheshire – was used in the series *Church in Action* six months later. That summer, Barnes quit the BBC after being granted grace leave during April and May and became vice-chancellor of the University College of North Staffordshire (subsequently Keele University). He died four years later, aged fifty-six.

Barnes was replaced by Gerald Beadle who had been Controller of the West Region and knew of Betjeman's work from there. Beadle continued to try to find something as substantial as *Discovering Britain* that Betjeman could pull off within his proven field of competence. The person who came up with the solution was John Vernon, who had produced the third of the three films that Betjeman had made after meeting Berkeley Smith. Vernon wanted to do a big fortnightly series on the social history of the English house and in July 1956 he convinced Berkeley Smith that they should take it on as a star vehicle for Betjeman. The offer was put to Betjeman, who accepted, and at the start of 1957 the historians Ellis Waterhouse and John Summerson were asked to act as consultants. The seven-part series would be called *The Englishman's Home*.

In April, after Betjeman returned from a guest professorship in Cincinnati, detailed discussions began on which buildings to film. The historical houses – Berkeley Castle, Castle Ashby, Uppark, Syon House – proved relatively uncontentious but Betjeman dug his

* Betjeman and John Piper had worked together on several county guides for Shell in the 1930s and two county guides for the publisher John Murray in the late 1940s.

heels in over the inclusion of twentieth-century buildings, which Vernon was committed to. Betjeman felt the twentieth century had no place in the series because its main concern was how to build mass housing rather than individual houses. In July, with Vernon still sure that it would nonetheless be 'fun' to have him talk about something he did not like, Betjeman turned to Berkeley Smith and threatened to drop out of the last programme unless the series stopped at Edwardiana. ('John, you must do this programme,' Berkeley Smith begged – or warned – in reply.) Even after Vernon had hit on the small but highly acclaimed private house of Farnley Hey, West Yorkshire, designed four years earlier in a Californian style by Peter Womersley, Betjeman resisted. A few days after the fourth programme in the series had gone out, in late August, he pulled out of promoting the final programme:

> I have been thinking about Farnley Hey and . . . I still do not want to do it . . . I only really like 'contemporary' in this country when it solves contemporary problems – like where to house slum dwellers and the homeless. I am not really interested in the house of a comparatively rich man. This sounds very left wing. But it's not. It's a socio-aesthetic objection. The way to show Farnley Hey . . . is with the architect himself explaining it to an inquiring interviewer. That inquiring interviewer I am not prepared to be. I am quite willing, for the sake of continuity, to dub a preliminary film shewing, let us say, the Pimlico estate and then sending you on with good wishes and goodbye to the contemporary house for the higher income groups.

Two days later he pulled out of the penultimate programme as well, which was to feature a Lutyens house of 1906,* on the grounds that the building was too altered internally and that an earlier house – Highclere (1843) by Charles Barry – would be better. He closed the fifth programme – Tower House, Kensington (1876–7) – by introducing the architect Lionel Brett, who'd agreed at one week's notice to take over from him.†

There was general agreement, following the series, that Betjeman

---

* Folly Farm, in Sulhamstead, Berkshire, owned by the Hon. Hugh Astor.
† Only the first of the seven programmes has survived. For technical reasons it was not possible to include it in this collection.

(and Brett) had done well and that Betjeman's stubbornness over Farnley Hey had at least been principled, even if it was inconvenient. He had now, however, been given a great deal of exposure and there was no great appetite to use him quickly again. When in 1957 he renewed his efforts to get an annual contract, Berkeley Smith was adamantly opposed. 'I cannot envisage any great increase by this department in the demand for John Betjeman's services,' he told McGivern. 'As far as we are concerned he is an architectural specialist and outside broadcast programmes of this nature are infrequent' – a judgement that glossed over the fact that Betjeman had been appearing in four different TV quiz shows during the mid-1950s* and was so popular outside the BBC that the Corporation habitually exploited him as a crowd-puller in its Christmas scheduling.

In 1958, in an attempt to give his career greater focus, Betjeman gave up doing studio shows for five years (except for *The Brains Trust*, which he continued to appear in until 1960) so that he could concentrate on what mattered more to him, in particular a long autobiographical poem that he had started work on. The poem, published in 1960 as *Summoned by Bells*, was an important piece of work. Written in blank verse – non-rhyming iambic pentameter – it has a wistful tone quite unlike the sardonic verses that he had been publishing in *Punch* and elsewhere during the 1950s. In *Summoned by Bells*, Betjeman discovered a language of personal revelation that inspired a new generation of film-makers looking for a new form of narrative to accompany their work. He now no longer had to sell himself; instead he found himself constantly in demand as a hero for a new breed of directors.

The last of his old-style films, with his rapid, rather hectoring style of speech, grew from an offer to present a film on the work of the National Trust that would coincide with an exhibition the Trust was co-sponsoring with London Transport at Charing Cross Underground Station in the summer of 1959. Working again with Peter Woosnam-Mills at Random, and with funding from National Benzole, Betjeman wrote and narrated a twenty-three-minute programme, 'Beauty in Trust', that looked at a handful of Trust

* *Animal, Vegetable, Mineral?*, *Who Said That?*, *The Brains Trust* and *What's the Object?*

properties. It was broadcast by the BBC while the exhibition was running, at the start of August. 'Beauty in Trust' was shot in colour – a first for Betjeman – and when the BBC started to trial colour transmissions, this was one of the 'trade test' colour films that it rented from industrial suppliers. Trade test transmissions, shown on BBC2 from 5 November 1962 to 24 August 1973, were never formally regarded as entertainment (so that the BBC could avoid paying royalties) but were broadcast to enable people in the TV trade and in retail outlets to get used to tuning to the new UHF 625-line signals. The test films nonetheless reached large domestic audiences. (Andrew Keys of the Test Card Circle★ has calculated that 'Beauty in Trust' was the fourth most frequently shown trade test film of all time, with 365 showings over eleven years, equivalent to at least one a fortnight.) The following year, National Benzole sponsored its second film in the series *Our National Heritage* – 'A Journey into the Weald of Kent' – and this became the third most popular trade test film, according to Keys, being shown 395 times in eleven years, with 128 showings – nearly eleven per month – in one year alone.

A complete change from these romantic, sunny evocations of England came from the pioneering young film-maker Ken Russell, who in 1959 was trying out for a job on the BBC's groundbreaking new series *Monitor*, launched by Huw Weldon the previous autumn. 'Betjeman was my choice, chosen in a panic when Huw rejected my idea of a story about Schweitzer in the leper colony,' says Russell. 'I admire the man completely and always make a point of re-reading him regularly.'† 'John Betjeman: A Poet in London' featured Betjeman in brooding black-and-white, mixing readings of his poetry with comments about London and himself. ('I can't keep sex out of my poems. It would be hypocritical for me to do so. Everywhere you go in London in public transport, you can't get away from the beauty of the gels.') Weldon liked the film, made Russell permanent and the following year asked him to direct another atmospheric film with Betjeman about what the *Radio Times*

★ The Test Card Circle is a UK-based group with 250 members around the world and a useful website. It is chaired by Stuart Montgomery, who points out that no viewing figures exist for test-card transmissions.
† Ken Russell in correspondence with Stephen Games, 2008.

called 'the fun palaces and pleasure domes of London' – Crystal Palace, Alexandra Palace, White City and Wembley – and how they had all degenerated and become BBC utilities.

Betjeman's warm relationship with Russell, a fellow maverick, was assisted by the difference in their ages, an element that erased much of the rivalry that Betjeman felt when working with people of his own generation. Younger producers – Russell, born in 1927, was twenty-one years his junior – respected him as a funny uncle with an established reputation; and for his part, Betjeman liked being surrounded by bright and energetic boys. Another favourite was Ken Savidge, based in Bristol and also born in 1927. Savidge, after working for the YMCA in the early 1950s, was given a job by Rupert Anand, Betjeman's favourite radio producer between 1949 and 1951, and then worked as assistant to BBC West's Director of Religious Broadcasting, the Revd Martin Willson, for whom Betjeman had written radio verses during the early 1950s.* (One began, 'The Reverend Martin Willson wrote / To me a most demanding note / Demanding of me Christian views / On current matters in the news . . .') In June 1958, Savidge produced Betjeman in a discussion programme in the religious strand 'Meeting Point' and went on to produce all but the first programme in an ambitious nine-part series called *John Betjeman's ABC of Churches*, which ran from 1960 to 1967. Sadly, little remains of that series or of other programmes that they made together.

In addition to younger men, Betjeman responded in the 1960s to the growing regionalisation of television that ITV had stimulated and that recalled the regionalisation of radio, and in particular Bristol, to which he had gravitated in the 1930s. One of the new corps of producers based outside London who took an interest in Betjeman's work was Malcolm Freegard, who had joined the BBC's Midlands region in Birmingham before moving to its new and tiny East Anglia television studio in Norwich in 1960. Freegard made programmes for a monthly studio-based series called *Outlook* that ran between December 1960 and July 1962; but in April 1961 he got out

---

* These have been newly edited by Kevin Gardner in *Poems in the Porch: The Radio Poems of John Betjeman* (Continuum, 2008).

of the studio and made a film (also for *Outlook*) that showed Betjeman taking a train journey from King's Lynn to Hunstanton. This nostalgic yet modern essay, realistic rather than idealised in the way that Random's films had been, provided an opportunity for Betjeman to employ the slower-paced and more meditative commentary style suggested by *Summoned by Bells* that he had first delivered for Russell. He also appeared in shot throughout. 'All Along the Line', later retitled 'John Betjeman Goes by Train', was followed by other regional productions for Freegard, including 'Something about Diss' (1964), in which Betjeman took the viewer on an exploration of a town he had never visited before ('All I know about Diss, up to date, is that it's near the headquarters of the British Goat Society,' he began). Here he acted not as an instructor, as in his Shell films, but as a slightly down-at-heel private sleuth, complete with a canvas shopping bag. Like Savidge's, nothing of Freegard's other work with Betjeman has survived. In spite of that, 'All Along the Line' must have influenced Betjeman's best railway film, 'Let's Imagine a Branch-Line Railway' (1963), lamenting the demise of the Somerset & Dorset line and the culture that went with it. It was echoed too in the later 'Metro-land', which was also structured around a train journey.

So pepped up was Betjeman by suddenly being in demand that he put in a fresh bid for a contract to BBC TV's number two, Harman Grisewood, an old Oxford friend. Naming Michael Croucher and Ken Savidge in Bristol, Roy Harris in Manchester, Malcolm Freegard in Norwich and Ken Russell in London, he said, 'I much prefer working for the BBC than the commercial chaps because it is there that I find sympathetic talent,' adding, 'I have worked with all these people and their minds are wedded and we could go on producing programmes.' He then went on to make a remarkable claim for his television work, saying, 'I, at any rate, find [it as] satisfying and stimulating as any work in prose or verse I have ever done.' He added that the films he had made for the BBC recently 'I regard as the major work of my life' – an attempt to ingratiate himself with Grisewood, certainly, but so against the grain of what he had always said hitherto as to deserve our attention.

Betjeman's renewed bid for a contract failed, as did all future bids, but later commissions from the BBC would bring him in contact with several producers for whom he would make distinguished programmes, including Julian Jebb (1967–72), Margaret McCall (1970–72) and Edward Mirzoeff (1969–77), producer of *Bird's Eye View* (1969–71), 'Metro-land' (1973) and 'A Passion for Churches' (1974). ITV wooed him with more mass-market programmes, including a series on the history of music hall* and another in which he visited London landmarks,† but the quality of its affiliates' productions was very much lower than what he was used to and by the end of 1960s he worked almost solely for the BBC.

The one exception to ITV's low quality threshold was the work he did with Jonathan Stedall at TWW, the ITV company that broadcast to Wales and the West of England. Stedall, born in 1938, was the same age as Betjeman's son, Paul, and had been to Harrow School, for which Betjeman had an unusual affection.‡ He joined TWW as a floor manager in 1961 at the age of twenty-three and was quickly made a director. Before leaving two years later, he was directing a specially devised flagship strand called 'Wales and the West', with Betjeman contributing a quarter-of-an-hour segment about the West Country and the playwright-novelist Gwyn Thomas contributing another about Wales. In the course of two intense periods of filming during the summer of 1962 and the winter of 1962–3, Betjeman created ten memorable programmes. He and Stedall went on to make a two-part series for the BBC called *Thank God it's Sunday* (1972) and a belated adaptation of *Summoned by Bells* (1976).

'At TWW, our brief was to do these fifteen-minute films and the places were chosen by Betjeman,' says Stedall:

> He knew the West Country intimately but there weren't clearly defined roles. What was lovely about working with Betjeman was he had ideas about shots and I had ideas about the script. It was very much a team effort. Unlike with some writers, he'd write the commentary in the cutting room, sometimes with me there, so we'd kick the commentary around together. He was in London, we were in Cardiff, so

---

* *Sing a Song of Sixpence* (ATV, 1963).
† *Betjeman's London* (Rediffusion, 1967).
‡ 'Why do you like Harrow?' Stedall asked Betjeman when they first met. 'Because it isn't Eton,' Betjeman replied. 'So why did you send your son to Eton?' Stedall asked. 'Snobbery,' Betjeman replied.

he'd come down for a few days at a time and I'd show him several
films at the same time. At most I had a fortnight, probably only a week,
and he'd spend maybe three days. He'd often imitate voices and I'd
encourage him. For a film we did about Bath he'd mimic the voice of
a property speculator. For a film we did about Clevedon he'd fantasise
about what old people in a hotel were thinking. I don't remember
being worried about his putting thoughts into people's heads because
there was nothing cruel in anything he said. I did some films later
with Alan Bennett and he did the same. I think the thing was, it wasn't
cruel – the whole tone is affectionate.*

Betjeman worked more quickly on TWW's low-budget films than
he did with Mirzoeff ten years later, when increased revenue from
colour licences suddenly gave the BBC increased latitude. 'He used
to write me these wonderful long letters, saying 'I see the film as
this and that . . .' says Mirzoeff:

> They were wholly unpractical. Thank you, John! Now we'll go and
> make the film the way it should be made. Sometimes he'd look at the
> film we'd taken and say 'Oh, that's jolly good.' Then he'd sit in the
> cutting room with his A4 pads, writing, for weeks and weeks, sitting
> in front of the editing machine, running film sequences backwards and
> forwards so their rhythms would sink in, waiting for inspiration from
> 'the Management' up above. There were days when he'd only write
> two lines and you had to press him to finish because of the finance
> people looking over your shoulder with slide rules: 'How long is this
> going to go on?' We had six to seven weeks of editing and then many
> more weeks of writing. It's inconceivable today. You're lucky if you
> can write a script in one day. It was a unique period and that's how he
> was able to find the poetry in the film. There was time.†

There was also help, Mirzoeff recalls:

> Sometimes the film editor, Ted Roberts, was able to overcome a block
> by supplying pastiche verse in the poet's own style. For the church fête
> at South Raynham, Ted suggested:
>
> > We must dip into our pockets
> > For our hearts are full of dread

---

* Jonathan Stedall in conversation with Stephen Games, 2008.
† Edward Mirzoeff in conversation with Stephen Games, 2008.

> There's all the more to pay for now
> The roof's been stripped of lead.

Betjeman was delighted – 'Oh, that's frightfully good' – but improved the final lines:

> At the thought of all the damage
> Since the roof was stripped of lead.*

Stedall remembers that some critics blamed Betjeman's television work for a collapse in the quality of his poetry – an uncomfortable subject for anyone who sees Betjeman only as a poet, but it discomforted Betjeman as well. In the middle of that decline he had written, 'I knew as soon as I could read and write / That I must be a poet'[†] but he was well aware that he was not producing work that in any way equalled what he had done in the past. Was television to blame?

Betjeman's childhood attraction to poetry had been bound up with anxiety and self-image: the idea of being a poet set him apart but also explained and justified his apartness:

> Misunderstood and not like other boys,
> Deep, dark and pitiful I saw myself
> In my mind's mirror, every step I took
> A fascinating study to the world.[‡]

But the best of his poetry – at Oxford and in the 1930s – was in fact the product not of Betjeman's apartness but of his sociability, for it was largely collaborative in its creation and practised on and with his friends to entertain them. Only exceptionally was that possible as his circle grew apart; instead he had to send his drafts by post. ('Dearest Spansbury,' he wrote to John Sparrow on Christmas Day 1947, 'I think "King's" is a corker of a poem and worth all the labour I can give on it and that you can; you have hit on the weaknesses in the last two lines, just as I knew you would, clever old thing.') It was with the isolation of being a 'professional' poet that the attraction

---

* *The Betjemanian*, vol. 19 (2007–8), p. 12.
† *Summoned by Bells* (John Murray, 1960), Chapter 2.
‡ Ibid., Chapter 8.

of poetry and the quality of his writing waned, until with his Poet Laureateship, from 1972, such work became entirely burdensome. (This is why his best later poems are often the amusing verses he knocked off for friends – verses that he disregarded and that are still not taken sufficiently seriously as part of his oeuvre.)

Looking at his television work, however, one finds welcome confirmation that his poetic imagination had not exhausted itself but had merely taken up residence elsewhere. Television, once it was able to fulfil its promise technically, was a new toy set to whose rules and equipment he responded eagerly. (Savidge talks of the pleasure Betjeman got from learning and deploying the language of TV equipment: small lamps called 'inky dinks', a type of microphone called an 'apple and biscuit' and various types of 'dollies' – 'Wembley dollies', 'Vinten dollies', 'Mole-Richardson dollies' – the wheeled platforms that cameras are moved around on.)* Even more crucially, television reproduced the collaborative nature of Betjeman's earlier poetry-making, not just in its production but in its reception. It provided a context that reanimated his words. He liked the sociability of developing his ideas with a trusted producer, he liked performing in front of crews, he liked having a national audience for his work and he liked the reassurance that newspaper reviews and TV ratings gave him of how well he had gone down.

As with all television programmes, the extent to which his writing was his own is to some degree indeterminate, as Stedall and Mirzoeff have shown. Betjeman didn't achieve the kind of editorial or directorial responsibility that he seemed to be asking for in the late 1950s but he was certainly the star around whom the programmes were constructed and he had creative input in the planning stage. How imaginative his input may have been can be seen from the handful of treatments included in the pages that follow. His accounts of how St Brelade's, Jersey, and Canterbury Cathedral could be filmed, for example, show that he was strong on visuals, understood how a sequence of shots could be set up and saw what the implications would be for what he did and what he said. He was

* Ken Savidge in conversation with Stephen Games, 2008.

also good on details. 'He certainly wasn't just a gifted amateur,' says
Savidge, 'which is a slightly pejorative phrase, I think.'

> He hated pretension when talking about direction and I remember
> he once sent up a fellow producer of mine whom he heard saying
> to the cameraman, 'I want you to go out and get me the texture of
> Cornwall.' Now that sort of thing Betjeman would have hooted at,
> and did. The other thing is, very simple things. He'd say, 'Wide angles:
> not much good. Beautiful scenery: not much good on television. The
> close-up is the thing. You must get close.' And in practical terms, if he
> knew we were doing a sequence that involved a lot of tramping on
> gravel, he'd always bring his golfing shoes to wear because he knew
> they'd be very effective from the recordist's point of view. Little things
> like that. But he never flaunted this understanding. You just gradually
> came to know as you began to work with him that it was there all the
> time and informed his every move, every suggestion.*

Mirzoeff recalls Betjeman's screeching with laughter at the jokes he
introduced into his script for *A Passion for Churches* but also agonis-
ing about how he ought to present his religion, especially in relation
to Roman Catholicism – a problem he solved, in the context of the
shrine at Walsingham, in a series of rhetorical questions: 'I wonder
if you'd call it superstitious? / . . . Or do you think that forces are
around, / Strong, frightening, loving and just out of reach / But
waiting, waiting, somewhere to be asked?') This sense of personal
accountability results in passages of religious verse that have 'a
complexity and depth of feeling unprecedented in his earlier films',
says Mirzoeff.†

Television gave Betjeman opportunities to explore language
in a way that few other poets have ever had. It also refreshed him
at a time when most other things in his life were depressing him.
'What makes Mr Betjeman such a delightful guide is not merely
the strength of his feelings but also his eye for the out-of-the-way
detail,' noted *The Times* of a programme Betjeman had made with
the BBC's Michael Croucher about Poole, in Dorset, in 1966. 'He
pointed out, for instance, two codfish, made in marble, decorating

* Ibid.
† *The Betjemanian*, vol. 19 (2007–8), p. 11.

one Georgian fireplace. His informality is also a great asset; he is
the first man one has seen on television standing on a suburban
bench and peering over a hedge to get a better view of the house
beyond.'*

Betjeman's television work operates in the same way: it provides
us with a perch to get a better view of him.

* *The Times*, 20 April 1966.

BETJEMAN'S ENGLAND

ENGLAND

BEAUTY IN TRUST

From the National Benzole series *Our National Heritage*
Random Film Productions Ltd
BBC Television, 4 August 1959
Producer: Peter Woosnam-Mills

• • •

Driving is no pleasure in this sort of thing. [We see traffic – mild by today's standards – driving through Betjeman's hated Great West Road in Brentford, west London, and passing the new Lucozade factory, which had opened in 1953 and was demolished in 2004.] I suppose all the noise and strains and frustration are necessary. After all, I am in a mechanical age and so I'd better put up with it. And it has its advantages. [A car horn parps.] Shut up, you neurotic ass. It has its advantages. For it makes the motor cars and the comforts of life. But the noisier the world grows in the cities, the more precious I find the places of tranquillity and permanence. This island isn't big and it's very overcrowded. Muddle like this makes me long for birdsong instead of traffic roar, flower smells instead of fumes.

In the end this road will take me to Cornwall: to north Cornwall, where I was brought up as a child, and to a part of it that has been kept in its natural state not by the government or by any private landlord but by the National Trust. Cornwall to be seen at walking pace, now there's time to breathe and see and smell and hear. Spring is the best time in Cornwall, when the hedges and turf are like acres of wild rock garden, when sea pinks colour the cliffs for miles.

There's always a breeze on these heights. It's only in the lanes between the high hedges that you can get out of it and even then there is wind enough to blow a gate shut. I remember the consternation there was when this piece of headland – Pentire – came up for sale; but local people subscribed to buy it and gave it to the National Trust, so that it is now an open space for ever for all to enjoy.

But it's not a useless open space. The National Trust owns Pentire farm, the old farmhouse on the left – and the newer house, in simple storm-resisting style, is already like the farm buildings: spotted with orange and silver lichens that grow where winds are salt. Farmers with the good Cornish name of 'Old' have looked after this land for generations and made a living from it. Their pasture and yards are sheltered from the great Atlantic gales: they're snug in a hollow of this windswept peninsula.

Cornish father and Cornish son. The edges of their farm are wild and wonderful, with the Atlantic Ocean tumbling all around them. Huge cliffs have hidden paths to secret caves, once only known to smugglers and where only seagulls dare to go today. And only seals can safely bask in these merciless waters, which are angry-looking even in the calmest weather.

The rocks are blue with mussels. The rock pools hold limpets and crabs, and their shattered remains strew the cliffs, dropped from the beaks of seabirds: birds like the oystercatcher, sailing there from peak to peak among the topmost pinnacles of Pentire Point.

Mouls Island and the Rumps. Here, on this outermost corner of the Celtic kingdom of Cornwall, it is thought that some race earlier than the Celts made a last stand before being driven backwards into the sea, for there are traces of pots here and of pit dwellings.

After such ancient and wild grandeur, I like a sudden and complete contrast of scene. Let's choose Claydon, near Aylesbury. The National Trust has owned it for less than five years. The Verneys, who gave it to the Trust, have lived in this mild and pastoral part of Buckinghamshire for five hundred years. The house you see was built by the second Lord Verney in 1752. It's plain outside but immensely luxurious within. Lord Verney was a genial spendthrift and a man of taste. He employed his friend Sir Thomas Robinson, a Yorkshire landowner-turned-architect, to design this spacious Saloon, with a ceiling by the famous stuccoist Joseph Rose.

But wait: see the contrast these chaste grey walls provide with the room that adjoins it and which we're going to enter now. Here Lord Verney employed a decorator named Lightfoot, about whom nothing is known except that he was thought to be a little mad. The walls have been coloured that Neapolitan yellow to show up the marvellous white carving with which Lightfoot decorated chimney piece, niches and door frame. He called it all his 'naturalistic' style and the sober architect Robinson didn't like it at all, though I must say I like it myself very much.

The Great Staircase at Claydon is one of the wonders of the late Georgian age. It goes up three storeys: the whole height of the house. Here, Lightfoot was again given a chance and showed his skill in joinery. The mahogany stairs are inlaid with rosewood, satinwood, ebony and ivory, not just underneath and at the sides but on the treads of the stairs as well. And up those stairs, a century ago, Florence Nightingale must have walked, for her sister married one of the Verneys and she often came and stayed here. The iron-work has metal ears of corn attached to it and any time anyone goes up the stairs the vibration sets the corn a-shaking, right up to the top of the house. And perhaps it's the ghost of Florence Nightingale that makes them shake now.

In an upstairs room is the most fantastic of all the wonders Claydon has to show. At this time, 1760, China was all the rage: Chinese patterns, Chinese figures and things like the Pagoda in Kew Gardens. Lord Verney had his own pagoda, carved by Lightfoot in the Chinese Room. All this carving is of wood, painted to look like plaster. It's the sort of thing Chippendale used to do to the frames of looking-glasses and pictures. It's Chippendale, only more so. And as we pass under this wild extravaganza, with its brackets and leaves and little wooden temple bells, we find a mandarin and his wife, carved on the ceiling, to welcome us to tea.

After art, nature: Wicken Fen, Cambridgeshire, which the Trust keeps as a nature reserve. You might think this mere, flooded to attract waterfowl, and these fringes of reeds, growing out of two feet of water, were dull: dull until you look at Wicken Fen in detail. A windmill water-pump: once these were all over the Fens.

Reeds grow out of water but the sedge you see here grows in swamp. Bushes would invade the sedge if it weren't cut every year. The dense fens, where sedge-warblers have precarious nests, are tall and if left uncut they rot and form soil, which bushes grow on.

Before corrugated iron was invented, reeds like these, with their round stems, and the more pliable sedge were used for thatching: the village post office at Wicken has reeds for the smooth part of its roof and sedge (which bends) for the ridges; and here's another Wicken cottage, thatched only with sedge.

The swallowtail butterfly, flitting about here, once bred naturally in the Fens but modern farming and drainage and various other things did it in until it was reintroduced to Wicken Fen, which is kept by the Trust in its natural state; and there it thrives.

The Fen is bright with flowers. In summer, purple loosestrife and the creamy meadowsweet abound, and the reed mace, scattering its pollen like powder.

A whole area as a nature reserve – a whole area of lilies, lodes and meres and marshes: that's one sort of Trust property. And as a contrast, another Trust property is a whole area of houses: a complete village. Lacock, in Wiltshire, was once a wool town. In medieval times, the main Bath Road went through it. Then its neighbours, Chippenham and Shrewsbury, became more important; but Lacock, under the ownership of the Talbot family, was kept intact. I like touring slowly through the streets, noticing details. That doorway, for instance: Corsham stone; and those carved Swiss rolls on the porch (I should think the date is Queen Anne). And the door scraper is to match, where a wool worker must have scraped his shoes about two centuries ago: old and practical – like this window catch, which is probably Elizabethan. The thick timber that supports this house is about 1380 and it's been filled in with brick and stone later. Of course, one's so used to fake half-timber, it's hard to believe the genuine, yet one knows that that's genuine, just as are the plants in the window.

Lacock isn't a self-conscious showplace: although the post office and the other shops fit in with their surroundings, yet they're practical and they're used. This door must have been there for at least four hundred years. It's Tudor – and look at those fern leaves in the wooden spandrel of the arch.

Stone was used at Lacock as easily as wood for walls and roofs and for doorways; and beyond this stone buttress is the blacksmith's shop, which is now used as a bus shelter.

The attraction of Lacock is that it is complete as a unit. Though the houses are all of different dates and styles and materials, they all fit in together: gabled cottages of the seventeenth century look perfectly at home beside the plainer houses of the nineteenth. And now they'll be kept in good condition for ever because the Talbot family who owned the village and other voluntary subscribers have handed the place over to the National Trust, with endowments for its upkeep.

The four little streets of Lacock were unconscious planning. English people once knew by instinct how to make a street exactly right. And as a contrast with this, the gardens of Stourhead, which are man-made landscape, are a piece of conscious planning. Originally, where we are walking now was a bare hollow in the downs on the Wiltshire–Dorset borders. The little stream in the valley was dammed in 1741 to make a lake. Henry Hoare, its owner, of Hoare's Bank, London, planted trees and built temples and grottoes on its shore so that every step you took should present a picture. His idea was to have the pictures he had collected on his Grand Tour of the Continent as a young man brought to life in his own Wiltshire valley.

His descendants, who gave these gardens to the Trust, belonged to the late Victorian age, which liked flowering shrubs such as azaleas and rhododendrons, while of course their ancestor, Henry Hoare, had preferred the more Classical scene, with water in the foreground and a temple in the middle distance. Thus Stourhead has become two gardens in one: a Classical landscape garden of Georgian times and a late-Victorian garden of blossoming shrubs. In spring, the two combine and make the lines of an eighteenth-century poet about Stourhead still hold good:

> Throughout the various scenes, above, below,
> Lawns, walks and slopes with verdant carpets glow.
> On the clear mirror float the inverted shades
> Of woods, plantations, wildernesses, glades,
> Rocks, bridges, temples, grottoes and cascades.

A landscape garden has to be laid out by an artist. That at Stourhead is the work of two: the planter of the flowering shrubs and the designer of the Classical temples. And here, the one is a setting for the other. And the old church of Stourton village at the head of the valley reminds us of the age before landscape gardening was invented.

From man-made scenery to the natural: Honister Pass, Cumberland. The Trust owns thirty thousand acres in the Lake District and I've often wondered what it is that has made these fells and streams and crags of Cumberland, Westmorland and Lancashire the playground of the Midlands and the North. I can't believe that it's because they've read Wordsworth that these boys bathe here – and, incidentally, defile the grass with their litter. (I wish they'd put it in the basket that's been provided for them.) Why do people come in their thousands every summer? And why, despite their tents and their caravans, does the scenery always prevail and seem big enough to hold them?

The crags, though some of them may be difficult enough to climb (and this isn't a particularly difficult one you're looking at now: Shepherd's Crag, near Derwent Water) – the crags are nothing like as adventurous as those to be found in the much larger and wilder mountains of Wales. So why, I ask myself, is the Lake District the most rambled over, scrambled over, camped over and admired and loved of all the natural scenery of England? Wordsworth knew: it's because everything here is of the right scale. The lakes themselves are all middle-sized: not too big so you can't see across them, but obviously not ponds; and it's also because they're full of variety, both on their shores and skyline. How pleasing, he said, to watch 'the stream pushing its way among the rocks in lively contrast with the stillness from which it has escaped'.*

An effect of size is not gained by magnitude but by proportion. Here, on Crummock Water, where you can usually catch a pike, all seems large enough; but it's the trees at the edge and the fold of

* From *A Guide through the Districts of the Lakes in the North of England* by William Wordsworth (1770–1850).

the hills beyond that give variety. It's the fields down to the shore that give friendliness to Derwent Water. And a circle of stones three thousand years old that gives mystery to the hills.

Over fifty years ago, here in the Lake District, Brandelhow was bought by public subscription. It was one of the first properties of the National Trust, which now owns over a thousand properties in England, Wales and Northern Ireland. St Michael's Mount in Cornwall was a gift from its owner, Lord St Levan. Lanhydrock, with its woods, seventeenth-century gatehouse and formal gardens, was given by Lord Clifden. And what do you do with a great country house like Cotehele if you inherit it and like it and can't afford to keep it up? Rather than let it become a ruin, anything. A fifteenth-century Cornish manor, it was accepted by the Treasury in lieu of death duties from Lord Mount Edgecumbe and the Treasury handed it on to the Trust.

But the National Trust is not a government department. It's a voluntary body for saving beautiful places. Ickworth, the Georgian Suffolk house of the Marquess of Bristol, is another gift from the Treasury in lieu of death duties. It was built by the Lord Bristol who was Bishop of Derry in the late eighteenth century. Blickling Hall, Norfolk, with its twenty-five farms and the money to keep it up, was left to the Trust by the will of the eleventh Lord Lothian.

However the properties come, by will or public subscription or, as in the case of Oxburgh Hall, Norfolk, partly as a personal gift from a member of the family, which has lived here for four and a half centuries – however the properties come, the idea is to keep these places as going concerns that are open to the public. And it's not always houses and landskip* that the Trust preserves. Avebury in Wiltshire is the biggest prehistoric temple in Britain: about 1500 BC. This was bought with money given by the Pilgrim Trust and a private subscriber.

Small manor houses – this is the one at Tintinhull, Somerset – are as attractive as big country houses. I don't know what it is that makes this garden so pleasant and peaceful and so obviously not

---

* Betjeman's favoured (eighteenth-century) word for 'landscape'.

looked after by a public authority but there it is: loved and cared-for and personal. The lady who created this garden still lives in a modest, early-eighteenth-century manor house – that at Tintinhull – as a tenant of the National Trust, to whom she gave it. There is a house that is lived in, enjoyed and welcoming.

When the tenant leaves a house, the soul goes out of it. Look on this picture – and on this. [We see an abandoned manor house.] Without the Trust, an essential and irreplaceable part of our rapidly diminishing national heritage of what is beautiful and old will go for ever to decay, the Devil and the demolition men.

THE ENGLISHMAN'S HOME

First in the thirteen-part series *Bird's Eye View*, looking at Britain from
   a helicopter
BBC2 Television, 5 April 1969
Producer and director: Edward Mirzoeff

• • •

There is a saying (you've heard it before): 'The Englishman's
home is his castle.' Well, I suppose – in a way – it is.

> The Celts in coracs crossed to Anglesey.
> Pre-Christians. Early Christians. Irish Celts.
> What were they like who dug these holes for huts,
> Roofed them with boughs to keep the winter out?
> What were they like, who lived in such a place?

The Ancient Romans too, who settled here at Rockbourne on the
downs before the Saxons called them Hampshire, Dorset, Wilts.
Patterned floors, remains of hypocausts: luxurious life, where never
luxury was seen again.

> Why did the Normans choose an Iron Age fort
> To build the castle of Old Sarum here?
> Why did the clerics – outlined in the turf
> You see their old cathedral over there★ –
> Why did they go away?
> Was it a water shortage or a feud
> That drove them down to build in Salisbury?
> We do not know. But when, across the waves
> From Ireland and the west, the shores of Wales
> Rise mountainous along those mountains' feet

★ The archaeological foundations of the cathedral throw a shadow on the ground.

We see the castles of an English king –
Edward the First – oh, then the answer's clear:
Attack, defence; after defence, attack.
Conquer, subdue and dominate the Welsh
With arrow, shot and battering ram and lead.
Harlech and Conway and Caernarvon, three
Grey bastions guard the northern coast of Wales.
Peaceful today. A poet of the Welsh★
Has thus translated from his native tongue:

> One night of tempest I arose and went
> Along the Menai shore on dreaming bent;
> The wind was strong, and savage swung the tide,
> And the waves blustered on Caernarfon side.
>
> But on the morrow, when I passed that way,
> On Menai shore the hush of heaven lay;
> The wind was gentle and the sea a flower,
> And the sun slumbered on Caernarfon tower.

Far over in England, how peaceful are names
Like Deeping St Nicholas, Deeping St James,
Long strings of rich soil and low houses of men
Where slow flows the Welland through Lincolnshire fen.

Villages, once Saxon or Danish, grew rich on ploughland.

> The earth is the Lord's, and all that therein is:
> the compass of the world, and they that dwell therein.†

Here at Chipping Camden in the Cotswolds the people prospered on the wool from sheep. They built themselves small substantial houses all along the market street. And at Nun Monkton, in the flat West Riding of Yorkshire, where roads and rivers meet, at the village pond and green is the picture people have of Merrie England, with dancing round the maypole on the grass.

★ Betjeman's friend, the poet R. S. Thomas (1913–2000). The poem is his 'One Night of Tempest'.
† Psalm 24:1 (Book of Common Prayer).

But life could be 'nasty, brutish, and short',* even for people at the top who lived in castles. Berkeley Castle, Gloucestershire, where the Berkeleys still live. Here on the night of September 21st, 1327, Edward II was barbarously murdered. You'll remember how Thomas Gray describes that fearful fate of the first Prince of Wales:

> Weave the warp, and weave the woof,
> The winding-sheet of Edward's race:
> Give ample room and verge enough
> The characters of hell to trace.
> Mark the year and mark the night
> When Severn shall re-echo with affright
> The shrieks of death thro' Berkeley's roof that ring,
> Shrieks of an agonizing King!†

A castle then. A castle still. But its walls are breached with windows that look at the world outside. A castle turning into a house – Stokesay, Shropshire: the timbered gate lodge is almost ornamental. Around the yard the wall is only a curtain wall. In that hall the lord of the manor eats at a high table above the salt. In that overhung bit, he and his family sleep.

> Across the hills, the borders of Wales are quiet,
> And over everybody is the King.

Compton Wynyates in Warwickshire. It was rebuilt by Sir William Compton, First Gentleman of the Bedchamber and favourite of the King. He dedicated that porch to 'My lord, King Henry the Eighth'.

> Yet if His Majesty, our sovereign lord,
> Should of his own accord
> Friendly himself invite
> And say 'I'll be your guest tomorrow night',

---

* From *Leviathan* by Thomas Hobbes (1588–1679), ch. 13.
† From 'The Bard' by Thomas Gray (1716–71). This extract is also known as 'The Curse upon Edward'.

> How should we stir ourselves, call and command
> All hands to work! 'Let no man idle stand.'*

Compton hid his house in a Warwickshire hollow – to be out of the weather and not to hide from enemies. Thomas Wolsey, a mightier man, Cardinal of England, built *his* palace at Hampton.

> Set me fine Spanish tables in the hall;
> See they be fitted all;
> Let there be room to eat
> And order taken that there want no meat.
> See every sconce and candlestick made bright,
> That without tapers they may give a light.
>
> . . . .
>
> Thus, if a king were coming, would we do;
> And 'twere good reason too;
> For 'tis a duteous thing
> To show all honour to an earthly king.†

It was not enough for Henry VIII, who deposed Wolsey and took the palace for himself.

The rich Elizabethans built to please themselves. Longleat in Wiltshire. Longleat is not a castle except in its square plan. Look: its outside walls are mostly glass and stone. The formal gardens are patterned like tapestries that hang on the gallery walls inside. On the roof the rediscovered gods and goddesses of ancient Rome – Elizabethan fancy carved again. Pleasure on the roof, pleasure in the garden, pleasure in the park. Mythical beasts from tapestries inhabit the waters and woods. Cars £1, with children free, no dogs.

Harlaxton Manor, near Grantham, Lincolnshire: the grandest Elizabethan house of all. But look at the date: 1837. Victorian-Elizabethan. But just as genuine-looking as the real thing and, I think, as impressive. This was about the last time that a private

---

* Anonymous, sixteenth century (*The Oxford Book of English Verse: 1250–1900*), but sometimes attributed to Thomas Ford (?1580–1648).
† Ibid.

unennobled citizen, Mr George Gregory, a landowner, would be
rich enough to build himself a palace. He and his architect Salvin
were inspired by the Elizabethans.

To earlier ages, earlier inspiration.

> Stay traveller! With no irreverent haste
> Approach the mansion of a man of taste.
> Hail, Castle Howard! Hail, Vanbrugh's noble dome
> Where Yorkshire in her splendour rivals Rome!
>
> . . . . . .
>
> Here the proud footman to the butler bows
> But kisses Lucy when she milks the cows.
> Here a proud butler on the steward waits
> But shares his mistress at the Castle gates.
> Here fifty damsels list my lady's bells
> And a whole parish in one mansion dwells:
> Chef, housekeeper and humblest houseboy, all
> In due gradation of the servants' hall
> Dependent on the slightest frown or smile
> Of him who holds the Earldom of Carlisle.
>
> . . . . .
>
> But what of wealth and pomp of Worldly state?
> To yonder Mausoleum soon or late,
> Up those broad steps will go great Howard's dust –
> A journey no man makes before he must.*

By now the garden becomes more than a tapestry: it's a place to
walk in when the weather's fair. The ingenious Monsieur Grillet in
1694, at Chatsworth in Derbyshire, with the aid of the first Duke
of Devonshire, turned the garden there into something as remarkable as the house. High on the moors was stored the water and he
trained it to cascade downhill through planted woodlands, down to
lesser ponds, and thence to burst from a temple. Step by step, formal

---

* Betjeman here adopts the style of Alexander Pope's 'Epistle to Lord Burlington'
and satirises the far more respectful poem 'Castle Howard' (1733) dedicated to its then
owner, Charles 3rd Earl of Carlisle.

and straight, it charged with rushing force and burst as fountains in the vale below.

> High to the heavens, behold the silvery shower,
> A dancing tribute to hydraulic power.

Big houses set the fashion. First, formality was all the rage: from the garden front at Melbourne Hall in Derbyshire, windows looked out to straight and formal lines, a vista made of shrubs and ordered beds. The fashion had come from France.

> Here at the fountain's sliding foot,
> Or at some fruit-tree's mossy root,
> Casting the body's vest aside,
> My soul into the boughs does glide:
> . . . . . .
> How could such sweet and wholesome hours
> Be reckon'd but with herbs and flow'rs!*

Belton, Lincolnshire. Formal on this side; and conscious wildness in the park beyond. Too much formality? 'Nature abhors a straight line,' said the eighteenth-century landscape gardener Capability Brown. 'I will make the Thames look like a small stream.' And so he did when he dammed the little River Glyme in a Cotswold valley and turned it into a mighty winding lake at Blenheim, Oxfordshire. It was given by a grateful nation to the Duke of Marlborough for his victories over the French in 1704. As for Vanbrugh's splendid palace, I think of the lines of Alexander Pope:

> 'Thanks Sir,' I cried, ''tis very fine,
> But where d'ye sleep, and where d'ye dine?
> I find by all you have been telling
> That 'tis a house but not a dwelling.'†

---

* From 'The Garden' by Andrew Marvell (1621–78).
† From 'Upon the Duke of Marlborough's House at Woodstock' by Alexander Pope (1688–1744).

A country house is nothing without its setting. In later Georgian days that setting had to be wild or changed to look wild. 'Nature abhors a straight line.' Curve of land and curve of groups of trees, curves on the surface of a landscaped lake. In Bedfordshire, Woburn.

> The sun shines out, no Mediterranean sun,
> For this is Stourhead where a chalky vale
> Planted with trees is turned into a scene
> Of temples, bridges, obelisks and rocks
> Commanded by the eighteenth-century taste
> Of a rich London banker, Henry Hoare.
> Instead of Claude or Poussin on his walls
> Showing a ruin dark against the light
> His garden walks became his gallery –
> The Temple of the Sun, the Pantheon,
> Reflected in the water, seen through trees,
> A Wiltshire valley changed to Italy.

On the shores of North Wales, overlooking Cardigan Bay, what fair Mediterranean port is this that stumbles to the sea? The port of Merioneth: Portmeirion. It's the work of a living architect, Clough Williams-Ellis, who has brought Italy and English eye-catchers to his native Wales. An architectural antique shop of the open air. The charm's deliberately plaster deep; colours are shown up by the grey Welsh skies, yet it looks no more strange or out of place than must another such Italian dream have looked two centuries ago when first it rose. This – Chiswick House: an Italian villa from the banks of the Veneto, built by Lord Burlington and his architect William Kent, copying much-admired Palladio in what was orchard land of Middlesex.

Country houses joined together to make the Royal Crescent, Bath: ancient Rome in Somerset, built in the mid-eighteenth century by a father and son, both called John Wood. The Royal Crescent was a good address. Façade only: you built your rooms behind – as many as you could. It didn't matter about the back. The front counted. You and your family had to be in Bath for the season, to attend assemblies and routs, to take the waters and fall in love, when the city of Bath was as smart as London, but all for a season – only a season.

Façades, façades, along the Somerset hills. And the smartest of all was the Circus. Bath led – but Bath seems to me to be in the crater of an extinct volcano. I prefer a part of Bristol that copied Bath: Clifton. High up upon the downs, built in the 1790s: a place to live in, not just to stay in for a season. Where East Indiamen returned from voyages.

> In some of the vaults below these Clifton terraces
> And crescents that hang above the Avon Gorge,
> The Bristol merchants stored their pipes of port.
> Bristol, the second city of England;
> Clifton, the fairest suburb of the West;
> Brunel's Suspension Bridge poised like an insect
> Across the Gorge. And there along the Gorge,
> The Avon winds by woods to Severn sea.

Seaside brings out the best in all of us. When England left her inland spas for sea, following royal fashion (not able to travel to Europe because of the wars with Napoleon), Brighton became what still it is: the best-looking seaside resort we've got.

> Those cheerful stucco squares and promenades,
> Those winding paths, romantic clumps of shrub,
> All in the curving Georgian landscape style,
> An intended contrast with straight seaside fronts,
> They were all the work of speculative builders
> Before spec. building got its dirty name.
> Spec. building of the thirties – 1830s.

The pleasure-loving Regent, George IV, liked Brighton better than his palaces. His favourite architect, John Nash, built for the King at Brighton an oriental pavilion. 'It is as though St Paul's Cathedral had gone down to the sea and pupped,' said the Revd Sydney Smith.

Outside Bristol, John Nash tried the cottage style with Blaise Hamlet, a model village on the big estate of Blaise Castle, so designed that every step you take when on the ground gives another subject for a watercolour.

On the great estate of Chatsworth, the sixth Duke of Devonshire in the 1830s wanted to improve the rolling vistas of his park – and glorious those rolling vistas are. He was a sovereign lord in his domain. He cleared away the old village that spoiled the view and only left a single house of it – but he built for his tenants a better-looking village further up the hill, a model village done in various styles, spelt 'Edensor' and pronounced 'Ensa'. And I can't see why this sort of thing is any more inhuman than what a council does today. And in the sixties, in the midst of it, Sir Gilbert Scott rebuilt the village church: uncompromising middle-pointed Gothic.

And so's North Oxford. Cradle of individualism, where professors – freed at last from the University statutes that forbade them to marry – bred families of first-class brains in all that gabled brick. So many rectories and not too close together. Each house is slightly different from its neighbour. A pleasant place of wide and shady roads: humane, High Church and Liberal. It gave birth to these swim-pool suburbs, far from industry. The sort of house that everybody wants: an acre and a garden and no cow. The Keston Park Estate, near Bromley, Kent.

'We'll house our workers not in flats but farms
And cottages their forebears might have lived in.'

So thought the Lever Brothers, who made soap and built Port Sunlight outside Birkenhead. A protest against Northern back-to-backs. They housed their workers in the eighties here. This was a very early garden village, with each house different. Work for each for weal of all and the Nonconformist conscience turned to Art.

New Anzac-on-Sea, just after the First World War. Eventually they called it 'Peacehaven': a garden suburb on the Sussex coast. We were told to laugh at it in days gone by as a dreadful example of urban sprawl and bungaloids and all that sort of thing but where you can still call your house your own and plant your garden with the plants you choose. The downland air is laced with a scent of sea; your house detached. Others mayn't like it but it's what you like.

Harlow in Essex, just after the Second World War. A new New Town. And as the guidebook says, 'You've come to live in a newly developed area of Harlow which incorporates the most up-to-date ideas and layout.' Indeed it does, with sports facilities, pubs, community centres, play areas and shopping precincts and a string quartet and public works of art and public woods and a church and houses designed by the Corporation architects, privately owned or rented from the Town. Do you think this is the way we ought to live? Perhaps we should and do as we are told.

Or do you prefer to live a country life with built-in urban joy? If you're in plastics or an account executive, handling quality consumer durables for the foreseeable future, New Ash Green, a neighbourhood unit development in Kent, is maybe what you need. The terrace houses with car courts, patios, and no loneliness can be obtained for about £6,000 each. A dream for some; for others *this* is home [we see tower blocks]: in Dockland, Germans bombed the little streets that had been homes for thousands. After that, partly to keep the rates up, partly to get as many as possible in a minimum space, out of this devastation slabs arose. Sometimes they called them towers and these replaced the liveliness of streets.

Now new high densities in open space: High Rise and Low Rise, towers and terraces. Planners did their best. Oh yes, they gave it all a lot of thought, putting in trees and keeping grassy rides and splendid views across to Richmond Park and landscaped streets and abstract sculptures – oh, Roehampton won the prize. It was all so well laid out. Just so much space from one block to the next. Perhaps this is the way we ought to live?

Where can be the heart that sends a family to the twentieth floor in such a slab as this?

> It can't be right, however fine the view
> Over to Greenwich and the Isle of Dogs.
> It can't be right, caged halfway up the sky,
> Not knowing your neighbour, frightened of the lift

And who'll be in it, and who's down below,
And are the children safe?

What is housing if it's not a home?

Thamesmead is to be built on Plumstead Marsh. Another town – how human will it be? New towns, new housing estates, new homes, new streets, new neighbours, new standards of living, new financial commitments, new jobs, new schools, new shops . . . new loneliness, new restlessness, new pressure, new tension . . . and people: people who have to cope with all this newness, people who cannot afford old irrelevancies, people who have to find a God who fits in.

A LAND FOR ALL SEASONS

Last in the thirteen-part series *Bird's Eye View* looking at Britain from a
    helicopter
BBC2 Television, 18 April 1971
Producer: John Bird
Series editor: Edward Mirzoeff

• • •

On yon unsheltered mountain height of Wales
The stalwart precipices free the gales,
While gathering clouds assume a threatening form
And valleys wait th'inevitable storm.
Under the winter's unrelenting sky
Caernarvonshire and Merioneth lie.
And few will think that there can ever be
An end to winter's reign of tyranny.
.   .   .   .

When snow and mist obscure the trees
And winter's grip is like a vice,
The farmer's ponds and buckets freeze,
Then he must up and break the ice,
And early in the morning rise
To bring his sheep their scant supplies.

Oh who would farm these barren slopes
When roads are blocked with drifting snows?
The farmer only lives on hopes
As through his wonted work he goes,
For all the yard is frozen mud
And not a sign of blade or bud.

The fleecy sheep are dirty grey
Beside the snow so white around,

But none so biddable as they
Now fodder hardly can be found.
So great their hunger scarce they hark
The shepherd dog's familiar bark.

. . . . . .

'Fled now the sullen murmurs of the North,
The splendid raiment of the Spring peeps forth;
Her universal green . . .'* No wildness fills
These long undancing rows of daffodils
In level Lincolnshire. Before they bloom
They will be gathered for an early tomb
In the deep freeze. Their resurrection day,
Will see them open miles and miles away
In florists' shops from Hull to Harringay.

. . . . . .

Ten thousand times ten thousand
At Spalding's annual show,
The regimented tulips
In ordered armies go.

. . . . . .

Upper Slaughter, Lower Slaughter,
In the Cotswold summer time,
For you and me, your son and daughter,
This familiar childhood rhyme.

. . . . . .

How often memory brings me
From Asthall up to Asthall Leigh.
The sound of cartwheels in the lane,
The smell of wallflowers after rain,
The River Windrush winding back
Upon itself, the grassy track
To Kitesbridge Farm, the family pew,
The gabled manor house, the yew,
The cottages, the village street,
The sheepdog panting in the heat.

. . . . . .

* From 'The Farmer's Boy' by Robert Bloomfield (1766–1823).

Where is the miner who tunnelled the hills,
The mother who milked the cow?
Sheep, sheep, nothing but sheep,
Never a shovel or plough.
Never an oven to bake the bread,
Never a family lately wed.
Sheep, sheep, nothing but sheep:
Where are the Welshmen now?

. . . . . .

Farewell to trees and hedges, man is free,
And in the coming season he will be
One of the millions racing to the sea.

. . . . . .

To Lancaster and Morecambe's annual show
Fatstock and fashion and the wrestlers go;
And here behold in simulated rage
Both Cumberland and Westmorland engage.
Famed Grasmere sports, they draw their thousands still
As athletes struggle up the craggy hill.

. . . . . .

We spray the fields and scatter★
    The poison on the ground
So that no wicked wild flowers
    Upon our farm be found.
We like whatever helps us
    To line our purse with pence;
The twenty-four-hour broiler-house
    And neat electric fence.

All concrete sheds around us,
    And Jaguars in the yard,
The telly lounge and deep-freeze
    Are ours from working hard.

★ This satire, based on the hymn 'We Plough the Fields and Scatter' by Matthias
Claudius (1714–1815), trans. J. M. Campbell (1817–78), was first published as a letter
in *The Farmers Weekly* and then as 'Harvest Hymn' in *High and Low* (1966).

We fire the fields for harvest,
   The hedges swell the flame,
The oak trees and the cottages
   From which our fathers came.
We give no compensation,
   The earth is ours today,
And if we lose on arable
   Then caravans* will pay.

All concrete sheds around us
   And Jaguars in the yard,
The telly lounge and deep-freeze
   Are ours from working hard.

   .   .   .   .   .

The sea is all cold and farewell to the sun,
The beaches are barren, the bathing is done,
Each holiday-maker has gone to his home
To varnish his dinghy and polish his chrome.
The winter's upon us, the countryman's dawn
With the pack and the field he will follow the horn.

* 'Bungalows' in the original.

REGIONS

SEASIDE RESORTS IN THE SOUTH AND SOUTH-WEST

Original title: 'Beside the Seaside'
Sixth in the thirteen-part series *Bird's Eye View*, looking at Britain from
  a helicopter
BBC2 Television, 25 December 1969
Producer and director: Edward Mirzoeff

• • •

> Oh, hear us when we cry to Thee,
> For those in peril on the sea.★
>
> They feared it most who knew it best,
> The sea that hits the rocky west.
> To merchantmen it might bring wealth,
> But it was dangerous to health.
> Far better live inland, and warm,
> Out of the perilous wind and storm,
> Safe from fresh air and suchlike harm
> In sheltered mansion, cot or farm.
>
> Quality sent its sons and daughters
> In search of health to inland waters.
> To Roman Bath or Cheltenham Spa,
> Where the Chalybeate fountains are.

To Cheltenham also came George III to be cured of biliousness,
until his physicians advised him to take the sea-bathing cure in
Dorset. So in July 1789 he went to Weymouth. It was then an unimportant fishing port, full of smugglers. The King stayed in a house

★ From the hymn 'Eternal Father, Strong to Save' by William Whiting (1825–78),
usually sung to 'Melita' by John B. Dykes (1823–76).

belonging to his brother, the Duke of Gloucester. A statue on the front commemorates his visit. 'God Save the King' on ribbons was hung on bathing machines, on the bonnets of the ladies, around the waists of the girls. Fanny Burney wrote, 'The King bathes, and with great success; a machine follows the Royal one into the sea, filled with fiddlers, who play "God Save the King" as His Majesty takes his plunge.'* The country rejoiced in the King's recovery. The sea was no longer unfashionable. Moreover it was healthy.

Where the monarch led, his subjects followed. To Lyme Regis, for instance, also in Dorset, came the genteel characters of Jane Austen's *Persuasion*. It was when jumping down on the Lower Cobb at Lyme – the Cobb is that stone wall that juts into the sea – that Louisa Musgrove, you will remember, sprained her ankle, closed her eyes and was taken by her companions to be lifeless. 'Rub her hands, rub her temples; here are salts, – take them, take them.'†

Grander folk went further west, to Sidmouth in south Devon. The Grand Duchess Helene of Russia set her double eagle there on Fortfield Terrace, whose cheerful stucco front looks on to a cricket ground and the cricket ground is swept by breezes from the English Channel. The wars against Napoleon stopped people going abroad – hence resorts like this.

Sidmouth is a sort of Cheltenham-on-Sea, the sea quite often as calm and gentle as the Thames. Behind that comely row of sunny lodgings, ornamental cottages were built, by men of means, out of sight of the water but within sound of the shingle shore. It was to Sidmouth that a younger brother of George IV came with his wife and infant daughter. He was the Duke of Kent. He despised the vulgarities of his brother's Brighton. He liked the country and the rock-strewn shore. One day in 1820 he got his feet wet here at Sidmouth, contracted pneumonia and died – there, in that ornamental cottage‡ he had built for himself, his wife and daughter, Princess Victoria. Could it have been her cradle memories of this

---

* From *The Diary of Fanny Burney*, entry for 8 July 1789.
† From *Persuasion* by Jane Austen (1775–1817), vol. 1, ch. 12.
‡ Woolbrook Cottage, now the Royal Glen Hotel.

southern shore that made Victoria, later England's Queen, build with her husband Albert, Prince Consort, this Italian palace – Osborne – on the English Channel? 'The dear Prince is constantly occupied in directing the many necessary improvements which are to be made,' wrote the young Queen Victoria in 1845.*

> It is impossible to imagine a prettier spot – valleys and woods which would be beautiful anywhere; but all this near the sea (the woods grow into the sea) is quite perfection; we have a charming beach quite to ourselves. The sea was so blue and calm that the Prince said it was like Naples. And then we can walk about anywhere by ourselves without being followed and mobbed. Drove down to the beach with my maids and went into the bathing machine, where I undressed and bathed in the sea (for the first time in my life), a very nice bathing woman attending me. I thought it delightful until I put my head under the water. And last not least, we have Portsmouth and Spithead so close at hand that we shall be able to watch what is going on, which will please the Navy.†

The Isle of Wight prospered. Ryde, so near to Osborne, grew in size. The whole island was fired by the royal example.

> Facing the Channel on the seaward side
> Rose Ventnor's lodging houses, tier on tier;
> The island's health resort in sunny pride
> By terraces descending to the pier.

The Royal National Hospital for Diseases of the Chest, built just west of Ventnor in 1868 – empty, now that they've found other cures for consumption. How many a pale face looked its last out of these windows? How many prayers were offered for sufferers? How many prayers were made by suffering patients? Echoes of weak coughs along deserted corridors. Empty.

---

* From a letter to Lord Melbourne on 31 July 1845, in *Letters of Queen Victoria*.
† Mostly from a letter to Lord Melbourne on 3 April 1845, in *Letters of Queen Victoria*. The reference to a bathing machine comes from a later letter, in 1847.

In a coign of the cliff between lowland and highland,
   At the sea-down's edge between windward and lee,
Walled round with rocks as an inland island
   The ghost of a garden fronts the sea.*

The sea as a cure for illness — 1868. In the next year the pier at Clevedon in Somerset was being built. The sea as a source of pleasure, for little steamer trips to Chepstow, Newport, Cardiff, Lynton and Lynmouth, Flat Holm and Steep Holm and other places of popular resort. At the opening ceremony they said, 'We believe it is the commencement of better times for our fair Clevedon.' It was. As the *Great Western Railway Guide Book* in 1884 said, 'An excellent esplanade faces the sea. Good beaches, gardens, shrubberies, and large modern villas built along the edges of the lofty sea-cliffs, with churches and chapels, public schools, lodging and boarding houses, hotels, dining rooms, public gardens and excellent shops.'

The sea as a source of pleasure. Steamer trips round the bay! These verses from long-forgotten songs remind me of the Victorian trippers' traditional fear of the sea:

Those horrible pistons, they make my heart thump
As the paddling wheels go round.
Are they churning the ocean up into a lump
Or will we all be drowned? Hey ho!
Or will we all be drowned?

·   ·   ·   ·   ·

Oh the paddle paddle steamer,
What a clever little schemer
That ever she inveigled me from shore.
Now I know I can't escape,
Perhaps we're sailing for the Cape
And I'll never see old England any more.
No more.

But if the truth be told, the man of wealth
Added some pleasure to his search for health.

---

* From 'A Forsaken Garden' by Algernon Swinburne (1837–1909).

Tropic Torquay overlooking historic Torbay: the balmy climate, the Palm Court Orchestra. This was the time of the holiday hotels with commanding names: Grand, Imperial, Majestic, Palace.

> Exclusive Bournemouth where the tide came twice
> And children played with children who were nice,
> Where parents dozed in after-luncheon ease
> And lovers longed to touch each other's knees.
> Hydraulic power delights the old and young.
> Steam traction! Let its praises now be sung.
> Steam down the valley, steam below the hill.
> The factories empty, lodging houses fill.
> The long expresses glided by the shore
> And towns grew where were never towns before.
> Compartments packed and holidays begun,
> It's Go Great Western to the coast and sun.

In fact it was the railways that made the mid-Victorian seaside resorts. On bank holidays they were crowded out.

> I want to take us off to somewhere where
> The sun shines brightly and the tourists tarry.
> Some people call it Weston-super-Mare
> And others call it Weston-super-Maré.
> Maré of course is Latin for 'the sea'
> And Maré is what here it's said to be.

> On this particular Whitsun, Weston's hey-day,
> Excursion trains arriving every minute,
> The town was cramm'd like rallies on a May Day,
> You wouldn't have thought more people could get in it.
> The roundabouts went round, the swings went swinging,
> The warm sea sparkled and the earth was singing.

> Yes, everything seemed paradise at Weston
> That Whitsun afternoon beside the sea.
> No one looked backward, everybody press'd on

To minerals and to ices and to tea.
Even the people walking on the pier
Were unaware of trouble waiting near.

How innocent and kindly was the funning,
All dedicated to the god of sport.
The driving and the diving and the running,
Fresh air and freedom – will they all be caught?
What thins the crowd, what darkens and what chills?
A mighty rainstorm from the Mendip Hills.

All put your macs on! Run for shelter fast!
Crouch where you like until it's fine again.
Holiday cheerfulness is unsurpassed,
Why be put out by healthy English rain?
Are we downhearted? No, we're happy still.
We came here to enjoy ourselves – *and* we will.

What's true of Weston's true of more than most,
No – *every* resort along the coast,
When everybody's feeling safe and warm,
Unheralded arrives the summer storm.
Those are the things the posters do not show,
Those are the headaches of the P.R.O.*

The model village shut and still it's raining;
Queues for the cafés and the sea-front's bleak.
Go to the pictures, then? I'm not complaining,
But didn't I see that film the other week?
As for our lodgings, we're in quite a fix,
They never want us back till after six.

Yet this is quite the friendliest place I've hit on,
The air's a tonic and the sea's a treat.
Of all the merry coast resorts of Britain

* Public-relations officer.

Its sunshine record would be hard to beat
Look on the bright side and we'll all feel better,
And if we're wet, well those out there are wetter.*

Escape – escape from the holiday crowds – over the Saltash Bridge.
Saltash Bridge by Isambard Kingdom Brunel, 1859: the first railway link between Cornwall and England. Not another county:
another country. For years, an all-day journey by train and a wild
reward at the end of it. No piers; no pierrots. With what delight did
late-Victorian artists bring their oils and watercolours to paint the
flaming gorse and amethystine sea.

> Have the rocks faith that thus they stand,
> Unmoved, a grim and stately band,
> And look like warriors tried and brave,
> Stern, silent, reckless o'er the wave?
> .   .   .   .   .   .
> Thy way, O God, is in the sea,
> Thy paths, where awful waters be;
> Thy spirit thrills the conscious stone:
> O Lord, Thy footsteps are not known!†

By train from suburbs of the big towns, by trap and wagonette, past
fern-stuffed hedges, from the oil-lit country station, schoolmasters
came with promising pupils, undergraduates on reading parties, doc-
tors with thin wives and freckled daughters. Lured by King Arthur
they came, Victorian romantics, to that holy island with its Celtic
cells and chapel – a sort of Lindisfarne of Cornwall: Tintagel.

> So all day long the noise of battle roll'd
> Among the mountains by the winter sea;
> Until King Arthur's table, man by man,
> Had fall'n in Lyonnesse about their Lord,
> King Arthur: then, because his wound was deep,
> The bold Sir Bedivere uplifted him,

---

* Refers to water skiers.
† From 'The Storm' by R. S. Hawker (1803–75).

> Sir Bedivere, the last of all his knights,
> And bore him to a chapel nigh the field,
> A broken chancel with a broken cross,
> That stood on a dark strait of barren land.
> On one side lay the Ocean, and on one
> Lay a great water.*

Cornwall is milder on its southern coast, which has a holy island too: St Michael's Mount. What Mont St Michel is to Brittany, this is to Cornwall. A monastic fort, later a fortress reached by a spit of land covered by water when the tide is high. Celtic saints came here and, later, Norman barons. Then King's men and Cromwell's men. Shrine, chapel, castle – later private house. A hundred years ago J. P. St Aubyn very well restored its outer walls and turrets. Victorians liked it. So do we, who gaze across its battlements today.

In best positions all along the coast rose the new castles of the newly rich. The well-appointed family hotels: the Headland, Newquay, 1891. Lifts to all floors. Electrically lit. Views of the sea from all the suites of rooms. The gaps between the large hotels were filled with boarding houses, tea places and shops, electric palaces and bright arcades.

Newquay became indeed the kind of place romantics avoided: Cornwall's holiday town. But once below the level of the cliff, and on the lovely beaches, what a wealth of rocks and sand and long Atlantic surf.

What people really came to Cornwall for was picturesque villages like this. That's Port Isaac.

Do you remember those Royal Academy paintings of King Edward's reign – sturdy fishermen pulling the lifeboat out, the Methodists on a Sunday after chapel, the red-cheeked fishergirl with sea-green eyes, the quayside chat, the widow in a whitewashed room, "A Hopeless Dawn",† an angry sea outside, the little climb-

---

* From 'Morte D'Arthur' by Alfred, Lord Tennyson (1809–92).
† A painting by Frank Bramley (1857–1915). Bought for the Tate Gallery by the Chantrey Bequest in 1888, it shows a young woman, whose husband is lost at sea, being comforted by her mother-in-law and her faith in God. The title comes from a line by John Ruskin (1819–1900).

ing lanes of slate-built cots, the wharves and sagging rooftops, the seaweed-slippery quay? Cornwall became an artists' paradise and the amateur photographer's as well. Those camera studies of weather-beaten skin, those sepia, slightly out-of-focus views of bollards on the quay . . . Posing for artists here in famed St Ives became quite an industry.

There's something in most of us that wants to be what we aren't: a Cornish fisherman, a Cornish boatbuilder or sailmaker. We wear navy-blue jerseys and sou'westers if we can. We want to be taken as natives. That's because we feel the need of solitude and roots. We listen guilelessly to sailors' yarns, oft told to tourists while the seagulls scream. The shrewd Cornish – independent, proud – cash in on the foreigners: and small blame to them.

Look at Polperro down there. Plenty of car parks on the way to the quay, and plenty of gift shops on the way to the car parks. It's economics, see. The Mermaid's Ditty Box, The Witch's Boutique, another car park and then Davy Jones's Diner with a nice smell of fish and chips. The Delinquent Piskey, home-made teas and Cornish clotted cream, and then we're at the harbour. There's not much money in fishing now. Ferrying visitors – there's that.

The Cornish have always been actors and singers – Henry Irving for one – so there's the literary side, and very popular it is with tourists on warm evenings. But bring your rugs and hot drinks just in case.

Minack Theatre, Porthcurno, rehearsing *The Thracian Horses*,[*] a witty comedy set in Classical Greece. I know no better-sited theatre.

> Nature has made the Minack Theatre famed.
> Let's go to Minehead and see Nature tamed.

'This is Radio Butlin's calling. The time is a quarter to twelve and lunch for first-sitting campers is available.'

---

[*] By the American playwright Maurice Valency (1903–96).

I floated over Butlin's between luncheon time and tea,
And wished that I was young again and as I used to be,
When anticipated pleasure was as boundless as the sea.

When Peter came from Peterborough, my goodness he was
    shy.
When Wendy came from Wendover she felt she'd like to
    cry.
But now they've formed a friendship that will lead to Lovers'
    Lane,
For they hold each other by the hand when travelling on the
    train.

Shirl and Sheila just are friends, for boys they do not care.
They tell each other secrets in the safety of the air,
Regardless of what's going on in chalets over there.

The twins inveigled Grandpa on the switchback by a trick,
But Grandpa had the laugh on them, for both the twins were
    sick.

'Hard luck, Norman! Never mind!
I think there's a consolation prize – Now next, all of you . . .'

Look at this competition. We've all come here to seek
The most cheerful, charming, chubby lass, Miss Venus of the
    week.
Which of them do you think it is? Then use your eyes and
    brains,
Miss Harringay, Miss Stoke-on-Trent, Miss Widnes or Miss
    Staines?

I'm glad I came to Butlin's. I hope you liked the fun.
There's some of it in all of us – or almost everyone.

We don't all want to be organised but if we aren't we seem to
sprawl everywhere. Look what's happened at Westward Ho!, north

Devon. We find a lovely bit of country and methodically we start to spoil it. It's not just true here, it's so along many miles of coast: too many, I'd say.

> Where yonder villa hogs the sea
> Was open cliff to you and me.
> The many-coloured caras★ fill
> The salty marsh to Shilla Mill
> And, foreground to the hanging wood,
> Are 'Toilets' where the cattle stood.
>
> . . . .
>
> Now, as we near the ocean roar,
> A smell of deep-fry haunts the shore.
> In pools beyond the reach of tide
> The Senior Service packets glide,
> And on the sand the surf-line lisps
> With wrappings of potato crisps.
> The breakers bring, with merry noise,
> Tribute of broken plastic toys
> And lichened spears of blackthorn glitter
> With harvest of the August litter.
>
> . . . .
>
> One day a tidal wave will break
> Before the breakfasters awake
> And sweep the caras out to sea,
> The oil, the tar, and you and me,
> And leave, in windy criss-cross motion,
> A waste of undulating ocean . . .†

Out there it's solitude: they can't build on the sea.

> 'They've taken our wind! Oh no, she's going about! Stand by
> to gybe! Ready about! Lee O! Starboard!'

★ Caravans.
† From Betjeman's poem 'The Delectable Duchy', first published in the *Cornish Review* in 1967 as 'One and All'. Some wording differs from the version later published in *A Nip in the Air* (1974).

Can the sea be solitude? No, it's being developed. [We see motor-boats racing across the water.]

> Hark to the song of the water hogs
> As they charge at us over the waves.
> Executive chases executive,
> Mercury, Volvo and Ford.
> 'Steady, old man, with the steering –
> Your company chairman's aboard!'
> 'The water's as still as a mill pond,
> We'll open it up like a flower,
> We'll drive and we'll thrust as competitors must
> And the prize of our driving is power.'

I'm glad that it's quiet again and I'm on foot. You know that sort of holy hush there is in the land on Christmas morning? The roads fairly empty, the sky almost free of aeroplanes, and you begin to hear and see and smell once more. The seaside can be like this if you find an unspoiled stretch of it like this one in north Cornwall. An enlightened landlord has saved this part; other bits have been saved by the National Trust and local authorities. The developers have taken more than their fair share of the coast. A third of it is already completely built up. We must keep the rest of it for the good of our souls.

George III took the seaside cure for biliousness; we need the seaside cure for relief from stress and tension. We need it to real-ise that there's something greater than ourselves – even if it only comes in little things: turf, scented with thyme and mushrooms, the feel of firm sand underfoot, the ripple of an incoming tide, a salt breeze, the smell of seaweed – that's where the cure is: at the sea's edge.

> And all the time the waves, the waves, the waves
> Chase, intersect and flatten on the sand
> As they have done for centuries, as they will
> For centuries to come, when not a soul
> Is left to picnic on the blazing rocks,

When seaside is forgotten. Still the tides,
Consolingly disastrous, will return
While the strange starfish, hugely magnified,
Waits in the jewelled basin of a pool.*

* This is a version of the last ten lines of Betjeman's poem 'Beside the Seaside' (opening line: 'Green Shutters, shut your shutters! Windyridge'), first published in the *Strand*, 1947. The lines 'When England is not England, when mankind / Has blown himself to pieces. Still the sea' has here been replaced by the single line 'When seaside is forgotten. Still the tides'.

THE HOME COUNTIES ON SUNDAY

The second of two films in the series *Thank God it's Sunday*
BBC1 Television, 17 December 1972
Producer and director: Jonathan Stedall

• • •

What do most Londoners do on Sunday? They leave it – most comfortably of all, of course, by rail from Fenchurch Street over brick arches. Who would want to stay behind in an inhuman slab of council flats, built in the priggish 1960s, when sea and country call? We leave by every means we can. Swift, swiftly eastwards through Stepney, Barking, Dagenham, Upminster. Electric railway, diesel, coach and bus. Car and motorbike, bypass and high road. Eastward and further east until the last brick is out of sight and then we see the wide, enormous marsh of Essex, London's nearest real countryside, and join the others speeding to Southend.

Hold on, what's that? A different sort of noise. And now we're in a different sort of train. We're travelling down Southend Pier by tram, for a mile and a third towards the coast of France. The longest pier in the world. Was it perhaps a mid-Victorian dream of bringing England close to France at last and getting there on foot? Or was it to build an elongated jetty for vessels making the Thames's mouth? At any rate, today upon the pier they sell a map that shows you where to find the different kinds of fish the estuary yields – and what's done with them.

Southward from Southend across the Thames you faintly see along the Kentish coast the oil refineries that work on Sunday. Give me Sunday here: sniffing the salt sea air and salt sea water, Sundays of patience waiting for a bite, Sunday the day when fathers push the pram, Sunday for lovers walking in the wind, Sunday for running to catch a lunchtime tram – and missing it. It doesn't matter here.

74

Time's of no consequence in kind Southend. An unpretentious, breezy, friendly place. I like Southend: East-London-on-the-Sea. Southend where Charlie Chaplin, as a child, saw the real sea and thought it was a wall of sky-blue water.

I can't like motor traffic on the Sunday struggle out of London, south through the Sussex Downs to the sea. Motor traffic. It smells nasty; it looks nasty. It's out of place in a human-scale village street. It's like a poisonous snake – a killer too. Not even a bit of nonsense like a nodding dog in the back window makes a motor car agreeable and driving a car makes the mildest man competitive and turns him into a fiend. All this for a first sight of the sea.

Early-morning Brighton waits in Sunday early-morning calm. Waits for the inflow of the human tide.

Seaside people are a friendly race because their job is looking after strangers and trying to make them happy – for a fee. I think that clever patron of the arts, the spendthrift Prince Regent, later George IV, with his pavilion, parties, mistresses, gave Brighton the cheerful smile that has never left its face. 'Old ocean's bauble' it once was called, and the name still suits it. It's a toyshop for London, open on Sunday – a place to lie back in and to look around and wonder who is who.

Of all the things this toyshop has to show, the favourite's the most dangerous toy of all: the English Channel. Oh, friendly and luxurious at the edge, delightful to the lazy and the tired. Look at it, breathe it, listen to it, but do not try to cross it. How comfortable the roar that rakes the shingle, the feel of rounded pebbles underfoot. The Brighton English Channel seems a friend.

And most people have come down for the day: swell bookies, shorthand typists, acrobats from Reigate, Purley Oaks and Thornton Heath. 'Old ocean's bauble!' Yes, indeed she is. Confectionery Brighton in the sun.

> Regardless of the sunlight on the sea,
> The businessman discusses stocks and shares.
> Regardless of the whisper of the waves,
> Ladies compare the prices at the sales.
> And some are old but still cling on to life,

> And some are young and wonder what it's for.
> For some this is the first time they've been down;
> For others, perhaps the last. For more and more,
> It's a first view of England and its coast.

I wonder what that lady used to do, so unattracted to the sleeping youth. [We see a close-up of an old lady sitting in a deckchair next to a young man.] A cook? A missionary? A woman don? And is she self-sufficient or afraid?

The joyous time of Sunday lunch is near: theirs is a set one in a private hotel. [We see a group of people walking up steps.] From this point we can survey the whole field of seaside sociology. Its 'income brackets' and that sort of jargon. These can't have come far in that uncomfortable position [we see a young couple on an easy-rider motorbike] or, if they've come from London, she must be absolutely mad about him. And all of us would rather go by bus [we see people in an open-top double-decker bus] than sit frustrated in a stuffy car, and all of us will want to view the sea.

What are the girlfriends talking of? Men or starfish? What the palmist said? Madam Gymkhana and her crystal ball? How different this than the bus to work – the 19, for instance, or the 22. A day of recreation and of rest. But oh, it is still travelling along.

On Sunday morning, Matins or Morning Prayer, the Mass or the Eucharist, whichever they like to call it, is over in Bosham Church. But still she paints [a lady watercolourist], forgetful of the time and food and other people. Absorbed in what she sees. She puts it down: happy, contented, quiet, competent.

Under those stones the local farmers lie. Their old brick houses mostly have been bought by businessmen who mess about with boats. The old church looks forlornly from the shore and a very curious thing it seems to see. What explanation can there be of this? [A man in a wetsuit launches a boat.] I wonder why that man is wearing tails.

That's going to leave a trail of misery behind it in the country lanes. [We see a boat trailer being pulled up the beach.] Those two rugged workers may well be retired admirals, such is the camaraderie of the sea. Just to anticipate any trouble:–

'Take a letter: from Wheelhouse Grange, Albatross Lane, Havant, to the Chairman of the Governors, BBC, London. Sir, I was disgusted to find the BBC had the effrontery to turn its cameras on to the private marine activities of the English coast and, what is more, on a Sunday morning when they should all have been in church. My aunt, who is not an expert oars-woman, was shown on the screen without her permission. My own picnic party, with my niece and daughter, was also filmed without permission, as was the party of my staff who were on holiday at Burnham-on-Crouch. How would you like to have the private moments of your family life shown to millions and commented on facetiously by a man with an unpronounce-able name? Is nothing sacred? There are many good sailors at the Yacht Club: why did you only select shots of incompetent amateurs? And why this emphasis on food and drink? Are you in the pay of the breweries, sir? What will foreigners think if this film is shown abroad as depicting the English way of life? Do we only live for pleasure? Surely on Sunday at least a rever-ent expression might have been shown somewhere. And I have one final and very serious complaint to make. The wife of my managing director kindly came down to the shore to meet me and your cameraman took the unpardonable liberty of filming her as she was getting ready for the bridge party to which we were going. Yours, etc.'

> A happy Sunday slowness haunts the Thames
> Between its Buckingham and Berkshire banks.
> The river of our contemplative youth,
> River for family parties, Cockney salts.
> Who with such skill can push the boat away
> And moor her safely into Boulters Lock?
> For Londoners are faithful to the Thames
> As the Thames has been to them for centuries.
> 'Sweet Thames run softly, till I end my song.'*
> So Spenser said it and we say it still.

* From 'Prothalamion' by Edmund Spenser (1552–99).

River and London mingle into one –
Riparian rights and lock-keepers and locks,
Sluices and weirs, punts and fishing permits.
Sweet Thames, the sliding wonder of our youth.

Fish on, fish on, until you find yourself
Or find yourself again, in years to come,
Alone among the strangers in the boat,
Or in the bosom of your family,
Who don't quite seem to know what they should do
With all those awkward bits of coiling rope.

Bear us along the river of our youth*
Into the long-remembered world of steam
Down here in Sussex, where from Sheffield Park
The Bluebell Railway runs to Horsted Keynes.
Here middle age remembers joys of youth,
And youth can share the joys of middle age.†
Deep down in Sussex listen for it here‡ –
The sound the poets hated makes by now
A melancholy music in the hills.

Whiter than the daisies are the flannels on the field. It's an heraldic
game, and cricket is the heraldry of Sussex.

And cricketers are large, large-hearted men
And boundaries are waiting to be saved.
(Thank God it isn't I who have to do it.)
I like to watch the calculated bowl,
The subtle curve along the cherished grass,
The hushed awaiting till the final kiss
Of wood on wood, directed from afar.

* A pleasure boat passes the camera.
† Little boys watch steam trains.
‡ The sound of a steam train.

Some Londoners most unwisely make for home,
Thinking they ought to make an early start.
Now we can take the dog out for a bark
And Alfriston becomes itself again
Under the shadow of the Sussex Downs.
If I may quote two lines of Thomas Gray
And leaving out the one that's in between:
'The lowing herd winds slowly o'er the lea
And leaves the world to darkness and to me ...'*

except for some late last Londoners who still savour the country
quiet. At half past six some villagers will go to Evensong. For
evening is a time when some of us are thinking of the evening of
our lives and of the vastness into which we go, or nothingness, or
of eternal bliss.

Whatever it is, for sure we've got to go
Alone, alone, and time will part us all,
And somehow, somewhere, waits the love of God.

Sunday is sad. But Monday's so much worse
For those of us who haven't any hope.
Faith, hope and charity. Oh, give me hope.

Her brief accomplishment is somewhere there,†
The painting that she did and tucked away.

The match is over, and the game they played
Was much more fun than work will be tomorrow.

Oh dear, oh dear, the agonies of youth.
Oh dear, oh dear, the trials of middle age.
But do they matter? There's the mystery.

---

* From 'Elegy Written in a Country Churchyard' by Thomas Gray (1716–71).
† The lady watercolourist walks home with her easel and her dog.

COUNTIES

BRISTOL

CLIFTON SUSPENSION BRIDGE

From the Shell series *Discovering Britain with John Betjeman*
Random Film Productions Ltd
ITV, 23 March 1956
Director: Peter Woosnam-Mills

• • •

Not enough people know how beautiful Bristol is. Here's Clifton, its hilltop suburb. Georgian crescents gaze across to Somerset hills. And by these Regency houses, be prepared for the splendid sight to be seen from their balconies. Get ready, round the corner and there it is – Clifton Suspension Bridge, crossing the Avon Gorge from the county of Bristol to the county of Somerset. It was designed by a young man of twenty-four in George IV's reign. He was Isambard Kingdom Brunel, the engineer of steamships and the Great Western Railway, and he died in 1859, five years before his great bridge was completed.

Those chains from which the bridge is hung come from London, where they supported a footbridge over the Thames at Charing Cross. Their ends are buried deep in the rocks on either side of the Gorge. In a strong wind the bridge sways like a ship at sea – a sign, incidentally, of its safety.

There are men at work here painting all the year round and heights mean absolutely nothing to them. I've seen these men walking along those two foot chains you see in the picture there, three hundred feet above the river and as unconcerned as if they were on a level piece of pavement on the ground.

The rocks of the Gorge are silvery white and interspersed with green woods and bushes. You can stand here for hours, watching the ships sail down the Avon with the tide, out to the Bristol Channel and the open sea.

People come here to admire the view. They like to watch the traffic buzzing along like children's toys, hundreds of feet below them.

But I prefer looking at the bridge itself. It stretches like a gigantic insect, delicately across the sky. From that dizzy height seventy years ago, a girl of twenty-four threw herself into the Avon. She was saved from death by the fashion of the times, for it was the age of wide skirts. As she floated gently down, her skirts billowed out into a parachute.*

I can never look at the Clifton Suspension Bridge without thinking of its great engineer: railwayman, bridge-builder, ship-designer, cigar-smoker – Isambard Kingdom Brunel.

Bristol and Clifton are 114 miles from London and 88 from Birmingham.

---

* Betjeman recounts a similar story in his film about Milton Abbey, p. 109.

BUCKINGHAMSHIRE

WEST WYCOMBE

From the Shell series *Discovering Britain with John Betjeman*
Random Film Productions Ltd
ITV, 25 November 1955
Director: Peter Woosnam-Mills

• • •

If there's a safe moment on the straight and hideous main road from High Wycombe to Oxford, look up at that extraordinary group on the hilltop. It was put there on purpose to terminate the view two hundred years ago and it's well worth climbing the hill to see, for here is the Mausoleum of the Dashwood family, who live in West Wycombe Park below.

And not only Dashwoods lie here. Do you see those square recesses? They contain urns intended for the hearts of members of the Hellfire Club, one of whose founders in about 1745 was young Sir Francis Dashwood. The Club was said to practise black magic and its steward was Paul Whitehead, a poet, whose heart was once in this urn.

After the wildness of youth, the penitence of age: Dashwood put in the Mausoleum these statues of his mother and his stepmother. And there's his own memorial. He was made a peer because, as he said, he was the worst Postmaster General in England.

Down the hill is the entrance to the caves where, disguised as monks, Dashwood and his wild and once famous friends celebrated the blasphemous rites of the black mass. There are a quarter of a mile of subterranean passages hollowed in the chalk, leading to damp and dripping halls, ghastly and cool.

I dare say the stories of the wickedness of the Club are exaggerated. They were young men of taste and wit. It's rather as though some young bloods today, with a few artists and poets, went off to wild parties at a country house; possibly no more than that.

People say they've seen ghosts of satanic monks here. Well, I've never seen one myself, though I must say I don't like the feeling of the caves.

The old church on the hilltop was greatly beautified inside by Sir Francis and on the top of the tower he built a golden ball. That devil Wilkes called it 'the best Globe Tavern I was ever in'* and Dashwood and his friends would sit and drink milk punch there, looking out over miles of chalky Chiltern hills and down to the dreaded tomb that one day must claim us all.

You can't miss West Wycombe, which is thirty-two miles from London. You see its Mausoleum and ball as soon as you leave High Wycombe on the Oxford Road.

* *The Public Advertiser*, 2 June 1763.

CHESHIRE

ADLINGTON HALL

From the Shell series *Discovering Britain with John Betjeman*
Random Film Productions Ltd
ITV, Spring 1956 (exact date unknown)
Director: Peter Woosnam-Mills

• • •

The main road from Manchester to London. On the right, the
Legh* Arms. The thunder of traffic. And half a mile to the left,
here's where the Leghs live: Adlington Hall, Cheshire: south front,
1757; pink brick and yellow sandstone.

But wait till you see through this arch to the older part of the
Leghs' house, in the courtyard. There it is, five hundred years
old: the Great Hall on the left. Inside, the Great Hall is dark with
woodwork and paintings. Do you see that long post in the middle
of the picture? That's the trunk of an oak tree that has been here
since 1315. It leans inwards from the prevailing north-west wind,
for it's a real tree and its roots are still in the ground. When they
built the hall round it in 1450, they carved it with an axe. Today
it leans towards the organ: Handel's organ, 1749. Handel is known
to have played this organ and he composed a hunting song for the
Legh of the time.

The Leghs have lived here for more than six hundred years and
they still do. They've painted the hall with the arms of families
who've married into them. The Leghs are Cheshire squires who
have quietly served their country and their county all these years,
producing no famous names but many good men. It's very English,
Adlington Hall.

Here's the Drawing Room and, characteristic of an English

* Pronounced 'Lee'.

87

manor house, it has much beautiful detail. This chandelier: 1751. And best of all, I think: the wood carving in pear wood. It probably really is by Grinling Gibbons. Look at this bird, coming in on the right, on its nest. And there's Ceres, over the door; and in a minute you'll see Neptune.

Well, I'll leave you looking at this carving and tell you where Adlington Hall is: it's five miles north of Macclesfield and fourteen from Manchester.

CORNWALL

BLISLAND*

From the first programme in the *Meeting Point* series, *John Betjeman's*
   ABC of Churches
A BBC West Region Film Unit production
BBC Television, 15 May 1960
Producer: Kenneth Savidge
Director: Dennis Towler

• • •

There's always a breeze on Bodmin Moor – and gorse and
heather and granite. Granite: hard and silvery grey. The
Cornish loved to carve it, as they did here on Jubilee Rock and
on signposts at the edge of the moor to the places in the wooded
valleys below.

People tell you inland Cornwell is dull. Don't you believe them:
but please keep this place we are going to a secret. It's hard to find
and it's so worth seeing when you're there on your own on a hot
summer day like the day I saw it.

Blisland with its cottages and its church on the edge of the
green. This granite farmhouse must once, I think, have been a
manor house. That chimney stack is something more than just for
a cottage. And what about those blocked-up windows and arches?
I think they must have been part of an old manor hall.

But the church: dedicated to St Protus and St Hyacinth. That's
why I've really come here. You wouldn't know from the outside
there was going to be anything special – but look at that gravestone.
It's to the memory of a rector who, at the beginning of this century,
gave all his money and knowledge and devotion to bringing back

---

* This part of the first programme in Betjeman's *ABC of Churches* was preceded by
Aldbourne, p. 255.

his church, here at Blisland, to what it must have looked like in the Middle Ages.

Now get ready for a surprise. See the outside – all rough, huge stone blocks of granite from the moor. And now wait: there's going to be a contrast. I turned first to the font, the door to the church. Here at Blisland its great cover reminds me that in the past, fonts were kept full of water and locked and only refilled once a year with fresh water.

And then I looked for the altar, to house which the church was built. Here at Blisland the altars are veiled by a rich screen of painted wood, partly made from the remains of an old screen and designed by F. C. Eden about fifty years ago. It stretches the whole width of the building, right across the three aisles.

Here at the South aisle we can walk right into the Chapel and from here we can look along the length of the East wall, past the high altar, to the Lady Chapel at the other end. And in the Lady Chapel F. C. Eden designed a reredos of carved alabaster, whose pink-and-amber-coloured stone contrasts with an old grey-slate monument of Elizabethan times.

And now look up: ribbed roofs like upturned fishing boats are all over the church. The richest of all of them, of course, is over the chancel. That has the best carving; and the plaster and wood-work are painted; and, according to Cornish custom, the angels are carved along the wall plates – and more modern cherubs over the high altar itself.

From where we are standing you can see back into the nave – the people's part of the church – and when they put in a pulpit here they wisely designed it in the Georgian style, to contrast with the rest of the building. Cornish passion-flowers and seashells carved by Lawrence Turner.

I think I like the look of this church best of all when it is being used – when, as here, you see human figures giving scale and purpose to the glorious decoration designed for the service of God. Blisland: a rich and unexpected shrine, deep in the heart of Bodmin Moor.*

---

* The programme continued with Crowcombe, p. 220.

DERBYSHIRE

BOLSOVER CASTLE

From the Shell series *Discovering Britain with John Betjeman*
Random Film Productions Ltd
ITV, Spring 1956 (exact date unknown)
Director: Peter Woosnam-Mills

• • •

In this part of Derbyshire, near Chesterfield, country roads suddenly end in coal mines. Bolsover Castle, which unexpectedly
appears on the horizon, is all the more dreamlike because of its black
industrial setting. When all the country round was woods and fields,
Charles Cavendish, a younger brother of the owner of Chatsworth,
built himself this semi-castle on the Norman ruins of an older
building. It was the first sham castle to be built in England.

Inside, it's a strange mixture of old and new. The walls and fireplaces look like an Elizabethan manor house and the stone-vaulted
roof is like a much older church, yet both were built at the same
time: 1612–16.

But it's William Cavendish, the son of Charles, who interests
me. He lived here too. He was a brave general, a poet and a famous
horseman, and he was the friend of Charles I.

That ceiling there is of pale blue with gold stars and he had it
copied from the Star Chamber in London where Judge Jeffreys tried
the enemies of the King.

Bolsover is empty now of people but full of ghosts. Most of all, I
think of the ghost of William Cavendish. He it was who built this
huge palace on to his father's house. Charles I showered titles on
him like rain – and there's his coat of arms, as Duke of Newcastle,
over the palace he built for receiving the great.

In this enormous hall he entertained the King to the biggest
feast that had ever been seen in England; but disaster came with

Cromwell. The loyal Duke fled abroad and his Duchess pawned her jewels to buy him food. Cromwell dismantled the castle; from the view-commanding terrace he took away the guns and defences. And when the King came into his own again and the Duke of Newcastle returned, he found Bolsover almost as desolate as it is today. Only the little castle his father had built remained intact. (There it is on the right.)

Bolsover is romantic three times over: for its history, for its beauty and for its position high in the air above the smoking coalfields of another age.

Bolsover is near Chesterfield and that's forty-six miles from Manchester and twelve from Sheffield.

HADDON HALL

From the Shell series *Discovering Britain with John Betjeman*
Random Film Productions Ltd
ITV, Spring 1956 (exact date unknown)
Director: Peter Woosnam-Mills

• • •

I like this part of Derbyshire: stone-walled and windswept. And here's Haddon Hall, the most lovable of all its great houses. On this side it's a fortress; on that, a Stuart manor house. Notice how unevenly the light is caught in the leaded panes. In this paved courtyard, you can see the steep slope. There are steps everywhere. Steps down to the Chapel, the oldest part of which is eight centuries old – as old as that Norman column on the right and the font below it.

But the Vernons were the people who built most of Haddon. They decorated these walls about four centuries ago in a style like the earliest printed books: in that stream [depicted on the wall] stands St Christopher, patron saint of travellers. In this Chapel, which is just as it was in Stuart times, lie the famous lovers John

Manners and his bride, Dorothy Vernon, the rich heiress. At this altar her sister was married on the day John Manners is said to have carried Dorothy away.

Up steps – always steps at Haddon – and here's the Drawing Room. Do have a look at its splendid plasterwork, put here in the seventeenth century by the Manners family, who've owned the Hall ever since.

Even more than the plasterwork, I like the view from the oriel window in this room. We're looking over the hills and dales of Derbyshire and its winding River Wye, spanned in the foreground by Dorothy Vernon's bridge.

The hooks that hang this tapestry back are original.

These steps – more steps – are made from a single oak. And here's the most beautiful room of all: the Long Gallery, built by Dorothy and John. The walls are of oak and carved walnut. The prevailing colour is silvery-grey, lit by gentle light through diamond panes. There's no need for me to say more: the Long Gallery speaks for itself.

Haddon Hall is forty miles from Manchester and sixty-three miles from Birmingham.

HARDWICK HALL

From the Shell series *Discovering Britain with John Betjeman*
Random Film Productions Ltd
ITV, Spring 1956 (exact date unknown)
Director: Peter Woosnam-Mills

• • •

Long Derbyshire lanes lead to the sudden strange vastness of an Elizabethan house: 'Hardwick Hall, more window than wall'* – a seat of the Duke of Devonshire. Do you see that 'ES' outlined

* Folk saying.

against the sky [in the four ornamental stone parapets on the roof]? It stands for 'Elizabeth Shrewsbury', called Bess of Hardwick: she built the house. And as we go upstairs to the principal rooms – in Elizabethan days the principal rooms were usually on the first floor – you'll see that Bess of Hardwick not only had a mania for building, she also had one for collecting tapestry and needlework. She collected four husbands, too, and each left her a fortune.

Bess and her last husband, Lord Shrewsbury, were made guardians of Mary, Queen of Scots; and perhaps it was this Queen who gave Bess a taste for French needlework. In the Gallery here, the tapestry is green and grey and dated 1574. And here's the High Great Presence Chamber: to me, the finest room in all England. That frieze along the top there isn't tapestry but plaster done in relief and painted and showing Venus and Diana and the gods. The tapestry below is Brussels: it shows the story of Ulysses. Let's look deep into it and see how, even when you get near enough to see the stitches, the figures stand out in high relief as though they were modelled.

The tapestry has been repaired with marvellous skill by the Dowager Duchess of Devonshire: she's worked on it for years [we see her in shot, working at the tapestry]. She found that the original blacks and browns of the backgrounds had often been dyed with rust and this had caused the thread to perish so that the backgrounds were more perished than the patterns. The Duchess replaced the warp with fine string or thread which she dyed, and since 1925 she's taught local people and others to help her in the work you can see her doing there.

There are more than a hundred pieces of tapestry at Hardwick and much of the work consists in fitting together again bits that had been cut up for patches.

Miles of delicate tapestry: that's one impression Hardwick leaves on you. The deep-green forests, the strange-shaped hills and animals and legends – all worked in the glowing dyes of Elizabethan fancy.

Hardwick Hall is near Chesterfield, which is forty-six miles from Manchester and sixty-five from Birmingham.

KEDLESTON HALL

From the Shell series *Discovering Britain with John Betjeman*
Random Film Productions Ltd
ITV, Spring 1956 (exact date unknown)
Director: Peter Woosnam-Mills

• • •

We are off* to admire the glory of the Curzon family. To make this park private, a main road was diverted by Act of Parliament; to leave this house on its own, a village† was swept away. These double steps, then, lead up to Kedleston Hall: rebuilt 1761 by Sir Nathaniel Curzon, first Lord Scarsdale; architect, James Paine.

Did I say James Paine? When this front was finished, he was out of fashion and Robert Adam was the coming man so Robert Adam designed this grand ceremonial marble hall for the Curzons of Kedleston. From this floor of Italian marble and Hoptonwood stone, see columns of Nottingham alabaster arise – red and cream – from the Curzons' own quarries. So skilfully are the pieces jointed together that the columns look like single blocks of stone. Such splendour had never been seen in this part of Derbyshire before; Dr Johnson said it looked like a town hall. Designs by George Richardson, the greatest plasterer of the day, decorate the ceiling. The marble chimney pieces and grates are all in keeping – and see, in the very midst of this one, where gods and goddesses of the ancient world stand gracefully, the arms of the first Lord Scarsdale, reminding us of the Curzons, who have lived at Kedleston for eight centuries.

Care has been taken over every detail. Look at this mahogany door: a keyhole would let in the draught, so cover up the keyhole with a face.

* Pronounced 'orf' by Betjeman.
† Kedleston.

And so to the State Drawing Room. The doorcases are of alabaster. Paintings by Veronese and Tintoretto hang on the walls. The crystals of the chandelier have that hint of blue in them peculiar to Waterford glass. This long sofa was designed for the room by Adam: its arms are mermen and they have dolphin tails for legs.

And even now you've only seen a tithe of the splendours of Kedleston Hall, which is four and a half miles north-west of Derby.

DEVON

SIDMOUTH

For the strand 'In the West Country with John Betjeman' in the series
  Wales and the West
ITV (TWW), 27 August 1962
Producer: Jim Douglas-Henry
Director: Jonathan Stedall

• • •

Thus Sidmouth looked a hundred years ago,
Still much the same it lies these hills below.
Still the old church tower rises in the trees;
But this quaint house's windows – what are these?
They're bits of church, saved from extermination
By the Victorians' so-called 'restoration'.

Still in the shadow of the tower repose,
'Neath handsome Georgian headstones, bones of those
Who built their mansions in this countryside,
Who came for health, bathed quietly here – and died.
Pause at this altar tomb where you can see,
Sculptured, the name of Mister Edward Lee.

And there's his house in 1823.
And here is it today. The change is small
Since George III was monarch of us all.

Mansions for admirals by the pebbly strand;
And cottages for maiden aunts inland
That go with tea and strawberries and cream.
Sweet sheltered gardens by the twisting stream:
Cob, thatch and fuchsia bells – a Devon dream.

Yon Gothic castle is the Royal Glen.
Princess Victoria, a baby then,
Played with her mother in this garden green;
And Sidmouth nurtured England's future Queen.

Why am I talking to this film in rhyme?
It suits the film, it suits the sunny clime,
It rolls with leisured ease these streets along,
It does to this verandah'd world belong.

Gothic or Classic, terrace or hotel,
Here does the backbone of Old England dwell:
Men who have served this country all their lives,
Mothers who smile to see their daughters wives!

From yonder balcony what eyes looked down
On some young lover strolling in the town?
And from this road what eyes have looked above
To yon bay window with this light of love?

Here with what happiness could I retire
And watch my own flame dying: love's young fire.

See, when the sun is at its noonday height,
Regency ironwork, elegant and light:
It stands out prim against the stucco's white.

Broad crescents basking in the summer sun,
A sense of sea and holidays begun,
Leisure to live and breathe and smell and look:
Unfold for me this seaside history book.

And when the architecture grows more slack
Among the little houses at the back,
Stucco recedes, Victorian bricks appear.
In Alma Terrace: shades of the Crimea!

Lunchtime is over, now the hour for rest;
And snores are gentle as the sun moves west.
In summer silence, bricks and blossoms swoon,
All on the drowsy Sidmouth afternoon.

Clocks in a hundred houses all chime three:
It's time to saunter to the town for tea,
To exercise the dog and have a chat
On this and this and this and that and that.

'Two and eleven? My goodness, what a price!
Now don't go there, dear; do take my advice.'
'Oh, everything is dearer now, I fear.
Do you find dear things so much dearer, dear?'

'Well I, you know, must think before I buy;
My pension's tiny and my rent is high.'
'Now wait two minutes, dear: wait while I shop
At Holmes's, here, and buy myself a chop.
You don't mind waiting? Well then, watch the meat;
I won't take long my purchase to complete.
Or go to Sellek's, just across the street;
I'll meet you there: I want to buy some paint.
I love these Sidmouth shopping streets: so quaint!'

'Oh, I must tell you, dear, you used to know
That corner cupboard where I like to show
My old Crown Derby? Well, it had to go.'

Ah, times must change and Sidmouth changes too;
If they did not, what *would* antique shops do?

'Since I have had to hold my purse strings tight,
Shop-window gazing is my chief delight.
Look, there's a real feature of the place:
That dear old shop that sells the Devon lace.
That dear old lady there is quite the same;

I'm getting old too − I forget her name.
It's time that I was going home to tea.
Come to the front, come dear, come there with me.'
'I'd simply love to: there's a glimpse of sea!'

And on the front, as Sidmouth teatime ends,
There's always such a chance of meeting friends.
'Uncle! − and Auntie Gladys! what a treat!'
'So this is Terence: doesn't he look sweet?
Well, weren't us lucky, all of us, to meet?'

As the waves thunder on the shingle shore,
'The wife and I lie back and have a snore.'
As the waves thunder on the shingle shore
I like to hear this pebbly backwash roar.
I lift my eyes to see the sunlight catch
Those Georgian cottages with roofs of thatch.

I like to stand upon the Esplanade
And look across to where some earthquake made,
Millions of years ago, those cliffs of red,
Bay beyond bay, from sandstone head to head;

Then to watch cricket on the fairest ground −
The scoring that excites all England round;
And although cricket bores me, here I find
The pleasant scenery helps to ease my mind.
Sun-smitten terrace, sound of ball on bat,
And in the quiet, the sudden cry: 'How's that!'
The keen sea air so keeps my brain awake
That even I can just some interest take.

And if on cricket I would turn my back,
To watch the wood go rolling to the jack,
Well here's the game that Devon used to play★
On Plymouth Ho!, four hundred years away.

★ Bowls.

Sunset and Sidmouth, sad, I say farewell
To your warm shallow vale where I would dwell,
Beyond that red, Edwardian hotel,
Pause on Peak Hill, look eastward to the town,
Then to the Connaught Gardens wander down
And in the shelter of its tropic bowers
I see its bright and outsize Devon flowers.

Farewell, seductive Sidmouth by the Sea –
Older and more exclusive than Torquay:
Sidmouth in Devon, you're the town for me!

NORTHLEW

From 'Northlew to Swindon'
For the strand 'In the West Country with John Betjeman' in the series
  Wales and the West
ITV (TWW), 17 September 1962
Producer: Jim Douglas-Henry
Director: Jonathan Stedall

• • •

Traffic changes everything – except cows, which never take any notice of traffic: wise creatures. Traffic changes everything. Let's go back, in this remote part of Devon, to the age before railways, to the time of carts.

Where are these old lanes leading? Each comes a cart's distance from some farm or hamlet to one secret hidden village. They're all leading to Northlew,★ which was once marked quite big on the old maps of Devon.

It's a very hard place to find, this once more-important place.

★ Betjeman spells this 'North Lew' in his script.

In fact you can only discover it with the aid of a one-inch map and somebody sitting beside you in the car to read it. Is it all deserted? No. But we don't want too many strangers' feet on these old causeways.

Northlew was once a marketplace to which all the many local lanes led, and like all old English marketplaces it has a market cross – there on the left – and like all market crosses, the cross is near the parish church. And Northlew Church is full of that carved woodwork that is characteristic of that age of faith in Devon when farms prospered and wool sold well and men gave their best – because everyone believed that Christ was God – to the grandest building in the parish: the church.

You can easily imagine the inside of this church as it was in the fifteenth century, the last time it was extensively rebuilt: the windows full of red, yellow and silver stained glass, twinkling lights on the several altars, the smell of trodden yew boughs rising from the floor and the carved pews filled with people whose only dwellings were cobbed-walled thatched hovels in loneliest Devon, with its white magic and mysterious silence. What did they know of the Reformation, when a visitor from as near as Okehampton or Hatherleigh was an event to be talked of for a week.

Northlew was once very nearly a town. First round that market cross, and then there wasn't much room afterwards for the market and it spread out into the square. Imagine that space filled with stalls and sheep pens. There are still rings in the village where ponies and cobs were tethered and it's still quite full on a fair day. Imagine the rich Devonian gossip that must have gone on round this parish pump.

Why is Northlew so deserted today? – for you can see it was once quite an important place. There's a Georgian shop front in what is now a private house. Bull's eyes or stationery? What was sold there? Could you buy *Doidge's Annual*, with its folding colour plates of Dartmoor and tales in Devon dialect? And in that upper window did they display crinolines and lace curtains or agricultural implements? Did toffee melt in the Devon sun amid groceries in this window? Here is quite a sizeable house that a farmer built for himself near the square so as to be on the spot for fair days:

early Victorian, I should think from the look of it, and well proportioned. Oh, and chapels too: they were mostly built in the last
century, when Northlew went on growing. One for Billy Bray, the
Bible Christian revivalist from Cornwall. [We see a chapel with an
inscription to William Bray.]

I don't say Northlew is decayed now; it just stays put, in comfortable peace. [We see a butcher in his apron, standing in his doorway,
enjoying the sun and the view.]

Some people would say that the coming of the railway ruined
Northlew. The London and South-Western opened a line in the
1890s from Okehampton to Launceston. Traffic changes everything. Steam power displaced horses and drained the trade away.
[We hear the sound of trains.] Listen to the warning note in the
valley, two miles away [a sign points to Ashbury Station and Bratton
Clovelly]: the note that emptied the market square.*

* The programme continued with an examination of Swindon (p. 258), which
Betjeman felt had much in common with Northlew.

DORSET

SHERBORNE

For the strand 'In the West Country with John Betjeman' in the series
 Wales and the West
ITV (TWW), 10 September 1962
Producer: Jim Douglas-Henry
Director: Jonathan Stedall

• • •

Sherborne lies in the Dorset hills in the valley of the Yeo, an
abbey town of golden ironstone: an abbey whose inside is a
surprise, a miracle of proportion carved out of a Norman fabric
and finished in 1490. And that stone reredos I've always liked: it's
Victorian. From the nave your eye runs down the fan-vaulted
roof and rests at its richest part over the choir and sanctuary. The
stalls of the monks survive, with medieval wooden carvings –
learning, work and concentration, and whipping – for here, on
this carved monk's stall, is the truth about Sherborne: it's a town
of schools.

Let's go and visit them. There's been a boys' school since Saxon
times and one of the more ridiculous school songs (it isn't sung any
more now) has these words:

When King Alfred was at Sherborne, he was just like you and me,
   He started at the bottom of the school.
He learned his Latin grammar and he learned his rule of three
   And he sometimes played the fool.

   Chorus
   So face life cheerily, as Alfred did of old,
   And if you're feeling gloomy, recollect

He went through it all before, and enjoyed it, what is more,
So what can you expect?*

What you don't expect in an English public school is such pleasant
old buildings. That's the part of the school refounded by Edward
VI in 1550, after the monastery of Sherborne had been dissolved. In
the monastic school was taught St Stephen Harding, who founded
the Cistercian order. And those are the old Abbey buildings, now
part of the school: the abbot's hall, now the school chapel; and on
the right the war memorial steps, built in keeping with the Abbey.
A Norman undercroft where you can read the school notices. And
though, thank goodness, I'm not a new boy any more at his first
term at a boarding school, sick with apprehension and longing to
be back at home, yet I don't see how I could fail to be impressed
by these brown ironstone buildings and to have been given a deep
subconscious sense of history at the most impressionable time of my
life, had I been to school at Sherborne.

Dark passages. Mouldering walls. Senior boys who seem as old
as one's father. Rules about where you can walk and where you
can't. And then what pleasure to move out into the narrow lanes
of this old-fashioned town, free at last to visit the shops, to walk
with friends, talking about the prospects for the next house-match,
makes of cars, perhaps even to notice architecture for the first time
– the public conduit at the bottom of Cheap Street where the monks
used to wash. Then to walk up Cheap Street in the soft Dorset air of
a summertime – exams over and peace of the heart – and to notice
the Georgian bay windows above the shops: that one, over the
Internationalist. Sherborne: town of schools, bookshops, antique
shops, tea shops, sports shops. It looks like a junior university city,
with every other house an old college. The merry whirr of the
dentist's drill on someone else's teeth. And here, at the top of the
town, we'll leave the boys.

So far you've only seen one of the nine schools of Sherborne. I
want to show you something more, as we start out from this bookshop.

* Betjeman quoted another part of this song in a review of light verse in the *New
Statesman and Nation*, 16 December 1939 (*Tennis Whites and Teacakes*, p. 176).

You see those girls?* Well, they shouldn't be wearing their school uniforms in the town: it's against the rules. They're pupils of Sherborne School for Girls. They should be wearing summer dresses when they go into town: it's a boarding school, you see. Uphill in the north of Sherborne are handsome Georgian houses, some of them owned by schools for the overflow and for staff. Let's follow our friends past these Dorset cottages, some of them converted into houses to which schoolmasters and schoolmistresses have retired, unable to tear themselves away from the town of beautiful youth and high-built pavements.

And there's the fine Edwardian tower of Sherborne School for Girls, surveying in golden stone its green playing fields and Celtic hills. Are these senior girls? And will they be caught, our three friends – reprimanded for being wrongly dressed in the town? No! No one has noticed.

Long Street, Sherborne. These are some more schoolgirls, from Lord Digby's School,† and I'd like you to see the eastern part of the town with them as they walk. The Red House – Georgian red brick – and brick is rare in this stone town. Seventeenth-century cottages – and you will notice the girls are wearing their uniforms: they're allowed to because it's a day school, Lord Digby's.

After those cottages, typical of much of Sherborne, here's the school itself. It now lives in this splendid eighteenth-century mansion of the Portman family, who used it as a halfway home between their Somerset and Dorset properties. Now notice those stairs and particularly those treads: they're in inlaid wood – the crest of the Portmans in walnut and sycamore. And when we get to the top of the stairs there's another surprise: the whole of the wall of the staircase hall was painted by Sir James Thornhill, who painted the inside

---

* The camera, which has been tracking three schoolboys, now furtively tracks three schoolgirls. It recalls Betjeman saying, in his film 'A Poet in London' (1959), 'Unfortunately I can't keep sex out of my poems. It would be hypocritical for me to do so. Everywhere you go . . . you can't get away from the beauty of the gels.' (See p. 151.)

† Dorset County Council leased the building in 1931 and offered it to Lord Digby's School the following year. The school remained there until its closure in 1992.

of the dome of St Paul's Cathedral in London. He was Hogarth's father-in-law.

In the art school at Lord Digby's, I'd like you to look at the picture this girl is painting: it's our farewell to Sherborne, the town of youth and the town of age. That picture is of the Almshouse of St John the Baptist and St John the Evangelist. It's still there, near the entrance to Sherborne Abbey and it's been there for five hundred years. It was founded by King Henry VI for twelve local men and for four local women and here they live with their memories of the Dorset of Thomas Hardy: 'Rime Intrinsica, Fontmell Magna, Sturminster Newton and Melbury Bubb'*. And there the screen divides the dining hall from the chapel; and here's the Prior, elected by the brethren, who's ringing the bell. The treasure of the chapel is the Flemish triptych of the fourteenth century. Sherborne bells for life's early morning. A bell for the sunset.

MILTON ABBEY

Original title: 'One Thousand Years at Milton – from Milton Abbey'
BBC1 Television (West Region), 3 March 1965
Producer: Kenneth Savidge

• • •

Three abbeys there are in Dorset: the Saxons founded Wimborne; then Sherborne; and the third one is Milton, round the corner here in a remote valley with no town near it like the others but, unlike the first two, just a park and a big country house.

You know what Dorset's like, don't you? Great big downs with junipers on them and hummocks and earthworks raised at the dawn of history.

* Betjeman here quotes the first line of his poem 'Dorset', itself an homage to Thomas Hardy's longer poem 'Friends Beyond'.

> Round about me bulged the barrows
> As before, in antique silence – immemorial funeral pyres –
> Where the sleek herds trampled daily the remains of flint-tipt arrows
> Mid the thyme and chamomiles.*

Once there was a bare down up here in this wood and a fort on it, something like the ones you have seen, and here a young Saxon king, Athelstan, grandson of Alfred the Great, had a vision that he would beat his enemies, the Danes.

The earthwork is still there, hardly visible today in the trees, and Athelstan *did* beat the Danes, at the Battle of Brunenburgh, and came back and gave thanks to God by building a chapel on the site where he had had the vision. That was a thousand years ago and there is still a chapel today, though it is Norman, as you can see from that South door.

And a flight of steep grass steps leads down from St Catherine's Chapel on the hilltop to the place where Athelstan founded an abbey and buried his mother's bones in it.

The Abbey, as you see it today, isn't of course the Saxon one that Athelstan founded. There was a Norman abbey here that was destroyed by lightning in 1309 and rebuilt after its destruction by Abbot Middleton.

And as you look at this sun-kissed flint and golden hamstone and at the flying buttresses and the long, tall windows, you will realise that this Abbey was rebuilt by the Benedictine monks, who lived in it in the fourteenth and fifteenth centuries, in the Perpendicular style. And if you want to see what sort of building Athelstan intended, then you must come inside.

There it is: there's some fourteenth-century artist's recollection of the *old* abbey with its three spires; and there's King Athelstan holding it.

Here we're standing at the entrance to the choir and the oldest part is up there at the East end of Milton Abbey and the reredos with all its niches. And my word! That's a real medieval wooden tabernacle for holding the Blessed Sacrament. It was a hanging

* From 'The Revisitation' by Thomas Hardy (1840–1928).

tabernacle and there is only one other such surviving from those days and that is in Wells Cathedral – and if you want to know what this East end probably looked like, here's old Sir Ninian Comper's drawing of what the East end looked like when that tabernacle hung in what was its probable original position.

Come through now and look at the great South window of the South transept, filled with good Victorian glass by Hardman from Pugin's design. The monks had this transept built and its richest vaulting is here under the bell tower but before they were able to build a nave, the Reformation came. A cunning Cornish lawyer called Sir John Tregonwell (that's his brass in the Abbey: you can see he was Cornish, incidentally, by the choughs on his arms) fixed up Henry VIII's divorce from Catherine of Aragon, and the Abbey and its lands were his reward. There was a little kiddie of his, who fell from the roof of the Abbey but wasn't killed because his skirts acted as a parachute.*

The next people to own the Abbey were some Swedes called Bancks – and that's their tomb.

And now come across to what is probably the most remarkable tomb in the Abbey, the tomb of a much maligned man: Joseph Damer, Lord Milton, later the first – and last – Earl of Dorchester. He is looking at his wife, who died in 1775.

You remember at the beginning we noticed that there was no town here: just the Abbey and a great house. Why is there no town? There was one in the Middle Ages: a flourishing town of considerable importance outside the Abbey here, with four inns, a grammar school, an almshouse and a brewery. The Abbey was its parish church and it stood on this site stretching down the valley. There is nothing left of it except a bit of stone in the grass there. That was where the old market cross stood – and this one cottage glimpsed through the trees: that gives you some idea of what it must have been

---

* Sir John Tregonwell's grandson, not his son, fell from the roof of the Abbey and his skirt apparently billowed out and broke his fall. A memorial tablet in the Lady Chapel recalls this with thanksgiving. It reads, '[He] gave in his will all the books within the vestry to the Abbey Church in thankful remembrance of God's wonderful mercy by his preservation when he fell from the top of this church.' He died years later on 20 January 1680.

like. But the plan suggests that it was a town of some size and this drawing shows you an imaginary reconstruction of it. But in 1780 all that was swept away by this man, Joseph Damer, Lord Milton. He gave each of the townspeople a new house and a bit of land. There's the village he built as it used to be in the early nineteenth century* and there it is when chestnuts grew between the pairs of cottages.

And that's the village today. He gave them a church and an almshouse and he sunk a well for them. He packed off the boys to a new grammar school in Blandford because they were always robbing his gardens. Milton Abbas was probably one of the very first model villages: the Welwyn Garden City of its day.

Now why did Lord Milton do all this: pull down a perfectly good medieval town and move it out of sight around the corner? Some people will tell you it was because it offended him having the town right next door to his house – that it spoiled the view. I don't think that's anything like a good enough explanation and, what's more, I don't think it does justice to Lord Milton. He was a patron of art and it's to him that we owe the surviving beauty of Milton Abbey.

Now Lord Milton, like many other eighteenth-century gentlemen, had been on the Grand Tour of Europe. He liked pictures, particularly the pictures of Claude and Poussin, and he saw that here at Milton Abbey, at the confluence of three valleys, there was a wonderful opportunity of doing what was considered frightfully good taste in those days: to make the view from your windows look like the scenes represented in the pictures on your walls. He saw that Milton Abbey could be made to look like a Claude if only those tiresome old cottagers and townspeople lived somewhere else. And I'm sure that's why he moved the whole town out of sight.

But before we look at the house, there's something I must tell you. If you had been an eighteenth-century earl and you wanted to make your wide domains look like a romantic Italian landscape, who would you have employed to lay them out? Well of course, this man Lancelot Brown, called Capability Brown. It was he who designed Milton Abbas village, climbing up the hill. (There's the

---

* We see an old postcard with a view of the village.

sort of garden he made.) And at Milton he saw the landscape possibilities. He planted the hills with trees so that they looked like promontories coming down to a lake. Of course, he must have a lake (and one appears in this view). But the disadvantage was that there was no water in this chalky part of Dorset, and the lake soon subsided and flooded the rest of the town.

Of course, Lord Milton went to the most eminent man in the profession for the new house he was to build beside the Abbey. That architect was Sir William Chambers, a Swedish knight – correct, haughty and Classical: he designed Somerset House in London. But he had his gay moments and was interested in gardening and the Orient: he designed the Pagoda at Kew. Chambers's problem was this: at Milton, Lord Milton wanted a Gothic house to blend with the Abbey. Chambers detested Gothic, so he designed a Georgian Classical house of beautiful proportions, in lavender-coloured ash, and he gave it Gothic details. Inside, it was all Classical. Chambers also detested Lord Milton, who, he said, treated him as though he were a footman. So, having finished the exterior, he left, having only designed a few ceilings and fireplaces inside the house.

Chambers very much disliked his rising rivals, the brothers Robert and James Adam, so he recommended a young architect who was improvident, unpunctual, amiable and a bit of a genius. This was James Wyatt, who had already designed, in the manner of the brothers Adam, Heveningham Hall, Suffolk. He designed Dodington House and Church near Bristol★ and Beckford's amazing Gothick abbey at Fonthill.

Let's go in and see what he made of the inside of Lord Milton's house, who by now had become Lord Dorchester.

This is the Ante-Room to the Saloon. Look at its frieze and domed ceiling and see how the frieze is repeated over the doors. And now let's go through into the Saloon. After you!

Let's have a symphony of Wyatt's exquisite plaster, marble and painted details over different parts of the house. I'll keep quiet while you look at Wyatt.

★ The Dodington estate, including St Mary's Church, has since 2001 been in the possession of James Dyson.

[We now see the Saloon ceiling in wide shot and detail, the Saloon frieze motif, the Ante-Room door, the sphinx frieze, various music motifs, a pilaster and pilaster detail, the fireplace and detail, the Portrait Room ceiling in wide shot and detail, the Portrait Room fireplace in wide shot and detail, the Library ceiling, Library mouldings, three medallions on the Lecture Room fireplace, the Lecture Room ceiling again, the Lecture Room frieze, a fireplace from Room 54, details of fireplaces in Rooms 101 and 100, and a wide shot and detail of the fireplace back in the Saloon. All of this is accompanied by Albinoni's Oboe Concerto in D Major.]

Here we are, back in the Saloon again. Lord Dorchester died and in 1856 a Danish banker, Baron Hambro, bought the house and this is how its Saloon looked when the Abbey was the Hambros' private house. Here is Baron Hambro's tomb in the Abbey. His descendants continued to live here until just before the war. His descendants lived to entertain King Edward VII and then the Abbey became a home for the sick, and now it is a school. This room, which used to be a chapel, is now the Dining Hall. It is part of the original buildings of the Abbey and was built in 1498. Look at that roof and carved beams. Aren't they pretty! Weren't they clever, those old medieval people! Although in the eighteenth century they were supposed to despise the Gothic, yet all owners of Milton respected it and Lord Dorchester, in the height of the Classical fashion, preserved the Abbey and this Hall in which we stand as part of his house.

Just think back over the owners and occupiers of this house and think of the way they've all left their mark. King Athelstan. Abbot Middleton. Tregonwell. Lord Dorchester. Baron Hambro. All these and other people in a thousand years have been abbots or lords of the manor at Milton Abbey.*

---

* Betjeman then introduced the headmaster of Milton Abbey School, who was asked three questions: 1. 'In a way, you are the logical successor of all the lords, squires and abbots who have ever lived at Milton for over a thousand years. Do you have any sense of continuity with them and of inheriting a particular tradition?' 2. 'We've seen that everyone who's lived in this house has had some influence on the Abbey. What influence do you think this school is having?' 3. 'What about the boys? Do they have any feeling of living close to a thousand years of history? Do they like the place?' His answers are not recorded.

Worship has gone on in this abbey for over a thousand years and despite changes in the music and the liturgy, there are some parts of the service that wouldn't be completely foreign to King Athelstan and Abbot Middleton. Let's go into the Abbey to hear the boys sing part of a setting of the Sanctus and Benedictus composed by the Milton Abbey School's music master.*

CHAPLAIN (*at altar facing west*): Lift up your hearts.

EVERYONE: We lift them up unto the Lord.

CHAPLAIN: Let us give thanks unto our Lord God.

EVERYONE: It is meet and right to do so.

CHAPLAIN (*turns east*): It is very meet, right and our bounden duty that we should at all times and in all places give thanks unto Thee, O Lord, holy Father, almighty, everlasting God. Therefore with angels and archangels, and with all the company of heaven, we laud and magnify Thy glorious name, evermore praising Thee and saying:

EVERYONE: Holy, holy, holy, Lord God of Hosts. Heaven and earth are full of Thy glory. Glory be to Thee, O Lord most high. Amen. Blessed is he that cometh in the name of the Lord. Hosanna in the highest.

* Trevor Doar.

ESSEX

BRADWELL-JUXTA-MARE*

From the Shell series *Discovering Britain with John Betjeman*
Random Film Productions Ltd
ITV, 4 November 1955
Director: Peter Woosnam-Mills

• • •

Here in this flat far-eastern part of Essex, a spit of land runs beside the River Blackwater out into the cold North Sea. It's a lonely place, the end of everywhere, with wide skies and roads that take sudden sharp turns by white-wood cottages till they reach the village church of Bradwell-juxta-Mare.

Here in the reign of George III the Revd Bate Dudley was made rector. He found the usual old English rectory: there it is on the left of the picture; and on the right is the stately Georgian house you see added to it. It's not really a big house but it seems big because it's so elegant in proportion and detail. That urn, for instance: notice how well placed it is beside this Venetian window; and this domed entrance hall, in white and Wedgwood blue. (I like the pattern of the fanlight reflected on the wall above.)

The house must have seemed a palace to the Rector's Essex neighbours. Why did he build himself so fine a place? Well, I suppose he had the money, for he was a rector and not a vicar and so he owned the tithes; but chiefly I think he wanted to remind himself of London and the fashionable world. He wrote comic operas for Covent Garden and Drury Lane. And here, on the windswept Essex

---

* This film was made in the wake of Betjeman's opposition to plans to build a twin Magnox reactor nuclear power station at Bradwell. Objections were unsuccessful and construction started in December 1957. Bradwell is currently being decommissioned, having become, in 2002, the first UK nuclear power station to be shut down. It had operated for only forty years.

marshes, he made himself a house that he thought would be worthy of his famous friends.

Robert Adam designed some of the decoration; Gainsborough painted the Rector and his wife in this house; and Mrs Siddons, the actress, came to stay here. The best artists of the day were used to paint Classical figures on plaster ceilings and inlaid plaster chimney pieces. Here in the drawing room, the most London-like apartment for many windy miles, Parson Dudley talked of literature and sport and duelling; and possibly, as he warmed his toes before the fire, he remembered the day when he killed his fox on the roof of Cricksea* Church, ten miles away. (In those days, fox hunting and culture weren't always separated.) But what he was like as a rector, the Lord only knows. Today, Tom Driberg[†] and his wife live in the house and keep up its atmosphere of hospitality and Georgian calm.

Bradwell is ten miles from Burnham-on-Crouch and forty-four from London.

STISTED MILL

From the Shell series *Discovering Britain with John Betjeman*
Random Film Productions Ltd
ITV, 18 November 1955
Director: Peter Woosnam-Mills

• • •

Roads like streams through elms and willows. This is Essex, a land of wooden watermills where, since Domesday, trout-filled brooks have pushed the dripping wheel; where still today – as

* Once Crixea, now better known as Creeksea, immediately west of Burnham-on-Crouch. (Betjeman seems to say 'Chicksea'.)
† Thomas Driberg (1905–76) was a famously rakish Labour Party MP (later Baron Bradwell) and a close friend of Betjeman's at Oxford. Throughout his life, Betjeman sought his advice about his poetry.

here at Stisted★ – you may find corn being ground in the old way. Listen to that noise: it's the same sound that Chaucer heard when he wrote *The Canterbury Tales* – the sound of water harnessed into power.

D'you see that sack in the miller's lorry? The millwheel provides the power that is hoisting it up to the top floor of the mill. Up here it's white with meal dust. The miller receives the unground corn and the huge, cumbrous and simple wooden machinery turns it into flour. Wooden cogs clack into wooden cogs as this great post, the main driving shaft of the mill, is turned by the waterwheel below. Stones weighing a ton each grind the corn in that barrel-shaped thing at the bottom of the picture. The hopper on the left holds the corn and shakes it out, to be crushed between the turning stones below.

Let's go and look at the millstone: it's of specially hard stone got from France. After grinding seventy or eighty tons, the surface is roughened with this formidable pick, called a 'thrift'. The flour runs out through the wide grooves on the stone and then the stone-ground flour is weighed in these huge and ancient-looking scales.

I can't leave Stisted without quoting a bit of Tennyson:

> I loved the brimming wave that swam
>   Thro' quiet meadows round the mill,
> The sleepy pool above the dam,
>   The pool beneath it never still,
> The meal-sacks on the whiten'd floor,
>   The dark round of the dripping wheel,
> The very air about the door
>   Made misty with the floating meal.†

You mayn't be able to get into Stisted Mill but you can see its outside and you can hear it. Stisted is in the Blackwater valley two and a half miles east of Braintree, which is forty-one miles from London.

★ First syllable rhymes with 'eye'.
† From 'The Miller's Daughter' by Alfred, Lord Tennyson (1809–92).

GLOUCESTERSHIRE
EASTLEACH TURVILLE

From the Shell series *Discovering Britain with John Betjeman*
Random Film Productions Ltd
ITV, 28 October 1955
Director: Peter Woosnam-Mills

• • •

In the Cotswolds, many main roads like this are dull: not a house in sight, hardly a tree. You can't believe any villages are near. Even the signposts seem to be telling lies: look at this one – 'Eastleach Martin'. [We see an old-fashioned, black-and-white wooden signpost at a crossroads that points to Barrington, Shilton, Filkins and Eastleach Martin.] It leads to my favourite Cotswold village. I'm not going to tell you how to get to it, 'cos it's a secret place and you have to be clever enough to use a large-scale map to find it. It's between Burford and Fairford, I will tell you that much, and the road suddenly descends into a wooded valley.

And here, from Eastleach Martin churchyard, you can look across to Eastleach Turville, which also has its own church.

The way to look at a village is to get out of your motor car and walk – and this place is full of beautiful footpaths. Let's cross from Eastleach Martin by a stone footbridge into Turville. (I like going slowly and stopping to stare.)

This fresh, clear, weedy water will soon join the Thames at Lechlade, which is really Leech-lade and takes its name from the River Leech. As you walk up the village street, the old cottages look as if they've been there since William the Conqueror's day, though they're probably not more than two hundred years old. The tradition of cottage-building in the Cotswolds has been passed down to the present day, so that these buildings seem ageless.

The Cotswolds are a country of dry walls, always built like this, and if you give them a hard enough push at the top, they'll fall over.

I always like to look at the post office to see what's going on in the village and I always buy the local postcards in case there's something I haven't visited. I notice today that they don't use the elaborate adjectives they used to: they don't call whist drives 'grand' any more; perhaps it's getting old-fashioned.

I said walking was the best way to look at a village and one of my favourite walks here is to Turville Church, which stands there with its saddle-back tower and has so stood for more than four hundred years. Baptisms, marriages and burials have been going on here, and in all these Cotswold villages, for centuries – to the sound of water, to the lumber of cartwheels, to the swish of cows' tails as they flick off the flies and drink the crystal River Leech.

If you can find the Eastleaches from Burford, well, Burford is seventy-four miles west from London and fifty-five south of Birmingham.

FAIRFORD

Original title: 'The Stained Glass at Fairford'
Arts Council Film
Made the by Realist Film Unit
ITV, Spring 1956 (exact date unknown)
Producer and director: Basil Wright

• • •

Fairford is a small country town in Gloucestershire. The River Coln flows through it from the Cotswold Hills to the Thames. The glory of the town is the church and the glory of the church is its famous stained-glass windows.

Stone. Honey-coloured Cotswold stone has been carved here for centuries. This statue of the risen Christ on Fairford Church tower is a thousand years old.

When people go into country churchyards they often forget to look at the splendid tombs of Queen Anne and Georgian times. Those around Fairford Church commemorate the sheep farmers and wool merchants who made the town prosperous in the days before the machinery of the North killed the Cotswold cloth trade.

Probably the sculptors of these table tombs and headstones were the sons, grandsons and great-grandsons of the masons who worked on the church in medieval days.

The older sculptors delighted to entertain with the figures they carved. Some of them may be portraits of bygone Fairford townsmen; other figures are designed to instil the fear of hell.

But people sculpted these figures to the glory of God rather than to their own glory and names were remembered in prayer instead of being carved in stone as they were down here in the churchyard.

Before we go into the church, take one last look at its outside. It was all rebuilt in the reign of Henry VII in the English Perpendicular style. It's a late and unusual example of it – I suppose the date's about 1497: a monument to its rebuilder, John Thame,* the richest local wool merchant, who lies here with his wife and asks us, in the lettering underneath it, to pray for his soul:

ffor Jhus love pray for me   I may not praye   nowe pray ye.
with A pater noster & an ave   That my paynys relessyd may be

(For Jesu's love, pray for me: I may not pray   now pray ye
With a pasternoster and an ave,   That my pains released may be.)

John Thame and his son Edmund after him rebuilt Fairford Church as a lantern for the windows.

Fairford glass is right at the end of the story of stained glass in the Middle Ages. There's a lot of white in it; and yellow, produced by silver. It's not like the earlier glass, which was all dark rich reds

* Or 'Tame'.

and blues and heavy leading. It's full of little pictures and details, such as you wouldn't see with the naked eye if you were standing on the floor of the church.

By the time the artists were at work on Fairford they were as interested in detail as in general effect. Here are some of these almost invisible details: birds flying round a fortified manor house, birds flying from a castle tower, a church tower (can it be Gloucester Cathedral?), a river scene with swans in the foreground, reed mace growing in the River Coln, and here the river again – and boating.

The inside of the church in the Perpendicular style of these times. And a lady in a smart fifteenth-century hat carrying a pair of doves in a cage. A cook's ladle held by a man looking out of a window and wearing a leather hat with the ears of the animal on it from which the hat was made. Soldiers in mail pressing in to look at an execution. Gideon in sixteenth-century armour kneels in anxious prayer. Around his neck are gold chains and his red shirt has a gold fringe.

The whole purpose of the Fairford windows is that they're a complete scheme for teaching the Christian faith. Their teaching is from the Scriptures and ever since they were put up, people have come to them for instruction, not just to admire their beauty.

The scheme of the windows is the order of the Bible. It starts in the Garden of Eden, goes on through the life of Christ and his mother to the Church after the Resurrection, and it ends with the Judgement that awaits us all.

In Fairford Church there happens to be this Matthew Bible of 1551 – earlier than the Authorised Version from which we're going to read:

> And the Lord God planted a garden eastward in Eden; and there he put the man whom he had formed . . . And the Lord God commanded the man, saying, Of every tree of the garden thou mayest freely eat: but of the tree of the knowledge of good and evil, thou shalt not eat of it. (Genesis 2:8–17)

Here are some of the leaves of the trees in the Garden of Eden, and this is the fruit of the tree of the knowledge of good and evil: apples, not oranges, although they look like them:

And [the serpent] said unto the woman, Yea, hath God said ye shall not eat of every tree of the garden? And the woman said unto the serpent, We may eat of the fruit of the trees of the garden: but of the fruit of the tree that is in the midst of the garden, God hath said, Ye shall not eat of it, neither shall ye touch it, lest ye die. And the serpent said unto the woman, Ye shall not surely die: for God doth know that in the day ye eat thereof, then your eyes shall be opened, and ye shall be as gods, knowing good and evil. (Genesis 3:1–5)

You can see on her face how Eve is tempted and how attracted she is by the apple held out by the serpent.

And when the woman saw that the tree was good for food, and that it was pleasant to the eyes, and a tree to be desired to make one wise, she took of the fruit thereof, and did eat, and gave also unto her husband with her; and he did eat. (Genesis 3:6)

Many of the pictures you are seeing will have black lines of leading across them or be worn away in places. The Fairford windows weren't damaged by Puritans but nearly five centuries of Gloucestershire wind and rain have cracked and weathered them like this so that only the colour survives. Many of the Old Testament scenes are obliterated so we'll go straight to the New Testament.

Here is the background to the Nativity. Through those arches you can see a park – perhaps Fairford park, which is near the church. In the right-hand arch a smart groom is standing, holding a horse.

Now when Jesus was born in Bethlehem of Judæa in the days of Herod the king, behold, there came wise men from the east to Jerusalem, saying, Where is he that is born King of the Jews? for we have seen his star in the east, and are come to worship him ... And when they were come into the house, they saw the young child with Mary his mother, and fell down, and worshipped him: and when they had opened their treasures, they presented unto him gifts; gold, and frankincense, and myrrh ... And when they were departed, behold, the Angel of the Lord appeareth to Joseph in a dream, saying, Arise, and take the young child and his mother, and flee into Egypt ... for Herod will seek the young child to destroy him. (Matthew 2:1–13)

There's the mother of our Lord, sitting on the grass, and on the left is the ass that has carried her, grazing the grass. Mary has our Lord sitting in her lap and she is offering him a date to eat.

> And [the two disciples] brought the colt to Jesus, and cast their garments on him, and he sat upon him. And many spread their garments in the way: and others cut down branches off the trees, and strewed them in the way. And they that went before, and they that followed, cried, saying Hosanna; Blessed is he that cometh in the name of the Lord. (Mark 11:7–9)

After the triumph of Palm Sunday, the humiliation of the Passion. A servant pours water into a basin for Pilate to wash his hands.

> When Pilate saw that he could prevail nothing, but that rather a tumult was made, he took water, and washed his hands before the multitude, saying, I am innocent of the blood of this just person: see ye to it. (Matthew 27:24)

Here Pilate and the High Priest are looking down on our Lord being scourged, and the soldiers are mocking as they stand round the scourged body. We can follow, all along this window, the walk up to Calvary: our Lord carrying his Cross and walking with bare feet on a stony path. Hanging from his girdle are pieces of wood, iron spikes in them to pierce and bruise his legs.

And there on the right we see the two thieves being led up to Calvary; and on the hill of Calvary, men are digging a hole for the third cross. In the centre light of the East window is our Lord on the Cross, his two feet pierced with a single nail. This man has a spear, which he is thrusting into the body of God: what were his thoughts when he did so? All the spectators – the enemies of Jesus – are mounted on horseback, while above them, in the heavens, angels weep.

> And they that passed by railed on him, wagging their heads, and saying, Ah, thou that destroyest the temple, and buildest it in three days, save thyself, and come down from the cross. (Mark 15:29–30)

But the friends of God have no horses: St John, the mother of God and Mary Magdalene.

And when Joseph had taken the body, he wrapped it in a clean linen cloth, and laid it in his own new tomb . . . And there was Mary Magdalene, and the other Mary, sitting over against the sepulchre. (Matthew 27: 59–61)

After the victory of the Cross, angels came and drew back the powers of evil. They descended into hell to preach to the spirits imprisoned. But in hell there is one soul looking out in despair because he has not been released and his torment is everlasting.

After the Crucifixion, the Blessed Virgin is supposed to have returned to her house and prayed for her son to come and see her – which he did, bearing the banner of victory in one hand and the wound prints in the other. This belief does not appear in the Bible but it is a very old one in the Church. When he first visited his mother, he then visited others.

And the angel answered and said unto the woman, Fear not ye: for I know that ye seek Jesus, which was crucified. He is not here: for he is risen, as he said . . . And they departed quickly from the sepulchre with fear and great joy . . . And . . . behold, Jesus met them, saying, All hail. And they came and held him by the feet, and worshipped him. (Matthew 28:5–9)

Here are the Apostles looking up at the Ascension. They are gathered round the base of a stone mountain which is narrow as a pillar, whose top has a grassy cap. Above it our Lord's feet can be seen, sticking out of the bottom of his garments, as he vanishes into the clouds.

And when the day of Pentecost was fully come, they were all with one accord in one place. And suddenly there came a sound from heaven as of a rushing mighty wind . . . And they were all filled with the Holy Ghost. (Acts 2:1–4)

After death, the Judgement.

For the trumpet shall sound, and the dead shall be raised incorruptible, and we shall be changed. (1 Corinthians 15:52)

The Archangel Michael is holding a balance in his hands for weighing souls, and his face is peculiarly sweet, almost feminine. A demon on the left is trying to weigh down the souls but their good deeds keep the scales tipped against the devil's advocate.

> So shall it be at the end of the world: the angels shall come forth, and sever the wicked from among the just, and shall cast them into the furnace of fire: there shall be wailing and gnashing of teeth. (Matthew 13:49–50)

A beautiful woman is being carried off to hell on the shoulders of a blue fiend. The creature pauses on the threshold, resting on his pitchfork, and glares into the everlasting fire. With scaly tail, dark against the sky, and the spiky backbone of a dragon, this red-faced fiend is thrusting into hell a woman who never thought she was going there. You can see the wheels of the cart which carries her, behind this horned demon. See impaled on spikes the damned, a dog-faced fiend with cruel snout in charge.

> And if thy hand offend thee, cut it off: it is better for thee to enter into life maimed, than having two hands to go into hell, into the fire that never shall be quenched: where their worm dieth not, and the fire is not quenched. (Mark 9:43–4)

Into the mouth of hell they swim, a hell with many heads: and there shall be wailing and gnashing of teeth.

> And he shall send his angels with a great sound of a trumpet, and they shall gather together His elect from the four winds, from one end of heaven to the other. (Matthew 24:31)
> There is joy in the presence of the angels of God over one sinner that repenteth. (Luke 15:10)
> He shall give his angels charge over thee, to keep thee in all thy ways. (Psalm 91:11)

.   .   .   .   .   .

> Hail Mary, full of grace. The Lord is with thee. Blessed art thou amongst women, and blessed is the fruit of thy womb, Jesus. (The Hail Mary, based on Luke 1:28–31)
> Blessed is the man that endureth temptation: for when he is tried, he shall receive the crown of life, which the Lord hath promised to them that love him. (James 1:12)

HAMPSHIRE

MINSTEAD*

From Programme 5 in the series *Meeting Point: John Betjeman's ABC of Churches*
A BBC West Region Film Unit production
BBC Television, 5 April 1964
Producer: Kenneth Savidge

• • •

M for Minstead in Hampshire, in the New Forest, with its ponies, forest roads, oak trees and there in a clearing of the forest, standing on a knoll a little way apart from the village, is the church of All Saints. It's completely unrestored outside. The core of the building is thirteenth century, to which has been added in 1774 that Georgian brick tower replacing an earlier thirteenth-century one. Brick and wood: materials from the forest in a county where there is little stone.

The exterior is like a series of cottages or like a badly drawn picture by a pavement artist or a picture in an early Victorian or Georgian child's book.

Before we go in, notice the headstones in the churchyard, all of different shapes – one over there is of wood, which is not very usual – and over on the other side of the church, the grave of Sir Arthur Conan Doyle, who lived in these parts for many years and whose book *The White Company* is set in this part of Hampshire.

Let's go nearer and have a look at the porch. The porch is dated 1683 and those initials up there, 'REM' and 'SCM', are probably the initials of churchwardens at the time. And the reason for putting up this porch is to shelter this fine stone doorway – built, oh, I suppose, about 1200 and a good example of what's called Transitional style:

---

* The text that follows is a draft script by Betjeman.

that is, between Norman and Early English. And now for the inside of the church itself. Ready?

Homely, cottagey, again like a bad drawing from some child's book — timbered with uneven plaster: a perfect example of how our churches looked in pre-Tractarian times. It's really a caravan adapted to Christian worship.

And notice that great oak three-decker pulpit. The idea was this: in this lowest deck the parish clerk read the service; in the middle deck the lessons were read; and the top deck was reserved for preaching. And in this picture you can see what a church like this would have looked like with a congregation in it. You know, it was all very practical. From this top deck the preacher could be seen and heard from practically anywhere in the church. Nobody was very far away from him. The people in that South aisle for instance: that aisle was built in 1790 for the Comptons who lived at Minstead Manor and it was added to in 1825 — and you can see where the box pews stop and the heavy Victorian work begins. And then the preacher could look back down the aisle and up to two splendid galleries, one on top of the other, built about the same time as the tower, with wooden benches and hat pegs for hanging beaver hats on, the top gallery known as the 'Gypsies' Gallery'.

And then coming down again we pass two family pews, the first one belonging to Lord Congleton, who lives at Minstead Abbey, and then over here in the chancel the family pew of Malwood Castle, now the home of the Southern Electricity Board, who light our ancient churches so beautifully! A family pew is really a sort of ecclesiastical opera box. You had your own private entrance to it from the outside: you didn't have to come in with the common herd. Inside it was very plush and often, like this one, with a fireplace. And when the sermon was particularly boring, as I expect they often were, your attention wandered away from the preacher and you'd gaze idly through the window to the oaks and parks of the forest where this church began.

WINCHESTER CATHEDRAL

Cathedral Crisis Appeal
Draft script (not broadcast)
BBC1 Television

• • •

[The broadcast is to begin with the sound of choirboys singing.]

> Dull would he be of soul who could pass by
> A sight so touching in its majesty.*

Well might the visitor who enters Winchester Cathedral echo
Wordsworth's lines as he gazes at the magnificent prospect of the
long nave and beyond it the choir and altar screen.

Winchester Cathedral was founded in 1079. Would you think,
listening to the wonderful sound of 'Carols at Christmas 1966',†
that this ancient building was in danger? Too easy, perhaps, to take
for granted a building as solid and established as this, in the ancient
capital of England.

Let's face facts. This vast roof is supported on twenty-four columns. Recently they discovered a crack running the whole height
of one of them. On examination, seven more were found cracked
or defective, representing a grave danger. A subsidence, which was
partly arrested at the beginning of this century, has remained a
threat and cracks have appeared in the South buttresses supporting
the nave.

This is a serious problem and when one considers this danger
one thinks of the priceless historical relics that are sheltered here:
Mary Tudor's chair (1554): she was married here to Philip of Spain;
William of Wykeham's tomb: the founder of Winchester College;

---

* From 'Lines Composed upon Westminster Bridge, September 3, 1802' by William
Wordsworth (1770–1850).
† A BBC television programme.

Isaak Walton's window: a window dedicated to Isaak Walton by the fishermen of many lands; the high altar screen, the beautiful fifteenth-century altar screen, destroyed and defaced at the Reformation and lately reconstructed and preserved; the Chapel of the Holy Sepulchre, with these medieval paintings at present being uncovered in its walls and roof.

This great heritage must be preserved for future generations. The baptismal font of the twelfth century with scenes from the legend of St Nicholas, the saint associated in our minds with Christmas: I'd like to feel that this font will be used to baptise children here for many, many centuries to come.

This is our responsibility. The preservation of this Cathedral ultimately depends on you and me and, with six days to go before Christmas, I would ask you to include Winchester Cathedral in your thoughts and send a Christmas present in memory of St Nicholas for the restoration of this great building.

I would ask you to consider: is this only an ancient monument or a museum piece – a relic of past days that we should allow to crumble to dust? Or is it a living portent for the future, a symbol of the ineradicable faith, hope and aspiration of man?

Will you think seriously about this and send me whatever you can afford? Send it to me at the Cathedral: John Betjeman, The Cathedral, Winchester, Hants. Thank you.

WINCHESTER CATHEDRAL

Cathedral Crisis Appeal
Broadcast script
BBC1 Television, 18 December 1966

• • •

You know the English cathedrals are I suppose the most beautiful series of buildings in Europe; and one of them, one of the best, Winchester, is in a very bad way at the moment. Now, when they asked me to make this appeal I said, 'Now, it's no use having my face and voice. What you must do is show people the building itself. Even if they know it, they'd like to be reminded of it.' So come and look at Winchester.

You remember the old city. Red Georgian brick, flint, chalk and those trout-full streams of Hampshire. And then the long, low Cathedral – the longest cathedral in England. Outside it's rather plain and quiet and, like everything in England, the surprise is when you get inside, then look.

Look at that mighty stone-vaulted arch. It's over the nave of Winchester Cathedral and it was built for this purpose: to shelter the pilgrims who came to Winchester to the shrines of St Swithun and St Berinus, which were right down at the end there beyond the high altar (and it was a very holy pilgrimage in England in the Middle Ages to go there).

And this nave you're looking at was built six hundred years ago by William of Wykeham, a Winchester man. There he is in his miniature cathedral within the Cathedral. You know, if Harold had won the Battle of Hastings, Winchester would have been more important than Westminster and Canterbury rolled into one. It would have been the capital of England. As it was, the Normans were determined to assert themselves. This Norman font of Tournai marble is a very splendid thing from France* and if you want to know what a Norman church looked like, well, there's a complete one in the cathedral paintings and all, in the Church of the Holy Sepulchre.†

In those days, England and France were one – part of Christendom. Round arches the Normans specialised in, and do you see that round arch there in the foreground beyond it – the much later, late-medieval nave roof that's over the tower crossing? And you see here the screen? That screen is there in order to shelter the choir so that the daily offices of the Church can go on, as they have done for over a thousand years, undisturbed.

* Tournai is in fact in Belgium.
† Also known as the Chapel of the Holy Sepulchre.

Let's come in and join the choir. They're preparing for Christmas, singing a Christmas hymn, and those stalls they're sitting in right to the back – to the right and to the left – they're the oldest choir stalls in England. They go right back to 1300. And look at that reredos behind the high altar of stone: I think the carving on it, which is Victorian, is very fine and just right for the Christmas hymn.

Now you heard the choir singing specially for you and you saw the masons at work keeping Winchester Cathedral standing. And that work of singing and prayer and building has been going on at Winchester for well over a thousand years, and now we've got to find £400,000 to keep it going; and I know it's the squeeze and I know we're all feeling poor, but so beautiful a building and such work we must keep, and I think you can do it best by sending anything, however small. You've been kind enough to listen to this broadcast: send anything to me and it doesn't matter how you spell my name: John Betjeman, the Cathedral, Winchester, Hampshire. Thank you so much. I know you are going to help.

KENT

FAIRFIELD CHURCH, ROMNEY MARSH

From the Shell series *Discovering Britain with John Betjeman*
Random Film Productions Ltd
ITV, Spring 1956 (exact date unknown)
Director: Peter Woosnam-Mills

• • •

Romney Marsh, on the Sussex border of Kent and close to the sea. Romney Marsh, where the roads wind like streams through pasture and the sky is always three-quarters of the landscape. The sounds I associate with Romney Marsh are the bleating of innumerable sheep and the whistle of the sea wind in old willow trees. The sea has given a colour to this district: it has spotted with silver the oak posts and rails; it gives the grass and the rushes a grey salty look and turns the red bricks and tiles of Fairfield Church a saffron yellow.

For a moment, when you see Fairfield Church there on the skyline, you think it must be a farm or a barn. There's no road to it – only a footbridge and a path. And in the church, you feel you're on an island in the marsh.

Inside, it's like walking underneath an upturned ship. (Those great beams are made of Kentish oak.) The communion rails go round three sides of the altar as they used to in many churches two hundred years ago; and since in those days, just as much as now, people were literate, they hired a local inn-sign painter to paint, in yellowish-gold letters on a black background, the Creed, the Lord's Prayer and the Ten Commandments.

The church is still kept up and used, though it's miles from anywhere, and that's what gives it atmosphere.

Another thing that endears Fairfield Church to me is that it's been spared electric light and the surgical basins in the roof that go with it. How pleasant those Victorian oil lamps are and how well they fit in with the scene.

Let's go into one of the high, white box pews. And sitting here in the quiet waste of marsh, islanded by grass in water, let's think ourselves back two hundred years. The place can't have looked very different. The parson read the service from that lower desk where the candle is, he climbed to the pulpit to preach, and if you found yourself not attending to the sermon, there was always a text to remind you of where you were and of the reverence due to this loved and lonely house of God.

Fairfield Church: it's about ten miles from Tenterden in Kent and therefore sixty-three miles south-east of London.

MEREWORTH CASTLE

From the Shell series *Discovering Britain with John Betjeman*
Random Film Productions Ltd
ITV, Spring 1956 (exact date unknown)
Director: Peter Woosnam-Mills

• • •

Kent is the most English-looking of our counties: hops and oast houses for beer, orchards, and timber-framed houses with old tiled roofs. How surprising it is, then, suddenly to see in it, not far from the main London-to-Maidstone road, an Italian villa – called Mereworth* Castle, built in the reign of George I. There's a little formal garden and then, all round, the undulating wildness of Kent.

As you come in at the front door, you can't help looking up,

---

* Pronounced 'Merryworth'.

however preoccupied you are. And under the great domed hall, we seem to be in a miniature St Paul's Cathedral.

The rooms are rich beyond all dreaming. Here in the Dining Room, the walls are tapestry: the chief colours are brown, red and green. They were made for the room 230 years ago but you can look into the richness anywhere and find greater richness still in the detail.

There were no fireplaces in Italian villas so Colen Campbell, the Scottish architect who designed Mereworth, put each fireplace very ingeniously across the corner; and look how he decorated this one: the wood is white and the figures are gilt.

But the finest room of all is this: the Great Drawing Room, which stretches down all one side of the house. What I like to do here is to lie on my back on the floor and imagine myself in a gondola, floating down under this carved and painted Italian sky. The frames around those goddesses on the ceiling are plaster, painted black and green and white and stippled here and there to look like gold mosaic.

But that which you see in the cove of the ceiling: do you think that's carved plaster? It isn't. It's painted flat on the wall and shadowed to seem as if it stands out in three dimensions. The sudden touches of brightness weren't fixed by us with electric light: they were painted like that on the wall by an English artist two centuries ago.

Just notice how that door is related to the height of a human figure. That's what makes it a great building: it doesn't dwarf us, it lifts us up and turns us into kings.

To find Mereworth from London, you only have to travel thirty miles. Go down the Maidstone Road* and turn right beyond the bottom of Wrotham† Hill.

* The A25.
† The road south of Wrotham Heath is Seven Mile Lane.

THE WEALD OF KENT

Original title: 'A Journey into the Weald of Kent'
The second film in the National Benzole series *Our National Heritage*
Random Film Productions Ltd
BBC Television, 26 June 1960
Director: Peter Woosnam-Mills

• • •

South-east London. Here's one of those blocks that used to be called 'industrial dwellings for artisans', built cheaply about a century ago. South-east London: it was bombed thoroughly and cruelly by Hitler and is still in want of repair. It's a place of small shops and friendly people. There's a different feel about it from the rest of London. Perhaps this is because it was originally in Kent and the name of the county is still remembered.

Along the Old Kent Road, thousands of Londoners go to the seaside every year. If only they turned off the main road for a moment, they could explore the Weald of Kent, which is that valley country you see at the foot of Wrotham★ Hill. It's really the centre of Kent and the reason why the county is sometimes called 'The Garden of England'.

Spring is a good time to start to explore the Weald. Spring – when the hop poles are bare and the young hops scarcely discernible against the brown earth, unless you stop and look closely. Now is the time to go down by-ways slowly. What looks so ordinary as you travel along this Kentish lane has much to show if only you're allowed to stop and get out and look. Even the commonest wildflowers shine. The Kentish poet Edmund Blunden well described this time of year down here:

★ Pronounced 'Rootem'.

134

When the young year is sweetest,
When the year is a symphony
Of sounds and sights and seeings.*

In spring, the middle of the Weald is bright for miles with apple blossom. The Weald of Kent itself runs through the centre of the county from Cowden† on the Sussex border east to Ashford. Oast houses, mills and roads, which wind like streams between the orchards. They don't call them orchards in Kent: they call them gardens – and the same goes for cherries and hop fields. Perhaps it's because you had to pay the parson tithe on a field or orchard but not on a garden. Here in Marden, cherries bloom at the end of April and are harvested in June.

Let's go and look at Smarden, another village deep in this district of nuts and hops, apples and cherries. There it is – and it's in a part where stone was hard to get. Stone was only used for the church, the most important building in the parish; the houses are mostly of timber, for that was plentiful. In Georgian times, they covered the old walls with weatherboarding like this, to keep out the wind and rain.

Smarden seems to have looked after its old cottages and repaired them instead of letting them fall down, as usually happens in villages. Because of this, we can trace the history of the place in its houses. It was once a prosperous centre of the cloth trade, which was the chief industry of Kent in the fifteenth century and later; and there, I suspect, is the house of the Tudor cloth merchant, who drew attention to his success by having this carving done on the bressumer of his gable. There are other such carvings in the village. And although the houses of Smarden have often been converted to other purposes than those for which they were built – this one, for instance [we see a half-timbered house which may now be a shop] – the houses are still there.

Here, right at the north end of the village, you can see the old Cloth Hall: seventeenth-century chimney stacks of brick, seventeenth-century tiles, but the outer walls of the Cloth Hall are

---

* From the poem 'A Pastoral', in *English Poems* (1925).
† Betjeman pronounces it 'Cow Den', to point up its meaning.

older: the oak beams filled in between with plaster; and a single oak branch, with a natural curve in it, has been used to support the projecting upper storey. Round the corner, you can see where the bales of cloth were let down by a pulley into wagons, which jolted off down the lane; and that lane still looks today very much as it must have done when Shakespeare was alive.

As we leave Smarden, by way of the churchyard, I'll quote Blunden again, whose poems are so full of Kent:

> From this church they led their brides,
> From this church themselves were led
> Shoulder-high; on these waysides
> Sat to take their beer and bread.
> Names are gone – what men they were
> These their cottages declare.*

Summer brings the cricket and Kent is a cricketing county.

> On the green they watched their sons
> Playing till too dark to see,
> As their fathers watched them once
> As my father once watched me.†

And here, probably, Blunden's father watched him play on the playing stool at Benenden. Most Kentish villages have a green and most greens have a cricket pitch and nearly always it seems that the tower of the church is somewhere near, watching the match. Here at Nettlestead, we leave the match and watch the church.

I'm always excited by a church I haven't seen before. What's it going to be like? That tower with its small windows, I should think, is Norman. Under these table tombs lie the bones of Georgian yeoman farmers. My goodness! – splendid windows in the nave: about 1450, from the look of them: very grand for so small a church. [We move inside the church.] Ah – obviously loved and cared for. Those are seventeenth-century monuments to some great folk,

---

* From the poem 'Forefathers' in *The Shepherd* (1922).
† Ibid.

either side of the chancel arch. Rather a vivid modern carpet in Mothers' Union blue. But here's something terrific: old stained glass, still in the windows designed for it – canopies, saints, little figures in the top lights, everything! We're told that the art of stained glass has been lost but that isn't true. People can make any colours now but what the people knew who made this glass five centuries ago was which colour to put against which to bring out the magnificence of each. For instance, those blue jewels, specially leaded into the border of the saint's robe, are shown up by the yellow and white of the border and the red of the robe itself. That's part of the secret of stained glass.

Now it's a Kentish summer. Beyond the oast houses is Sissinghurst Castle: at least, it's not a castle now but there must have been something much bigger here once. What you're looking at is just the entrance block to a large Tudor mansion. And there was a great house here. It was built by a man named Baker – 'Bloody Baker' he was called locally, because of all the Protestants he persecuted in the reign of his friend and employer Queen Mary. I think blood must have soaked into the brick for it's certainly the most marvellous colour. Kentish Tudor brick is the best-looking brick in England and nowhere do I know it better than at Sissinghurst, for here the brick has been specially moulded for window arches and mullions, doorways and chimney stacks. And just about at the time of year that we were making this film – in fact on 15 August, but in 1550 – Queen Mary *did* come to stay, as Baker's guest. She must have passed through the entrance courtyard, which still remains, and she may have looked up at that brick chimney stack and then walked on and come to this gateway tower.

The point about Tudor gardens is that they were enclosed. They were the tapestries that hung on the walls of the house in winter, translated, as it were, into real herbs and flowers. Tudor gardens were secret places in a frame of high brick walls. Lady Nicolson has restored this part of her garden at Sissinghurst back to what the Tudor gardens here must have been like when the great house was still standing.

Here's quite a different way of treating a garden. Nothing secret or enclosed. The country around is part of the garden of the house.

Whole woods and fields have been landskipped★ to give it a setting. It's Mereworth Castle,† built in 1720 by the son of a rich nobleman who'd been on the Grand Tour to Italy and wanted to bring Italy back to Kent. He employed a Scottish architect, Colen Campbell, to design it for him and everything has been sacrificed to magnificence on the ground floor. For instance, the only stairways are hidden behind the walls of this great circular Entrance Hall. They wind up to the Gallery on the bedroom floor; and the upstairs bedrooms are nothing compared with the ground-floor rooms – and over each of these are carved the symbols that show their various purposes: music and embroidery above the entrance to the Long Gallery, the most splendid of all the rooms. It stretches along the whole south front of the house. The idea, you see, was this: when the Kentish skies were grey outside, you had your own private sky to look at, with its gods and goddesses in the clouds; and the plasterers and decorators and painters of these great ceilings took great pride in making it difficult to discern which was carving and which was painting. That urn, for instance, with the decoration around, is painted to look as three-dimensional as possible, so as to blend in with the carved wood of this chimney piece below, which is the real thing. And the light thrown up from snow in the park, in winter, outside, would be heightened by the touches of gold on those leaves and on that goddess.

The richest of all the rooms in Mereworth is quite small: the Card Room. Watch that floor of inlaid parquet: in the eighteenth century, the usual scheme for decoration inside was dark floor, medium-coloured walls and light ceiling, and the Brussels tapestries around this room represent the four continents. You're looking at Asia. And then from Asia up to a sky with winds at the corners and, in the clouds, the gods of Olympus.

Outside the house, the Classical fantasy is kept up. From this temple portico, you look across to another temple – and all Kent outside is planted to seem as much as possible like those oil-painted landskips people brought back from the Grand Tour in

★ See p. 41.
† See 'Mereworth Castle', p. 132.

Italy: that John Fane probably brought back when he built this house. That formal garden in the foreground is Victorian: I think, really, there should be grass coming right up to here where we're standing.*

At the end of summer the hop harvest begins in the Weald. It's really a festival for East London, as Londoners for generations have come down here to pick the hops.

For something so near to London, it's strange that there should be anything as remote, hidden and peaceful as Bayham Abbey. It's on the Sussex border and the building was started in about 1250. (That's the nave.) And it's rather a relief to find a ruin that is quite unofficial like this and not too tidied up and stuck about with notices. Along these cloisters, about six centuries ago, the White Canons must have walked. Here in this silence it's possible to imagine them, in their white habits, leading the austere life peculiar to their branch of the Augustinian order. We know that they were much liked locally, for when the Abbey was dissolved the people round about rose up and drove out the Commissioners of Henry VIII. From this Chapter House, which we're now coming into, they must have walked out into their great Abbey church, which still adjoins it, with its choir and transepts and its carved corbels and mouldings now open to the sky.

Now autumn is here and hedges glow with red and gold, as vivid as Kentish brick and tiles. We started to look at the Weald in spring; in autumn, Blunden's lines are still true: the year is still sweet and the Weald a symphony of sounds and sights and seeings.

* In the portico of one of the temples in the grounds.

CANTERBURY*

'Canterbury At Christmas'
Proposed treatment

Letter to Peter Hunt (producer)
25 August 1967

• • •

43 Cloth Fair, London EC1

Dear Peter,
    I have worked out a shape for a Canterbury film at Christmas. There have been some general considerations to bear in mind. One is that you have told me that whereas Easter is being devoted to a film on St Peter's, Rome, Christmas is to be given to Canterbury. I think it would be a pity to imply any sort of rivalry. I am therefore keeping most of the film parochial, with only a final reference to the fact that there are many more millions of Anglicans in other parts of the world than there are in the British Isles.

I do not think it is even worth going into the unfilmable abstract matters of episcopacy, the validity of Anglican orders, or the relationship between, let us say, the huge Episcopal Church of America, the churches of the Philippines, and Anglican mission churches in Africa and India with Canterbury. For most people this is implicit and the joy of being Anglican is that definitions are left, in the English way, capable of various interpretations. Love only lives in liberty.

Next, I wanted to avoid too much 'ye olde' and, though we will have to mention pilgrims modern and ancient, this film must not look like something for the British Travel Association. I do not know how we are going to avoid this.

* Broadcast in a different form as 'A Tale of Canterbury'. A Rediffusion Network Production. ITV, 25 December 1967. Director: John Rhodes.

I have made three visits to Canterbury looking at things rather than people and the treatment is meant to be something that you can give to an official of the Cathedral – the Canon, the Dean or the Registrar – for him to suggest who would be the right characters living in Canterbury, and whom he knows, who can take part in a film as expositors or interviewees.

If it is necessary to have me in the film as a connecting link and as an interviewer, I shall be very grateful to be given film dates. Please remember that I will be away on my much looked-forward-to annual holiday from October 7th to the 24th. The later the film is made the better, since the crowds in the city this August when I visited there have been great.

Yours,
John

The See of Canterbury

We will have to open with pilgrims, though the pilgrimage in this film is one through time in the city of Canterbury itself rather than along roads to the city. We could open with medieval illuminated manuscript pictures of pilgrims, very bright in colour – all red and gold and blue: perhaps two or three. Cut to the words 'Pilgrim's Way' on an enamel notice-board on the by-pass into Canterbury from London. There is a fine view beyond it of the West front of the Cathedral in the distance.

Now let us get in a mini-bus with Americans on a tour of the city. Mini-bus tours go from Buttermarket from 10.30 till 3 every day and take three-quarters of an hour. I do not know the company that runs them but there is a gramophone record that the driver puts on and that tells us what we are going to see, and the speaker on the record has a nice Canterbury kind of voice. We should have mini-bus and voice takes at Kent University looking down on to the city and at Christ Church College, which is 1960s 'with-itry', with the Cathedral beyond. In the new shopping centre there we should drop the Americans in a shop full of souvenirs.

The next sequence is of Canterbury as a living city like any

well-preserved English county town. We should travel on the top
of a bus down St Peter's Street and notice the old houses, mostly
Georgian facings above the modern shops. We should look at the
Petty Sessions House, the entrance to the gaol and the Georgian
terraces by the Dane John mound. If need be I could walk past some
of these, talking. Somewhere in this sequence we should interview
a citizen who likes the city and who sees the Cathedral as part of it.
Ideally it should be a shopkeeper with a picturesque shop interior
– for instance, Cheshams* the second-hand book shop, if the man
there is regarded as suitable, or anybody our Canterbury adviser
likes to suggest: perhaps the Mayor or the Town Clerk.

When we have left this conversation we go into the smaller
side streets of the city – for instance, Guildhall Street where one
sees above the shops in Sun Street the Cathedral looking a little
bit nearer, Butchers Row,† Mercery Lane and the charming view
down Black Griffin Lane to the School of Art on the other side of
St Peter's Street. We should also go down by the Friars and find a
back garden on the way to the Blackfriars River Tours where there
are weeds and fences and, again, views of bits of the Cathedral over
the rooftops. Sound should be bells and footsteps and barking dogs
and children playing. We should end this sequence with the most
beautiful view down a narrow lane to the Cathedral so as to give
a sense of the Cathedral being the climax and end of our journey.
I think one of the best is from somewhere along the High Street
towards the Parade. These shots should not be static but, if possible,
should give the impression of walking.

Now we come to the water sequence and the sense of the
Church. This can be done by stepping down from the High Street
into the Hospital of St Thomas, where there is a Pilgrims' Crypt
and a Chapel up steps, all small enough and capable of being lit,
and here we could show the tokens medieval pilgrims used to carry
on their way to Canterbury: there is a collection of them in the
museum; and then we step out on to a kind of balcony where the
river is immediately below us. Here I think we should make a water

---

* Cheshire's.
† Butchery Lane.

journey through the city, past the bridges and old houses, because that is the way the stone came to build the Cathedral, and the water is weedy and in many places very charming. The Blackfriars River Tour could show you. We could have a lovely green Ophelia-like sequence with tile-hung houses and back gardens, ending finally near the walls of one of the little churches of Canterbury.

The next sequence is of one particular city church in Canterbury. To me, the most suitable – and I have seen them all – is St Alphege, because it is like a Kentish country church, is comparatively unspoiled, has some medieval glass and is in a charming street; and I should like, in this church, to meet the incumbent so as to get an idea and for him to talk about Canterbury generally. I would ask him questions about which [churches] were High and which Low and which were restored, whether they were full and how they compared with the Cathedral. He could then take me to the Archbishop's Palace, whose entrance gate is within sight of St Alphege Church. This would introduce us to the Archbishop as Bishop of the Diocese of Canterbury: in fact he might prefer to speak of the different churches of Canterbury and Kent and how they work and the difference between the Cathedral and the parish churches.

You will notice that up to now we have only had glimpses of the Cathedral and I think we should keep up this tension and I would like a visit, next, to the Dean or one of the canons so that we could see inside his house and talk to him about the work of the Cathedral itself. Then we should see King's School, Canterbury, and we should also see the choir entering through the cloisters, so that one gets a sense that there is to be a service in the Cathedral.

At last we come to the Cathedral and there is no doubt that the change of scale here is breathtaking. We come in the obvious way under Christchurch Gate and see the West front and Bell Harry Tower deliberately set at an angle so that you can see two sides of the Cathedral at once. I would prefer to do what everybody does after this: that is to say, instead of taking a walk round the outside, going straight in and seeing that soaring nave and then to go or zoom in on a transparency to the choir, with a distant view of the glass. (See my alternative suggestion following a regular worshipper at the end of this treatment.)

Then a detail of the glass. Then cut to a detail of glass of the same date at Bourges and Chartres – to an exterior of Chartres and of Bourges and then to exteriors of the East end of the Cathedral so that we can show that the older part of the Cathedral, in the time of Henry II and the martyrdom of Becket, was part of western Christendom when France and England were one kingdom and not consciously separate countries. We can then look at the outside of one of the Canterbury Quire [Choir] Romanesque windows and out to a travelling shot inside part of the Quire aisles and ending on St Augustine's throne in the Corona.* This would be a place to mention St Augustine, though I cannot myself see much visual appeal in the vestigial relics of his time that are preserved. It all makes it a bit 'museum-y' – although I am sure I may be wrong and shall be delighted to be corrected. One might tell the story here about the York and Canterbury precedents.

There is to be an ordination service in the Cathedral conducted by the Archbishop, I think about October 13th. It would be marvellous if part of this could be filmed because it would link with my idea for a final sequence, which is of the Archbishop, whom we had seen in his study in the Palace in his everyday clothes, fully robed and giving the blessing at the high altar in the Cathedral.

From this, go to the westward view from the high altar on a transparency; zoom into the light, white nave beyond the Quire [pulpitum] screen. Now come down the pilgrims' steps† into the nave. It will be very satisfactory if we can get the majesty of the nave with natural light. It is a much lighter part of the Cathedral than the Quire and the West window has glorious glass. Our final shot should be that most awe-inspiring of all views in Canterbury – I think almost in England – which is as you stand at the South-West door and look eastward. From this, fade or dissolve into eastward-looking interiors of Anglican cathedrals abroad. The Church Information Office must know of colour transparencies of such interiors as those of Brisbane, Australia; St John the Divine, New York; and some modern cathedrals recently put up in Africa.

---

* The Eastern Tower.
† Known as the Pulpitum Steps.

There is a book called *Anglican Cathedrals Abroad*, published by the SPCK and written by the Revd B. F. L. Clark, but the illustrations here are in black and white. From there I think one ends again looking westward and then at the Archbishop at the altar as he finishes giving the blessing; and then possibly back to our vicar at St Alphege saying a part of the Book of Common Prayer which is considered suitable.

If there is space within this framework and if some things are considered unsuitable, I would rather like to have a shot of one of those old people who come daily to the services of the Cathedral – a retired priest or a priest's widow or a verger's widow. I would like to follow him/her from their house across to the West door and then up the steps to a stall in the Quire where they are used to sitting every day. It might be as effective a lead into the Cathedral as the one I have given. And from where he/she sits one could look up at the stained glass in the clerestory of the Quire and then into the stained glass of Chartres, and so on.

I fancy the proportion in the film should be one-third city, one-third Cathedral and churches outside, one-third inside. It is possible that the interiors, except for the glass sections, could be less than the exteriors. I have not worked out details about the choir school nor King's School. In fact, if this framework is approved, the finding of characters I must leave to your research department, and I may say that the people will be less *affairé* down at Canterbury when the holidays draw to a close.

LANCASHIRE

HALLI'TH'WOOD

From the Shell series *Discovering Britain with John Betjeman*
Random Film Productions Ltd
ITV, Spring 1956 (exact date unknown)
Director: Peter Woosnam-Mills

• • •

We're in the cotton district of Lancashire on the outskirts of Bolton, and in the middle of this industrialised scenery you unexpectedly find this house: Halli'th'wood,* which is the birthplace of the cotton-spinning industry. It's a fifteenth-century yeoman's farmhouse, bought by Lord Leverhulme in 1900 and given to the Corporation of Bolton. It's now a folk museum and though I don't generally like museums, this one is well worth seeing for the beauty of its half-timber and also for its inside, where the fine cotton-spinning industry started.

The farmers and small squires who lived here for generations were great men for gadgets. This kitchen is full of them. For instance, here's one: a spit, that works by a weight and is geared through a pulley that turns it slowly.

Samuel Crompton lived in this house in the 1760s. He spun by hand – I suppose on a thing like that [we see a traditional spinning wheel] – until his gadgety mind was set going (by things like that spit we saw) and he invented the Spinning Mule, which changed all this part of Lancashire. Crompton's Spinning Mule was so unpopular that people wanted to come along and break it up, this monster of automation, so he had to hide it up here in the attic; and that's where it stood – there. And there's the monster itself that could do the work of sixteen men.

* Betjeman pronounces this 'Horlithwood'.

Lancashire cotton spinners lived by streams, where they used water power and lived in little communities called 'folds'. (This is a model of a fold in the Bolton Museum and it seemed to me such a good model that it's worth looking at, as most of the real folds around Bolton have tumbled down. You can find none as complete as this one.)

Crompton caused this sort of world in Bolton today. From his machine grew the landskip* of long streets, tall chimneys and rubbish dumps around the great mills. All this from a half-timbered farmhouse in a Lancashire valley.

Halli'th'wood is just outside Bolton.

* See p. 41.

LONDON

A POET IN LONDON

A segment from *Monitor*
BBC Television, 1 March 1959
Director: Ken Russell

• • •

[Betjeman is seen walking through a City bomb site, under a grim grey sky.] Most of my verse is about London and Cornwall. (Can you hear me above the traffic roar of the City of London?)* I've written quite a lot of verses because this part is associated with my childhood. I can remember when where we are now was the Manchester Hotel. And where this bracken and rosebay grows, once, down in the passages, which are tiled – you can still see the tiles – once, people hurried along with trays of tea; and now all that remains is this and the bombed ruins there of Aldersgate Street Station.

Long after the amalgamation of all the independent railways, Aldersgate Street Station in the City of London remained a memorial to unwilling co-operation. On one side of the station to this day, steam trains come in early in the mornings from the suburbs and go out in the afternoon to the suburbs; and on the other side electric trains are constantly and efficiently whirring to Hammersmith and round on the Inner Circle.

And that huge station had up at the top, as you went out, a refreshment room that I can remember before the war: it had plate-glass windows and on the plate-glass windows in China letters were the words 'Afternoon Teas a Speciality'. A very nice place to have tea. And then last year, or maybe the year before, they took the enormous cast-iron roof off the station and that took away a lot of

---

* Supposition. The first half of this sentence is lost in a bad edit.

its personality and a lot of the feeling of the old City people who used to use it when people wore silk hats and travelled in a very respectable manner in non-smoking carriages. This is 'A Monody on the Death of Aldersgate Street Station':

Snow falls in the buffet of Aldersgate station,
   Soot hangs in the tunnel in clouds of steam.
City of London! before the next desecration
   Let your steepled forest of churches be my theme.

Sunday Silence! with every street a dead street,
   Alley and courtyard empty and cobbled mews,
Till 'tingle tang' the bell of St Mildred's Bread Street
   Summoned the sermon taster to high box pews,

And neighbouring towers and spirelets joined the ringing
   With answering echoes from heavy commercial walls
Till all were drowned as the sailing clouds went singing
   On the roaring flood of a twelve-voiced peal from Paul's.

Then would the years fall off and Thames run slowly;
   Out into marshy meadow-land flowed the Fleet:
And the walled-in City of London, smelly and holy,
   Had a tinkling mass house in every cavernous street.

The bells rang down and St Michael Paternoster
   Would take me into its darkness from College Hill,
Or Christ Church Newgate Street (with St Leonard Foster)
   Would be late for Mattins and ringing insistent still.

Last of the east wall sculpture, a cherub gazes
   On broken arches, rosebay, bracken and dock,
Where once I heard the roll of the Prayer Book phrases
   And the sumptuous tick of the old West gallery clock.

Snow falls in the buffet of Aldersgate station,
   Toiling and doomed from Moorgate Street puffs the train,

For us of the steam and the gas-light, the lost generation,
    The new white cliffs of the City are built in vain.*

[We see new City buildings – then the area round one of London's rail termini: perhaps Paddington.] What people don't realise who build these big modern blocks in the City, these huge new white cliffs, is what an awful time these people who have to work in them have in getting to them. The struggle that business girls, young business gels, fresh from home, have to go through in order to reach these big cliffs. I'm always touched by the sight of people struggling to get to these places; and they live, very often, in furnished rooms in large houses originally built for large families and now turned into flats. You can see them all over London, particularly in the inner steam-railway sort of suburb, and this poem I wrote about 'Business Girls' in Camden Town.

From the geyser ventilators
    Autumn winds are blowing down
On a thousand business women
    Having baths in Camden Town.

Waste pipes chuckle into runnels,
    Steam's escaping here and there,
Morning trains through Camden cutting
    Shake the Crescent and the Square.

Early nip of changeful autumn,
    Dahlias glimpsed through garden doors,
At the back precarious bathrooms
    Jutting out from upper floors;

And behind their frail partitions
    Business women lie and soak,

* 'A Monody on the Death of Aldersgate Street Station' by John Betjeman, first published in *Punch*, 16 March 1955.

    Seeing through the draughty skylight
    Flying clouds and railway smoke.

    Rest you there, poor unbelov'd ones,
    Lap your loneliness in heat.
    All too soon the tiny breakfast,
    Trolley-bus and windy street!*

Unfortunately I can't keep sex out of my poems. It would be hypo-critical for me to do so. Everywhere you go in London in public transport, you can't get away from the beauty of the gels.

    The sort of girl I like to see
    Smiles down from her great height at me.
    She stands in strong, athletic pose
    And wrinkles her *retroussé* nose.
    Is it distaste that makes her frown,
    So furious and so freckled, down
    On an unhealthy worm like me?
    Or am I what she likes to see?
    I do not know, though much I care.
    Eithe genoimen†. . . would I were
    (Forgive me, shade of Rupert Brooke)
    An object fit to claim her look.
    Oh! would I were her racket press'd
    With hard excitement to her breast
    And swished into the sunlit air
    Arm-high above her tousled hair,
    And banged against the bounding ball
    'Oh! Plung!' my tauten'd strings would call,
    'Oh! Plung! my darling, break my strings.
    For you I will do brilliant things.'

* 'Business Girls' by John Betjeman, first published in the *Observer*, 28 September 1952.
† A simple transliteration of 'εἴθε γενοίμην' which is what Betjeman wrote, quoting Rupert Brooke's 'The Old Vicarage, Grantchester'. In both Brooke and Betjeman the meaning follows: 'would I were'. The Greek is wrongly spelled in the *Collected Poems*.

And when the match is over, I
Would flop beside you, hear you sigh;
And then, with what supreme caress,
You'd tuck me up into my press.
Fair tigress of the tennis courts,
So short in sleeve and strong in shorts,
Little, alas, to you I mean,
For I am bald and old and green.★

Finally, some of my verses are connected with childhood and memories of it that we all share in common. My own childhood wasn't quite as successful as that of those beautiful tennis-playing gels we've just seen. And the other day I went back to Hertfordshire† – my verse is always about places – and in Hertfordshire I recollected painful times when I went wrong, shooting with my father. That brought forth these verses:

I had forgotten Hertfordshire,
   The large unwelcome fields of roots
Where with my knickerbockered sire
   I trudged in syndicated shoots;

And that unlucky day when I
   Fired by mistake into the ground
Under a Lionel Edwards sky‡
   And felt disapprobation round.

The slow drive home by motor-car,
   A heavy Rover Landaulette,
Through Welwyn, Hatfield, Potters Bar,
   Tweed and cigar smoke, gloom and wet:

★ 'The Olympic Girl' by John Betjeman, first published in *A Few Late Chrysanthemums*, 1954.
† Betjeman pronounces Hertfordshire without the 't'.
‡ Lionel Edwards (1878–1966) was a painter who specialised in hunting scenes, often depicted under brooding, cloudy skies.

'How many times must I explain
    The way a boy should hold a gun?'
I recollect my father's pain
    At such a milksop for a son.

And now I see these fields once more
    Clothed, thank the Lord, in summer green,
Pale corn waves rippling to a shore
    The shadowy cliffs of elm between,

Colour-washed cottages reed-thatched
    And weather-boarded water mills,
Flint churches, brick and plaster patched,
    On mildly undistinguished hills –

They still are there. But now the shire
    Suffers a devastating change,
Its gentle landscape strung with wire,
    Old places looking ill and strange.

One can't be sure where London ends,
    New towns have filled the fields of root
Where father and his business friends
    Drove in the Landaulette to shoot;

Tall concrete standards line the lane,
    Brick boxes glitter in the sun:
Far more would these have caused him pain
    Than my mishandling of a gun.★

[Betjeman recites this poem from memory, with the intonation of a
vicar, sitting cross-legged on a park bench, resting on one crooked
arm. Behind him, children play and take no notice of the camera.
He stresses 'One can't be sure where London ends'. During his
reading, the scene switches to Hertfordshire and a field that is being

★ 'Hertfordshire' by John Betjeman, first published in *Punch*, 3 October 1956.

153

turned into a building site. Our last view is of him walking away from the camera into a misty emptiness.]

LONDON'S EXHIBITION SITES

Also titled 'Journey into a Lost World' and 'The Architecture of
    Entertainment'
Segment from *Monitor*
BBC Television, 28 February 1960
Director: Ken Russell

• • •

I've always been fascinated by exhibitions and the architecture of exhibitions, and here we are on the National Festival of Britain site of 1951 and can you remember how tremendously modern it seemed and contemporary and there's something very sad now, looking at it, how quickly contemporary rusts and decays, how the concrete cracks and the pools that were meant to swim with goldfish are muddied over and have got a little oil on the surface, and how those masts over there, dashed off with a pencil with such *joie de vivre* in 1949, now in 1960 seem rather pointless and sad but also infinitely romantic.

These national exhibitions have been blossoming and perishing for a hundred years. They only exist now in old photographs and bits of broken celluloid.

Exhibitions were born from fairgrounds. Barnum and Bailey's circus, 1896. Brighton ten years later. That horse boxed like that in 1920 on Hampstead Heath. [Archive footage shows a boxing horse on a fairground stage.]

But the first national fair in the world was the Crystal Palace, erected in Hyde Park and re-erected, pane by pane and piece by piece, on this hill in Sydenham, south London – the first great pre-fab in the world. What hopes its promoters had in instructing us in the arts, as we wandered from style to style. Brass bands for Sousa, ladies' choirs for Spohr, and Handel dominating all. And then the fireworks reflected in these walls of glass – and the greatest display of flames: the conflagration of 1936.

And still more fireworks at the Alexandra Palace, north London's dusty answer to the south: fireworks and the first great airships. From a balloon on a morning in 1873, the Palace looked splendid. Ketèlbey and the Shilling Concerts: a cut-price Handel from the North. Then came 1914 and the Great War. The People's Palace became the People's Ward – a military hospital. Even the roller-skating rink. Even the puppet theatre. And outside, German prisoners of war behind the mild barbed wire. The Palace, less palatial at the corners now,* is still in use. They call this place the Lung of North London and here it stands, airy and remote, protected by an English lady sphinx.

With Good King Edward came the reign of pleasure. Who would have believed that this was Shepherd's Bush? – the White City, where they held the Franco-British Exhibition of 1908. I just remember it – or do I dream I do? I'm fifty-three. It was like a dream – a white city, covered now with greyhound tracks and factories and office blocks. And was this watery high street ever Shepherd's Bush? And the cold air under that waterfall: I can just remember it. It smelt of chlorine as the boat drew near.

White City Station, run by the London and North-Western Railway. Wembley, 1924: a dream of empire, made in concrete. The Festival of Britain, 1951. A phoenix from the ashes, light-hearted on the surface: a worried government, breaking into mirth.

The picture palaces came from the fairgrounds and the fair-ground style still remains in super-cinemas of the suburbs: Naples in Brixton at the Odeon Astoria. Forthcoming attractions are heralded from little stages above the screen. The gardens of Seville in Finsbury Park. Cathedrals with their altars to the stars. Marlene Dietrich, Rudolph Valentino.

---

* Because of a BBC mast at its south-east end.

'Change and decay in all around I see.'★ Where has it all gone? Not everything has vanished. The trumpets of the 1860s can still be heard at the foot of Sydenham Hill in London. Science flabbergasted the Victorians: these prehistoric monsters [we see full-scale models of dinosaurs]† were originally raised to the glory of Darwin and the age of the world.

How desolate seems Wembley-on-the-Hill. Was this where, in 1924, my father walked to Pears' Palace of Beauty?

The Alexandra Palace. I think it was in 1930 that I was walking there alone when I heard the voice of Gracie Fields, somewhere, somewhere. There was no one about, and in the end I found her in the theatre, rehearsing to the empty stalls. I wonder if that theatre is still there.‡

Fantasy to fantasy. This is where the Crystal Palace stood before it was burnt down. I am climbing through the ruins of dreams. How odd it is that the BBC should choose these places – Ally Pally, the White City, Wembley, Crystal Palace – still to make our dreams for us today. This Crystal Palace mast is at the moment beaming out this very programme. New dreams grow on the ruins of old dreams.

Dreams. Dreams.

★ From the hymn 'Abide with Me' by Henry Francis Lyte (1793–1847).
† Designed by Benjamin Hawkins in 1854 for the ornamental park in which the Crystal Palace was relocated.
‡ It survives, but is totally derelict.

MARBLE ARCH TO THE EDGWARE ROAD

'Contrasts: Marble Arch to the Edgware Road – A Lament'.★
Treatment, 2 October 1967

• • •

I am taking it that this is film and not videotape and that the commentary, whether prose or verse, will be dubbed after the film is made. I gather that even if I don't see all the rushes, I will see a rough cut.

The area covered will be from Marble Arch to Edgware. The time will be from dawn in November to dusk on the same day. The utmost length of the film is presumably half an hour. The sound, which is most important, will be in terms of traffic, road drills and conversation, with a surprising injection of Handel when we reach Edgware and the church of St Lawrence, Whitchurch, where Handel was organist when that church was the private chapel of the Duke of Chandos, and in the parish of Edgware. Handel's Harmonious Blacksmith is buried in the churchyard.

Dawn

Terrific traffic noise, Seddons, Scammels, Atkinsons and other articulated vehicles, some with statics on them; and seen between them, now and then, a faint suggestion of familiarity in the outline of Oxford Street, Marble Arch or Hyde Park.

A tyre going over the mark in the road where Tyburn stood. The outside of Tyburn Convent. The inside of the Annunciation Church – Gothic and soaring at first, quiet after all the Scammels

★ The programme that this treatment gave rise to was first broadcast on BBC1 Television, 31 January 1968. Producer: Julian Jebb. Editor: Tony Woollard.

and then the sound of Anglican Mass and the sight of Baroque vestment and decoration in the Gothic.

Breakfast

The interior of the Cumberland Hotel. An impressed family from the country in Lyons' luxury modern.

Shops opening, and in this first shopping sequence we want to stress American names and the international anonymity of places like Park West★ and the sculpture over Marks & Spencer.

Tea up

Workman at morning tea break on that dreadful complex going up where the Met† used to be. The smooth voice of a planner and his smooth face talking about plot ratio and the like. Fade into exterior of the Met, then interior with singing (there must be some stock). Out into the complex again and smooth talk going on.

Morning Coffee

This is the chance for a flat sequence. We should have two interviews, one with an old-fashioned person in an Edwardian corner/domed block, called 'Mansions' or 'Gardens', and before entering we should go through a sequence of mansions, courts and gardens until we find ourselves looking down from one of them on to the Edgware Road. We should then have a sequence of 1930s and post-war 'with-itry' flats – it doesn't matter where they are along the road – and here we should interview a rather foreign person in a flat where the curtains are crisscrossed; and we drink advocaat, or something like that, in decoration that suggests pre-Hitler Germany, or pre-Dollfuss Vienna.

★ A 1930 block of flats.
† The Metropolitan Music Hall, built in 1897 by Frank Matcham, closed in 1963 and was then demolished.

Early Lunch

A barman talking about the change since his time, or a young barman, indifferent to who people are, talking about his hours of work. Anyhow, the bar of a rather dreary public house opening on to the Kilburn High Road. A shopping sequence here which can be scarcely distinguishable from Hong Kong or Singapore, with the wares displayed on the pavement, until you look up and see the Venetian Gothic above some familiar name like Sainsbury's or Boots. Another approach to this might be through that public house alongside Kilburn Station, which looks nice and old-fashioned from the outside, and we might approach it by coming up from Kilburn High Road Station, where the contrast between that wooden-and-glass corridor is so marked with the scenery outside, Stone's Radio, etc., and this might be the chance for some disgruntled landlord to remember the glorious Kilburn of his past.

Lunch

Captions* of the electric tramway system to Cricklewood. Captions of the Plough, Cricklewood, before rebuilding. Quotations from *Diary of a Nobody*† about bona-fide travellers. A shot of the exterior of the Plough and then of the interior of its banqueting hall, and here the proprietor, Mr Shon, or one of the staff, might talk.

After-Lunch Siesta

A sequence of the most fearful industrial shots and a mutilation of the Welsh Harp reservoir, so that one gets a sense that there was once country here. In fact, the old Welsh Harp pub and its chucking out of customers might be an enjoyable conclusion of this, as

* Betjeman uses the word 'caption' to mean 'transparency'.
† The comic novel by George and Weedon Grossmith, first published in book form in 1892 after appearing in *Punch* in 1888–9, about the snobberies and embarrassments of lower-middle-class suburban life.

the public house turns its back on all the wild garden down to the edge of the Welsh Harp. Around the Welsh Harp there is a lot of country mixed up with rubbish dumps, particularly at Kingsbury. We should then go to the revolting clock on Sectrick and from there to the flat of Mrs Grahame White, 49 Berkeley Court, Baker Street, W1 (Hunter 2142) and the trophies and photographs she has in her seventeen-room, beige-and-green flat, of her husband and Hendon Aerodrome. The Aerodrome must account for the presence of so many precision-instrument and motor-car factories from the Hyde to Colindale and we could here, in the middle of this, cut in Mr Coleman, the funeral director, in his last remaining Middlesex cottage in this land of factories and institutions. We could end by trying the door of the Bald Faced Stag and finding it shut, unless we find, as a result of our visit on Wednesday, that it is an Arts & Crafts gem.

Tea

If we can find photographs of Middlesex hills and farms between Kenton and Edgware, we should intersperse these with that bus journey to Alperton that we took and we should have schoolchildren boarding the bus and we should look down on those carefully tended gardens with their roses and gnomes. In fact that gnome and garden shop just beyond the Hyde should give us the idea of venturing out into what once was rural Middlesex.

A tea trolley in the Green Shield Stamp building in Edgware, or in any anonymous post-war office building, and a sense of typewriters and corridors. There are, as an introduction to this, two enormous buildings just erected between Cricklewood and Edgware that would lead in to the Green Shield building that defaces Edgware itself. People pouring out of the Underground station, back from work. Edgware High Street a complete rural contrast. Not just Landau's, which we saw and which is excellent and unselfconscious, but also the parts beyond where we went, where there is a whole genuine half-timber sequence, and we should also see the exterior of Edgware Parish Church (very Low) but it is not worth close inspection inside. I think we should go to villas such as we have seen already from the children's bus, to St Lawrence, Whitchurch, hear the organ, see the paintings, having looked at the grave of the Harmonious Blacksmith. Cut to North London Collegiate College and a view down to the lake. The lake itself and reedy islands. Open the wire-netting door with a key and be taken by our chartered accountant, through a Canons Park Close or Way, to a house and bridge in a nice comfortable neo-Tudor drawing room as sunset fades over the elms and the kiddiz climb the stairs to slumberland.

I suppose you could go back to Marble Arch at night. And it is night at teatime in November.

Narrative

How beautiful the London air,
How calm and unalarming
This height above the Archway where
The prospects round are charming.

Oh come and take a stroll with me
And do not fear to stumble.
Great Cumberland, your place I see,
I hear your traffic rumble.

See Oxford Street on my left hand,
A chasm full of shopping.
Below us traffic lights command
The starting and the stopping.

And on my right the spacious park,
So infinitely spacious,
So pleasant when it isn't dark
But when it is – good gracious!

What carriages below these skies
Came rolling by on Mondays.

What church parades would greet the eyes
Here in Hyde Park on Sundays.

And trodden by unheeding feet
A spot which memory hallows:
Where Edgware Road meets Oxford Street
Stood Tyburn's fearsome gallows.

What martyrdom this place has seen,
What deeds much better undone,
Yet still the greatest crime has been
The martyrdom of London.

For here where once were pleasant fields
And no one in a hurry
Behold the harvest Mammon yields
Of speed and greed and worry.

The rights of man, the rights of cash,
The left, the right, the centre;
Come on, let's off and make a dash
And meet it where we enter.

The road that no one looks upon
Except as birds of passage:
Oh Edgware Road, be our abode
And let us hear your message.

.   .   .   .   .   .

Ho for the Kilburn High Road!
Ho for a sumptuous feast.
It's your road and it's my road,
And Ireland meets the East.

Let's mount the Sixteen bus with care,
It's empty, wide and free.
It will take us out of everywhere
To the days that used to be.

Forget the littered pavements,
The chainstores row on row
And the super-super-cinema
Where our parents used to go.

With Shoot-up Hill before us
We leave the hemmed-in town
And raise a country chorus
To Cricklewood and the Crown.

There stood a village marketplace
Where now you buy your yams,
And I like in memory to trace
The red electric trams.

However far their journeys made
They always waited here
And in this terracotta shade
Their passengers drank beer.

        .   .   .   .   .   .

The sisters Progress and Destruction dwell
Where rural Middlesex once cast her spell.

Dear vanished county of such prosperous farms,
Where now are gone your weatherboarded charms?

Still in my dreams I see your sudden hills,
Your willowy brooks and winding lanes and rills,

The red-brick Georgian mansions' garden wall,
The little church, the spreading cedar tall –

(See the Welsh Harp with undulating shore
And hear beyond the road's arterial roar).

Your swinging signboards, barns with curly tiles,
Your little lakes on which the sunset smiles.

Keats and Leigh Hunt in better lines than these
Have praised your misty fields and towering trees.

Constable's brush with light and liquid fire
Immortalised this unforgotten shire.

Dear Middlesex, dear vanished country friend,
Your neighbour, London, killed you in the end.
. . . .
One after one rise these empty consecutives,
Now we have come to the uppermost floor.
Where in the car park are Jags of executives?
Where, far behind them, the bikes of the poor?

Ghosts of the future are waiting to settle here,
Click of the typewriter, buzz from the boss:
The tea-trolley's tinkle and hiss of the kettle here,
'Hurry up Myrtle, he's ever so cross.'

Pig trough of light will hang down from the ceiling,
Holiday postcards this bareness adorn;
Brave indoor plants give a tropical feeling,
Eyes will look lovingly, hearts will be torn.

Somewhere they'll raise, where the views are extensive,
Beige, pink and soundproof, a partition wall.
On fine figured walnut and leather expensive,
Here may be sitting the top man of all.

LONDON ON SUNDAY

The first of two films in the series *Thank God it's Sunday*
BBC1 Television, 10 December 1972
Producer and director: Jonathan Stedall

• • •

The empty Sunday city, Royal Exchange,
Cornhill, Throgmorton and Threadneedle Streets,
Without their central roar. The Underground
Alone is open, St Mary Woolnoth shut;
And Smithfield Market lacks its loads of meat:
A used cathedral of departed flesh.
Just here and there a solitary bus
Sets out for places that were once in fields:
Remoter parishes of Middlesex.

Now London City, here within its heart,
On Sunday is a village once again.
We who are left in it may wonder what
Those boys are up to: I suspect no good.
At empty offices the tourists gaze.
Linguaphone English is the language here.

Commerce relaxes on her pediment,
For this is Sunday and the trustful Sikh
Will find that all the City doors are shut.
Sikh and ye shall not find. Forgive the joke:
It isn't all that funny; life is sad
For foreigners in London's Sunday streets.
For Sunday is the day for morning prayer,
A compensation for the council flat
And loss of status. Church remains the same:
A reminiscence of the good old days

Our parents lived in and of Sunday roasts.
Church is a change from lonely sitting rooms,
For rich or poor the aches of age come on.
Church is a chance once more of making friends
And meeting the Eternal here on earth.

Hyde Park on Sunday, on this day of rest.
How often this begins with gentle rain.
It percolates the leaves of spreading trees,
Dislinks the little bands of new-made friends,
Unties the lovers' knots, depresses dogs
And gradually seeps through our leather soles.
And still we try, the hopeful and the young,
And still we try to make the best of it.

In London's sentimental Soho Square
See the varieties of Christ's religion.
St Patrick's, through its proud Palladian porch,
Welcomes us to the ritual of Rome.
Irish, Italian, Spanish, French, Maltese:
We are all one within its round-arched walls,
This faithful crib of an Italian church.
And in another corner of the square
French Protestants say goodbye till Sunday next.

Steady on just and unjust falls the rain.
Across the soaking acres of the grass,
Over wet pavements and by dripping boughs,
We pilgrims plod to the last shrine of all –
The best-attended and the most revered,
The sacred altar of the Sunday press.
What's in? What's out? What's on? We ought to know,
For if we don't we won't be thought informed.
Willingly we make offerings at the shrine.

On Sunday too we ask relations round
Or maybe buy them flowers. Or maybe not.
And Sunday is the day for sleeping-in.

The newest feature of our Sunday streets,
On double time upon the day of rest:
The deafening dawn chorus of the drills.

The sudden quiet of a London village –
Chiswick, upon the Thames's northern bank,
Where amateurs express themselves in paint:
A constant searching for the picturesque.
Chiswick Old Church, grouped with a Georgian house,
Looking across the reaches of the Thames.
The trappings here are landsmen's nautical.
It's cocktail time in view-commanding rooms
And some of us will turn our thoughts to gin
(Pink gin, of course, which goes with naval men);
Others have minds more wholly set on fish.

Rowing its sense of solitude away
The swift pulsating eight divides the stream
And rests, anticipating bitter beer.

He likes his Sunday mowing of the lawn.
More satisfying than what people do
On weekends in their offices. Pleasant smiles
Of Peace* and hybrid tea-rose mix with scent
Of new-cut grass, and thoughts of Sunday lunch
Come wafting outwards from the dining room.
Oh happy, hungry Sunday!

                    Hunger here†
Is of the mind and so it does not see

* A rose.
† People are queuing to get into the Victoria & Albert Museum.

Your most impressive terracotta porch:
Victoria & Albert, Kensington,
Designed in nineteen-one by Aston Webb.

Say which of these are mad on modern art?
Are these girls keen on della Robbia?
And which are only sheltering from the rain?
And did Norwegian stavekirks summon him?
Albanian head-dress? Jacobean chairs?
Or some rare form of *deutsche Kunstgeschicht*?
God knows, God knows. And some perhaps have come
To meet a friend and don't like art at all.

Meanwhile in Natural History next door
Stuffed elephants and elks and crocodiles,
Spiders and beetles, worms and centipedes,
The wonders of creation pinioned down
In awful stillness, wait our casual gaze,
Arrested as the stream of life flows on.

Southwark, the lost cathedral of the south,
Swallowed by tall Dickensian-looking wharves,
The river brown and dark and full of fear.
St Paul's triumphant, riding over tides,
Serene and cheerful on the northern bank.
The darkness under bridges leading on
Once more into the glory of the dome.

Poor tourists, filled with various footling facts.★
How old? How many? When? And why? How long?
They do not know that 'twixt the river banks,
Between the City and the Surrey side,
Dwell different peoples, different ways of life.
He who knows Southwark doesn't know St Paul's,
And Westminster's a stranger to Vauxhall.

★ Tourists are being lectured to on a boat tour down the Thames.

Facts tell you nothing, only people do,
Poor tourists, shipwrecked on a sea of facts,
Not safe and sane again till you're at home.

A London afternoon clears up at times
And sun shines down the lengths of Regent's Park,
Two centuries ago a foggy marsh,
Flat fields of dairy farms and cattle ponds,
But now the Sunday exercising ground
Of lone enthusiasts who can overcome
Matters of balance with a reel and string,★
Matters of breathing – solitary art†
Culled in the gorgeous East. And summer days
On daisied lawns at father's vicarage
Are here relived for children. Summer days
Among your level acres, Regent's Park.

Most Londoners are countrymen at heart
And live again their childhood time of flowers
Within a stone's throw of the London Zoo;
And strange as many creatures seem therein,
Strange as delightful and lumbering bears
Who pace the Mappin Terraces,‡ and strange
As we must look to bears when viewed through bars,
And strange as yon reluctant elephant
Thinking of what beside that bitter wall?
Thinking perhaps of Regent's Park outside
When love was young and he was not alone,
Oh strange and sad is youth.

                           The eager runner
Remembering when he won the mile at school
But now with nobody to run against.

★ Someone is seen with a yo-yo.
† A man is practising yoga, standing on his head.
‡ Opened in 1914, the Mappin Terraces at London Zoo are an artificial 'mountain' habitat for bears and goats.

Oh strange and sad he is, but not so strange
As those aspiring buttocks and the toes★
Pointing so bravely to the London sky
But so unsurely to eternity.

London is such a host of villages.
High on its northern heights stands Highgate Hill,
'Enfolding sunny spots of greenery',†
Where Coleridge lived, and steeply shelving slopes
From Waterlow Park provide a Sunday walk
Slowly downhill to waiting Kentish Town.

What banker once in far Stoke Newington
Built here his Georgian mansion by the Church?
And he who feeds his sole remaining friends,
The London sparrows, does his mind recall
The gentry once who had their tea out here
Before the happier children of the poor
Invaded thy seclusion, Clissold Park?

How little known are London's lesser parks!
All visit Hyde Park, Green Park and the Mall,
But Londoners prefer their local hills
And London's full of tended open space.

Who outside Lambeth goes to Brockwell Park? —
A country house once and still countrified,
With views from spreading lawns across the Thames
From the safe haven of its Surrey hill.
These are the places where the locals come
And lose themselves in harmless hopeful dreams,
Or muse away those merry, merry days
At the Palais de Dance in 1924.
Or maybe spend a sheltered afternoon

★ The yoga man again.
† Line 11 of 'Kubla Khan' by Samuel Taylor Coleridge (1772–1834).

In scent of flowers walled in from diesel fumes,
While others on this Sunday afternoon
Plan out the garden that they do not own
But hope they will do when their ship comes in.
'We couldn't plant it here, but as it is
We've got this public playground for the kid.
It might be worse.'

        And who would ever think
That drab south London, with its slabs of flats,
Could make a marshy swamp in Peckham Rye,
Islanded from the traffic noise by fields,
Blossom into a paradise of streams.
God bless the gardener's genius and his eye!

On Golders Hill, in what was Middlesex,
The air's so fresh it's better than champagne,
Or Coke, or beer, or even lemonade.
A draught of health upon a sandy soil
Where the dread tree-rat,* that attractive pest,
Drives the red squirrels out and eats our fields
And woods and gardens.

They will remember her,† the older ones,
The theatregoers of King Edward's reign,
But will the young have even heard her name? –
The dancer who brought fame to these fair slopes
When crowds would come to gaze upon her house.
She of the twinkling legs and sinuous arms,
The great Pavlóva who once lived up here.
Or is it Pávlova? I'm not so sure.
Sunday's a day when we can listen in‡

---

* The grey squirrel.
† Anna Pavlova whose house was near one of the entrances to Golders Hill Park.
‡ Two men in the park are overheard reminiscing about Pavlova and mispronouncing her name.

And sometimes from a neighbour hear the truth.
Pavlova, are you listening with us now?

Most of us want a cottage of our own –
Well built; if possible before the war,
Or in the twenties when the standard still
Was so much higher in the building trade
And architects took trouble over walls
And pitch of roof, handles and window frames
And stairs, and views from both the front and back.
And Hampstead Garden Suburb has the lot.
I used to laugh at it when I was young,
Thinking it stood for beaten pewter jugs,
No vice, no meat and only vegetables,
No alcohol of course. And I recall
A rhyme like this about it:

> O wot ye why in Orchard Way
> The roofs be steep and shelving?
> And wot ye what the dwellers say
> In garth and garden delving?

> 'Hand-woven be my wefts, hand-made
> My pottery for Pottage,
> And hoe and mattock, aye, and spade
> Hang up about my cottage.'*

But now I think I'd rather settle here
Than anywhere in London. Clip my hedge
Ready for visitors at sherry time,
For Sunday's when we like to make things smart

---

* The rhyme is in fact an early satire by Betjeman, 'The Garden City', but not included in his *Collected Poems* compiled by Lord Birkenhead in 1958 nor in subsequent revisions. Some of the lines quoted here differ slightly from the first and third stanzas of the original version. There is also a second stanza: 'Belike unlike my hearths to yours, / Yet seemly if unlike them. / Deep green and stalwart be my doors / With bottle glass to fryke them.'

And give the things we like a lick of paint,
Ready for business in the coming week.

On Sunday evening rain begins to fall;
On Sunday evening we feel all alone.
Unhappy rumours flicker through the mind,
News seems futile and the coming week
A long, long avenue of unpaid bills.
We can't keep up the struggle any more:
No wonder many of us take to meths.

London today has newer Evensongs*
To usher Sunday out, and here they are:
The priests processing with the acolytes.†
The members have a dedicated look
Of those who think of others than themselves.
The grave churchwardens in their uniform‡
Pace on and on beside them and before.
Hymns and responses are not quite the same
As those we know in church or chapel choir.
Banners are hardly Mothers' Union type;
The saints not mentioned in the calendars
Of Rome or Canterbury but concerned
With suffering and injustice to mankind.

The newer Evensong is one of hope
And generosity and loving care –
Though some prefer the older service still.

* Betjeman here describes an anti-Vietnam War demonstration taking place around
Piccadilly.
† Older and younger political activists.
‡ The police.

METRO-LAND

BBC2 Television, 26 February 1973
Producer: Edward Mirzoeff

• • •

> Child of the First War, forgotten by the Second,
> We called you Metro-land. We laid our schemes,
> Lured by the lush brochure, down byways beckoned,
> To build at last the cottage of our dreams.
> A city clerk turned countryman again;
> And linked to the metropolis by train.

Metro-land: the creation of the Metropolitan Railway, which as you know was the first steam underground in the world. In the tunnels, the smell of sulphur was awful.

When I was a boy, 'Live in Metro-land' was the slogan. It really meant getting out of the tunnels into the country, for the line had ambitions of linking Manchester and Paris and dropping in at London on the way. The grandiose scheme came to nothing. But then the Metropolitan had a very good idea.

Look at these fields. They were photographed in 1910 from the train. 'Why not', said a clever member of the board, 'buy these orchards and farms as we go along, turn out the cattle, and fill the meadow land with houses?' You could have a modern home of quality and distinction; you might even buy an old one, if there was one left.

And over these mild Home County acres soon there will be the estate agent, coal merchant, post office, shops and rows of neat dwellings – all within easy reach of charming countryside. Bucks, Herts and Middlesex yielded to Metro-land. And City men could breakfast on the fast train to London town.

Is this Buckingham Palace? Are we at the Ritz? No. This is the Chiltern Court Restaurant built above Baker Street Station:

the gateway between Metro-land out there and London down there — the creation of the Metropolitan Railway. The brochure shows you how splendid this place was in 1913, which is about the year in which it was built. Here, the wives from Pinner and Ruislip, after a day's shopping at Liberty's or Whiteley's, would sit waiting for their husbands to come up from Cheapside and Mincing Lane. While they waited they could listen to the strains of the band playing for the *thé dansant* before they took the train for home.

> Early Electric — punctual and prompt.
> Off to those cuttings in the Hampstead Hills.
> St John's Wood, Marlborough Road,
> No longer stations — and the trains rush through.

This is all that is left of Marlborough Road Station. Up there the iron brackets supported the glass-and-iron roof. And you see that white house up there? That was where Thomas Hood died. Thomas Hood the poet. He wrote

> I remember, I remember,
> The house where I was born★

and the railway cut through his garden. I remember Marlborough Road Station because it was the nearest station to the house where lived my future parents-in-law.

Farewell old booking hall, once grimy brick; but leafy St John's Wood, which you served, remains: forerunner of the suburbs yet to come, with its broad avenues, detached and semi-detached villas where lived artists and writers and military men; and here, screened by shrubs, walled-in from public view, lived the kept women. What puritan arms have stretched within these rooms to touch what tender breasts as the cab-horse stamped in the road outside. Sweet secret suburb on the City's rim: St John's Wood.

Amidst all this frivolity, in one place a sinister note is struck — in

★ From 'I Remember, I Remember' by Thomas Hood (1799–1845).

that helmeted house* where, rumour has it, the Revd John Hugh Smyth-Pigott lived: an Anglican clergyman whose Clapton congregation declared him to be Christ, a compliment he accepted. His country house† was called the 'Agapemone' – the Abode of Love – and some were summoned to be brides of Christ. Did they strew their Lord with lilies? I don't know. But for some reason this house has an uncanny atmosphere: threatening and restless. Someone seems to be looking over your shoulder. Who is it?

> Over the points by electrical traction,
> Out of the chimney-pots into the openness,
> Till we come to the suburb that's thought to be
>   commonplace,
> Home of the gnome and the average citizen.
> Sketchley and Unigate, Dolcis and Walpamur.

Beyond Neasden there was an unimportant hamlet where for years the Metropolitan didn't bother to stop. Wembley. Slushy fields and grass farms. Then out of the mist arose Sir Edward Watkin's dream: an Eiffel Tower for London. Sir Edward Watkin, railway king and chairman of the line. Thousands, he thought, would pay to climb the tower, which would be higher than the one in Paris. He announced a competition: five hundred guineas for the best design. Never were such flights of Victorian fancy seen. Civil engineers from Sweden and Thornton Heath, Rochdale and Constantinople, entered designs. Cast iron, concrete, glass, granite and steel, lifts hydraulic and electric, a spiral steam railway. Theatres, chapels and sanatoria in the air.

In 1890 the lucky winner was announced. It had Turkish baths, arcades of shops and Winter Gardens. Designed by a firm of Scots with a London office: Stewart, MacLaren and Dunn. It was to be 150 feet higher than the Eiffel Tower. But when at last it reached above trees and the first stage was opened to the crowds, the crowds

---

* Also in St John's Wood. The house has more recently been the home of Charles Saatchi and of Vanessa Feltz.
† In the village of Spaxton, Somerset.

weren't there. They didn't want to come. Money ran out, the tower lingered on, resting and rusting, until it was dismembered in 1907.

This is where London's failed Eiffel Tower stood: 'Watkin's Folly' as it was called. Here on this Middlesex turf; and since then the site has become quite well known. It was here I can just remember the excitement and the hope: St George's Day, 1924 – the British Empire Exhibition at Wembley, opened by King George V. Ah yes, those imperial pavilions – India, Sierra Leone, Fiji – with their sun-tanned sentinels of Empire outside. To me they were more interesting than the Palaces of Engineering and Industry, which were too like my father's factory.

That was the Palace of Arts, where I used to wait while my father saw the living models in Pears' Palace of Beauty. How well I remember the Palace of Arts: massive and simple outside, almost pagan in its sombre strength; but inside . . . ! This is the basilica in the Palace of Arts. It was used for displaying the best church art of 1924: A. K. Lawrence, Eric Gill, Mary Adshead, Colin Gill and so on. Today it's used for housing the props of the pantomime 'Cinderella on Ice' and that kind of thing. And really it's quite right, because church and stage have always been connected.

The Pleasure Park was the best thing about the Exhibition. The King and Queen enjoyed it too: there they are.

> Oh bygone Wembley, where's the Pleasure now?
> The temples stare, the Empire passes by.
> This was the grandest palace of them all.

The British Government Pavilion and the famous Wembley lions. Now they guard an empty warehouse site.

> But still people kept on coming to Wembley.
> The show-houses of the newly built estates.
> A younger, brighter, homelier Metro-land:
> 'Rusholme', 'Rustles', 'Rustlings', 'Rusty Tiles',
> 'Rose Hatch', 'Rose Hill', 'Rose Lea,' 'Rose Mount', 'Rose Roof'.

> Each one is slightly different from the next:
> A bastion of individual taste
> On fields that once were bright with buttercups.

Deep in rural Middlesex, the country that inspired Keats, magic casements opening on the dawn. A speculative builder here at Kingsbury let himself go in the twenties. [We see an extraordinary development of flats that look like castles, built by Ernest Trobridge (1884–1942).]

And look what a lot of country there is: fields and farms between the houses, oaks and elms above the roof tops.

> The smart suburban railway knew its place,
> And did not dare approach too near the Hill.

Here at the foot of Harrow Hill, alongside the Metropolitan electric train, tradesmen from Harrow built – in the eighties or nineties, I should think, from the look of the buildings – these houses; and a nice little speculation they were. Quiet, near the railway station, with their own church and public house, and they're named reverently after the great people of Harrow School: Drury, Vaughan and Butler.

Valiantly that Elizabethan foundation at the top of the hill has held the developers at bay. Harrow School fought to keep this hillside green but for all its tradition and elegance it couldn't wholly stem the rising tide of Metro-land. The healthy air of Harrow in the 1920s and '30s when these villas were built: you paid a deposit and eventually, we hope, you had your own house with its garage and front garden and back garden. A verge in front of your house, and grass and a tree for the dog; variety created in each façade of the houses in the colouring of the trees. In fact, the country had come to the suburbs. Roses are blooming in Metro-land, just as they do in the brochures.

Along the serried avenues of Harrow's garden villages, households rise and shine and settle down to the Sunday-morning rhythm. This is Grimsdyke in Harrow Weald. I've always regarded it as a prototype of all suburban homes in southern England. It was designed by the famous Norman Shaw a century ago. Merrie England outside; haunting and romantic within.

With Norman Shaw, one thing leads to another. I came out of a low entrance hall into this bigger hall, and then one doesn't know what is coming next. There's an arch, and if I go up there I'll see goodness knows what. Let's go and look. There's a sense of mounting excitement. Have I strayed into a Hitchcock film?

SECRETARY: Ladies, good afternoon and welcome to the Byron Luncheon Club. I would like to give a very warm welcome to our speaker, Mrs Elizabeth Cooper.

Applause.

MRS COOPER: I would like to thank you, Madam Chairman, first of all, for inviting me to this beautiful lunch, a beautiful room and a bevy of beautifully dressed and beautifully hatted ladies. I think it's the most beautiful house in Harrow: one of the most interesting both architecturally and historically.

Dear things, indeed it is. Tall brick chimney stacks, not hidden away but prominent and part of the design; local bricks, local tiles, local timber. No façade is the same. Gabled windows gaze through leaded lights down winding lawns. It isn't a fake: it's a new practical house for a newly rich Victorian: strong, impressive, original.

And yonder gloomy pool contained, on May 29th, 1911, the dead body of W. S. Gilbert, Grimsdyke's most famous owner and Sullivan's partner in the Savoy Operas. After a good luncheon he went bathing with two girls, Ruby Preece* and Winifred Emery.† Ruby found she was out of her depth and, in rescuing her, Gilbert died of a heart attack – here, in this pond.

---

* Also known as Patricia Preece. She was an artist and became the second wife of Stanley Spencer.
† Not Winifred but Isabel Emery. Ruby Preece was her pupil and perhaps her lover.

Funereal from Harrow draws the train.
On, on, north-westwards: London far away
And stations start to look quite countrified.
Pinner, a parish of a thousand souls,
Till the railways gave it many thousands more.

Pinner is famous for its village fair
Where once a year, St John the Baptist's day,
Shows all the climbing High Street filled with stalls.
It is the feast day of the parish saint,
A medieval fair in Metro-land.

When I was young there stood among the fields
A lonely station once called Sandy Lodge,
Its wooden platform crunched by hobnailed shoes,
And this is where the healthier got out.

One of the joys of Metro-land was the nearness of golf to London
– and Moor Park, Rickmansworth, was a great attraction. 'Now,
eye on the ball; left knee slightly bent, slow back . . . Missed
it! Well that wasn't up to much. Perhaps the clubhouse is more
exciting.'

Did ever golf club have a nineteenth hole as sumptuous as this?
Did ever golf club have so fine a hall? Venetian decor, 1732.

And yonder dome is not a dome at all
But painted in the semblance of a dome;
The sculptured figures all are done in paint
That lean towards us with so rapt a look.
How skilfully the artist takes us in.

What Georgian wit these classic gods have heard,
Who now must listen to the golfer's tale
Of holes in one and how I missed that putt,
Hooked at the seventh, sliced across the tenth
But ended on the seventeenth all square.

Ye gods, ye gods, how comical we are!
Would Jove have been appointed captain here?
See how exclusive thine estate, Moor Park.

Onwards, onwards, north of the border, down Hertfordshire way.
The Croxley Green Revels – a tradition that stretches back to 1952.
For pageantry is deep in all our hearts, and this, for many a girl, is
her greatest day.

Large uneventful fields of dairy farm.
Slowly winds the Chess, brimful of trout.
An unregarded part of Hertfordshire
Awaits its fate.

And in the heights above, Chorleywood village, where in '89 the
railway came.

And wood smoke mingled with the sulphur fumes,
And people now could catch the early train
To London and be home just after tea.

This is, I think, essential Metro-land.
Much trouble has been taken to preserve
The country quality surviving here:
Oak, hazel, hawthorn, gorse and sandy tracks,
Better for sport than farming, I suspect.

Common and cricket pitch, church school and church: all are
reminders of a country past.

BOY: Mrs Hill, we've got eight rounders now.

In the orchards beyond the Common, one spring morning in 1900,
a young architect, Charles Voysey, and his wife decided to build
themselves a family home. I think it was the parent of thousands of
simple English houses. 'All must be plain and practical.' That sloping buttress wall is to counteract the outward thrust of the heavy
slate roof. Do you notice those stepped tiles below the chimney

pots? They're there to throw off the driving English rain. And that lead roof ridge is pinched up at the end for the same reason. Horizontal courses of red tiles in the white walls protect windows and openings. It's hard to believe that so simple and stalwart a house was built in Queen Victoria's reign.

Voysey liked to design every detail in his house – for instance, that knocker: Voysey. A typical curious-shaped handle: Voysey. And this handle or iron hinge with what seems to be his signature tune, the heart: it's there at the end of the hinge, it's here round the letterbox, it's also round the keyhole and it seems to be on the key. That's a Voysey key. And in the house he did everything down to the knives and forks.

The plan of the house radiates out from this hall. Extreme simplicity is the keynote. No unnecessary decoration. The balusters here for the stairs – straight verticals – giving an impression of great height to this simple hall. But as a matter of fact, it isn't a particularly high house; in fact it's rather small. I knew Mr Voysey and I saw Mrs Voysey: they were small people and in case you think it's a large house, I'll just walk – I'm fat, I know, but I'm not particularly tall – and I'll stand by the door here and you compare my height with the ledge and the door.

A round window on the garden side of the house. A typical Voysey detail, this pane that opens to let in the air from beechy Bucks, which is just on the other side of the road, over there.

Back to the simple life, back to nature, to a shady retreat in the reeds and rushes of the River Chess. The lure of Metro-land was remoteness and quiet. This is what a brochure of the twenties said: 'It's the trees, the fairy dingles and a hundred and one things in which Dame Nature's fingers have lingered long in setting out this beautiful array of trout stream, wooded slope, meadow and hilltop sites. Send a postcard for the homestead of your dreams to Loudwater Estate, Chorleywood.'

> O happy outdoor life in Chorleywood,
> In Daddy's swim-pool, while old Spot looks on
> And Susan dreams of super summer hols,
> Whilst chlorinated wavelets brush the banks.

O happy indoor life in Chorleywood,
Where strangest dreams of all are realised.
Mellifluating out from modern brick
The pipe-dream of a local man, Len Rawle;
For pipe by pipe and stop by stop he moved
Out of the Empire Cinema, Leicester Square,
The Mighty Wurlitzer
Till the huge instrument filled half his house
With all its multitude of sound effects.

Steam took us onwards through the ripening fields –
Ripe for development – where the landscape yields
Clay for warm brick, timber for post and rail,
Through Amersham to Aylesbury and the Vale.
In those wet fields the railway didn't pay;
The Metro stops at Amersham today.

In 1931 all Buckinghamshire was scandalised by the appearance high above Amersham of a concrete house in the shape of a letter Y. It was built for a young professor by a young architect, Amyas Connell. They called it 'High and Over'. 'I am the home of a twentieth-century family,' it proclaimed, 'that loves air and sunlight and open country.' It started a style called Moderne – perhaps rather old-fashioned today. And one day, poor thing, it woke up and found developers in its back garden.

Goodbye, *High* hopes and *Over* confidence.
In fact, it's probably goodbye England.

Where are the advertisements? Where the shopping arcade, the coal merchant and the parked cars? This is a part of the Metropolitan Railway that's been entirely forgotten. Beyond Aylesbury it lies, in flat fields with huge elms and distant blue hills: Quainton Road Station. It was to have been the Clapham Junction of the rural part of the Metropolitan. With what hopes this place was built in 1890. They hoped that trains would run down the main line there from London to the Midlands and the North. They'd come, from the

Midlands and the North, rushing through here to London and a Channel Tunnel and then on to Paris. But alas, all that has happened is that there, a line curves away to the last of the Metropolitan stations in the country in far Buckinghamshire, which was at Verney Junction.

And I can remember sitting here on a warm autumn evening in 1929 and seeing the Brill tram from the platform on the other side, with steam up ready to take two or three passengers through oil-lit halts and over level crossings – a rather bumpy journey to a station not far from the remote hilltop village of Brill. The houses of Metro-land never got as far as Verney Junction.

Grass triumphs. And I must say I'm rather glad.

MANCHESTER

HEATON HALL

From the Shell series *Discovering Britain with John Betjeman*
Random Film Productions Ltd
ITV, Spring 1956 (exact date unknown)
Director: Peter Woosnam-Mills

• • •

A drive to Heaton Hall, in the misty suburbs of Manchester. (Here's the portico of the old Town Hall, brought here forty years ago.)

And there's the house, designed by James Wyatt in 1772 for the first Lord Wilton. I wish the Corporation had bought the furniture too when they so wisely bought Heaton Hall from the fifth Earl in 1901 but they did the next best thing: they made it a museum of Georgian craftsmanship. Glass, for instance – like this goblet with Sunderland Bridge, a triumph of cast-iron engineering, engraved upon it. Here too is a wonderful collection of silver from Stuart to late Georgian times. (I like this thing: it's called a taper stick. It can be used for lighting cigars and cigarettes today but in 1780, when it was made, it was a table light.)

The chief rooms of the house, like this Music Room, are so well proportioned, they hardly need furniture to enhance them – but let's look at this organ: a two-manual, made by King George III's organ-builder. The range of stops is well ahead of its time. Classical figures in pale greys and greens adorn its panels; those pipes are made of pure tin to give sweetness of tone and they're gilded for display. This mahogany piano with decorations in satinwood veneer was made in London in Wardour Street by Stodart* in 1784. I can think

---

* Robert Stodart of Kailzie, Peebleshire, (1748–1831), piano-maker to George III, contributed significantly to the design of the concert piano.

of no better way of enjoying the porcelain-like beauty of Heaton Hall than to the accompaniment of eighteenth-century music.

The grand staircase. Notice the balusters and the candle stands and these scagliola columns. The age of elegance.

And now Heaton Hall is open to the public as one of Manchester's seven art galleries. It is four miles north of Manchester.

NORFOLK

KING'S LYNN TO HUNSTANTON

Original title: 'John Betjeman Goes by Train'
A section in 'All Along the Line' in the *Outlook* series
BBC TV East Anglia, with participation from the British Transport
    Films Unit
BBC Television (East Anglia Region), 17 April 1961
Director and producer: Malcolm Freegard

•   •   •

We are leaving the London line – do you see? – from King's Lynn to Hunstanton:* we are travelling to the sea.

Do you know, this is like a dream come true. I've always wanted to do this on a train: to be able to go on one of these country-line journeys, looking at the scenery, far better than you can ever see it by road, and telling you what it's like and pointing out the things to left and right of us.

Now we're coming out into the open flat land at the mouth of the Wash: flat on all sides. It might be Lincolnshire but it isn't: it's Norfolk but it's the part of Norfolk nearest Lincolnshire – long lines of level drains, then the grey North Sea.

Now we're coming out of the flat land into the royal country of Sandringham and guarding it is Wolferton Church, the usual Norfolk church with a tall tower and a tall nave and chancel – [the engine sounds its whistle] the driver liked that bit – and then we come to Wolferton Station, different from all other stations in England.

As soon as you step on to the platform at Wolferton Station† you

---

* Pronounced 'Hunston'.
† The station is no longer in use. It was closed in 1966, sold in 1967 and opened as a museum in 1977. In the 1990s it was converted into a private residence.

realise that it was built in the time of railways when no expense
was spared. I mean, look at this carved stone from a local quarry – a
lovely brown colour. Little bits of it there, big bits of it there, careful pattern and red brick here to contrast – and then there, the style
of a Norfolk manor-house porch. It looks to me from the carving
and the style of it generally as though it was done in the time of
King Edward VII and I expect it's the addition to the station that
was built in his time. And there, through the arch, you get a proper
Sandringham vista: a medieval-style lantern of the reign of King
Edward – and, beyond, a station lantern in Queen Victoria's grandest manner, with a crown on top. There are station lanterns like
that all over this station.

There are no posters on Wolferton Station and you'll notice how
the signal box is made to fit in with the style of the cottage to which
it's attached. And there in the distance is Wolferton Church; and
here, nearer, on the corner, is the stationmaster's house, 1897, looking proudly down on to the platform opposite – 1894 and earlier,
in a half-timbered style.

Of course this station is much more spick and span than any
other. It has won thirty prizes in the Eastern region for being so –
and I'm not surprised. And it's not just the outside. Look here, at the
public waiting room and booking office. Leaded windows. Framed
pictures, of prizes and things, round the wall. A pelargonium on
the round table. A patterned carpet. A fireplace. It's just like home
– and all clean and shiny.

Now we've left the hilly, heathery part, which looks like
Scotland and Surrey mixed, and are coming into a part that rather
looks like the Norfolk Brecks, though it isn't the Brecks – that's
to say, it's silver birches and, surprisingly enough among the silver
birches, red farms and flint churches.

I'll get out here at Snettisham and sit on the platform for a bit
and wait for the next train.

It's unadulterated north Norfolk. I can think of few pleasanter
places to hang about in on a sunny afternoon like this than Snettisham
Station. And by the way it's called 'Snett-sham' though it's spelled
'Snett-i-sham' and it's a complete contrast with Wolferton Station.
A remote country place it is, though Snettisham's a much bigger

place than Wolferton itself, and it's got all the little characteristics that I like about a country station. In the hedge behind me there's written 'Snettisham' in box letters and 'GER', still cut year by year there; and even on this seat, the thing that's supporting me, it has 'Great Eastern Railway' in cast-iron work.

And at the end of the platform, where the line curves away to Lynn, there's a lilac bush in full bloom and beside it an eighteenth-century Norfolk farmhouse in that rich plum-coloured brick that you get in these parts, with an annexe to it and a garden wall with wallflowers. And on the other side, where the trains go to Hunstanton, two stations away, deliciously and unexpectedly in the shelter is a poster that says, 'Come to Bavaria'.

As we leave the station, notice the change of buildings: the engine shed, rather like a Primitive Methodist chapel; the wall, completely Georgian in proportion though it was probably built in Queen Victoria's reign, forming a pleasant group with Ken Hill Wood behind, and beech trees and the appearance of a park.

We are mounting a hill. The country's becoming as though it were quite far inland. Until suddenly – there – is the long level land below the North Sea. Once this was marsh land but in 1953 there were terrible floods. It doesn't seem to have disheartened people, the flood.

Here we are, straight as a die, heading straight for the terminus. If the diesel goes too fast we'll go right through the barrier, out through the hotel and into the sea.

There's the green at Hunstanton, just outside the station: a nice outline except for that concrete lamp standard – and here, the sea. I'm glad that there were children on the train: that was right. The train brought the children home from school to the sea and it's brought me to this bracing wide Norfolk coast.

DISS

Original title: 'Something about Diss'
BBC East Anglia
BBC Telelvision (East Anglia Region), 25 March 1964
Director and producer: Malcolm Freegard

• • •

Ah, Norfolk. Diss. Here's the station. Where's Diss? All I know about Diss, up to date, is that it's near the headquarters of the British Goat Society. That's all I know at the moment. I must go and find Diss.

[To a driver who takes his bag] Yes, thank you so much.

I say, what's that over there? The Jolly Porters? A very unexpected place to find an inn. [He tries the door. It won't open.] Too early. Perhaps there's some more of Diss round at the back of the house. [He goes round the back.] Anyone in? Hello? [A shirt flutters on the line.] No luck. [He gets back into the car.] Well, can you take me into the town?

Now do remember this: nowhere in England is dull, not even the road from the station on a wet day. How far is Diss? Just a mile from here.

[He observes the passing scenery as they drive and comments on what he sees.] Industry. That's the tar refinery. It's always rather rough-looking near the station. And now we're turning into Victoria Road. The railway came, you see, in 1847 – hence 'Victoria' Road. There's been more modern development since. And there's still bits of country coming right up into the town. Right up to the gasworks. And where there's a gasworks there must be a town. Oh yes, a new estate. Victorian villas. Earlier Victorian villas. And now round the corner and there's Diss. A nice little Georgian terrace on the left. Another Georgian house.

Hello, what's that? Some sort of lake or something? Yes, the Mere. This must be Mere Street, the chief shopping street of the town. There's the coaching inn. Elizabethan, I should think, with that overhanging upper storey. [He gets out of the car.] I think I'll put my luggage here and go through the yard at the back and see if I can find that Mere again. Let's just have a look.

Here's the yard. Yes, there's the Mere, with the houses of Diss all round the edge of it. That's pretty, that place down at the water level.

Now we'll start off and explore. The first thing to do – oh, a medieval carved angel on a shop – the first thing to do is to go to the bookshop and make straight for the stand of postcards. There's generally some local views and they show what the people in the town are most proud of. I'll take – yes, I'll take those. Is there a local guide? Oh, there's the local paper – actually printed here at the back of this shop, the *Diss Express*. And a guide. I'll take both, thank you very much. Now we'll go off to the town.

Now let's have a reading from the local guidebook:

> Though a busy country town, Diss has a wholesome charm all its own, which has wooed and won many a stranger. The Victorian era saw the heyday of the country market town. Many, nay most of them have lost much of their importance to the principal county towns, but not so Diss.

The marketplace. There it is on a Friday. I like the Shambles, there on the right with their Georgian columns, and the little glimpse you get of the parish church. There is the church before Victorian restoration and exactly the same view today. This East Anglian napped flint looks marvellous: it shines like crystal in the sharp spring sunlight, contrasting with the silvery stone. Look at that gargoyle with a spout in its mouth: fifteenth century. It was in the fifteenth century that John Skelton, tutor to Henry VIII, was rector here. Skelton was the poet of birds, beasts, flowers, love and jokes. (He must have looked at that flint.) He called himself 'Rector of Hell'. Here's his church. Listen to some of his lines:

> Ye may hear now, in this rhyme,
> How every thing must have a time
> . . . . . .

Time to be sad, and time to play and sport;
   Time to take rest by way of recreation;
Time to study, and time to use comfort;
   Time of pleasure, and time of consolation:
    Thus time hath his time of divers manner fashion:
Time for to eat and drink for thy repast;
Time to be liberal, and time to make no waste;

Time to travail, and time for to rest;
   Time for to speak, and time to hold thy peace;
Time would be usèd when time is best;
   Time to begin, and time for to cease;
    And when time is, [to] put thyself in press,
And when time is, to hold thyself aback;
For time well spent can never have lack.*

It's easy to discover Diss of the Middle Ages in the houses round here by the church – I mean, that inn through the arch there, called the Saracen's Head. Or come outside from the churchyard and look out at the traffic and, just opposite, there's a narrow alley called Drapers Row – and it's always worth going up alleys in old towns: you never know what sort of a building you aren't going to discover. For instance, in this one, in Drapers Row, on the right there, there's a medieval house – the one with the bicycle leaning against it: you see how the first storey hangs over? And then turn left at the top of the alley and go across to Market Hill, walk past the draper's, and I'll show you another bit of medieval Diss.

Do you see there's a corn chandler's shop coming up? And on the corner there's a beam. And carved on it, the Annunciation on the left there and the Nativity on the Right: Norfolk's devotion to Our Lady – Our Lady of Walsingham.

And now the guidebook again:

The business life of Diss turns very naturally upon the surrounding agricultural district and its market and Diss still depends primarily on the farmers. Erected in 1854, the Corn Hall was given to the Council

* 'Ye May Hear Now, in This Rhyme' by John Skelton (c. 1460–1529). Lines 3–9 were omitted by Betjeman.

by Rear Admiral A. H. Taylor in 1956 and has since been redecorated in pastel shades, with toilets and kitchen added. The weekly corn sales, which rate among the most important in East Anglia, are held here every Friday.

Now I'm going to show you something. Come down the hill here: you see that brick wall, next to the Corn Hall? That is an inn, the Greyhound; and, you know, Diss doesn't show itself at once: you have to go and look to find the treasures – and where they are, they're not faked up: they're genuine. See that plasterwork in the Greyhound: Jacobean at the very latest. And then come into what must have been part of the huge room, probably originally hung with tapestry or painted, and goodness knows what sort of roistering in Elizabethan days or Jacobean days went on behind that door.

After the roistering, reaction: Puritanism. Diss, like all East Anglian towns, is full of Nonconformist chapels. The older ones are hidden down alleys. The Plymouth Brethren's meeting house, 1830, with a little graveyard at the back: Gospel simplicity. The Unitarian chapel, down by the edge of the Mere: very elegant. (It's now a Masonic hall: a bit of New England, here in Norfolk. I should think it was built about 1800.) There's the Quaker meeting house: very simple. The Baptists rebuilt themselves in the 1860s, on the other hand, in a very grand manner: sort of Lombardic.

And with Nonconformity goes thrift. The prosperous merchants of Diss built themselves new houses with large gardens sloping down to the edge of the Mere. There's one, right down by the Mere itself – Park House, there it is: I should think about 1840. And right at the top of the town, away from Park House, there's Mount Street and this late-Georgian door of a lawyer's house, and from it you can look down a charming country-town street, still very like that old photograph there; and that one. On the right is Mount Pleasant: chief house of the town, where Admiral Taylor lives. There's Admiral Taylor welcoming his son. The Admiral's ancestors built this house in the eighteenth century. They were brewers and Unitarians. Notice the trouble taken about the detail: that dentil cornice, white paint against red brickwork, and a splendid great garden window. And on the other side of Mount Street, see that bit of country? It's still the same today: a bit of country coming right into the town. A little park.

From the elegant quiet of the professions, let's go down into the town and to the shops. Look at the chemist's there: Gostling. Perfect mid-Victorian. Notice the lamp: the same sort of lamp over the same firm [comparing the modern-day shop with an old photo]. And that chemist's,* a Georgian exterior. And here are the drapers' shops, founded in 1847. Notice the name: Bobby's. It's the same family as all those Bobby's stores on the south-coast towns but they're now part of a big combine while the Bobby's in Diss still belongs to the family. Look at that woodwork: the mahogany counter, the oak shelves, all about 1850 – and there's Mr Bobby himself. He's been a draper in Diss all his life, as have his father and grandfather before him. Have a look at the detail of that Victorian carving.

All this time, there's been something I haven't pointed out to you. It's the kind of thing you come to take for granted, strolling about in a town like Diss: the happy inconsequence of everything. The way old houses go well with less-old ones, like that one on the left and the one beyond on the right. The sudden glimpse, as you're coming down Denmark Hill, for instance, between two buildings and you see the Mere down below you. And the way gardens look over red-tiled roofs. And how, from the middle of the town, you can look over sharp roofs to the country and the church. And on the whole, an absence of traffic – at any rate heavy through-traffic. Real quiet. The sense of a happy, self-contained, friendly community.

Diss. It would be a very nice place to live. Not too big. Not too small. A good train service. And no main road.

But look what's happening. The old houses in the back streets of the town, instead of being repaired are being allowed to fall to bits. Instead of being enlarged, that's what's happening to them [we see smashed window panes]. Some, I grant you, aren't worth preserving [we see two small, plain, brick-fronted, late-Georgian cottages in a terrace]; others are [we see white-plastered cottages with pantiles] and you could buy them very cheaply and turn them into comfort-

* Gibson.

able places to live in. It's been done. I mean, look at this row of cottages. They've let them fall to bits on the left here; and then on the right, there's one that's been put into repair. And here are others. They're not right into the centre of the town but they're very near it: much nearer than the council estate. And look at those: they're the real Diss, on the Fair Green.

What you don't want in Diss is copybook contemporary architecture, like this: out of scale, out of texture and very soon out of date [we see a mock-Georgian brick gateway with coach lamps, and a tall, cubist building behind it with Crittall windows]. I mean, look at those real Diss houses and compare them with that thing [we see a terrace of old cottages and then a rectangular box with a 'modern' version of sash windows]. And those [we see terraces of typical 1950s council housing] could just as well be in Slough or Southall.

Let's go down to the Mere and say goodbye to Diss.

There's something I want to tell you before we go. It's very serious. There are rumours of an overspill coming to Diss. That means thousands of industrial workers from the North of England and London will be settled down on rich agricultural land outside the town. It means that supermarkets will appear in the streets, that there will be strangers everywhere; and I suppose you can say it is prosperity of a sort: it'll mean money. But it will be the end of Diss – the end of what is home for four thousand people. Is it really in the public interest, to use a Civil Service phrase, to overwhelm a balanced, prosperous community with a strange one? Are the Treasury, the Board of Trade and the planning authorities to trample on our hearts? It can't be right.★

★ The overspill that Betjeman feared did not take place but the population has since almost doubled, to around 7,000.

A PASSION FOR CHURCHES

Working title: 'Failed in Divinity'
BBC2 Television, 7 December 1974
Producer: Edward Mirzoeff

• • •

I was eight or nine years old when I used to come here to the Norfolk Broads on the River Bure, sailing and rowing with my father. And I think it was the outline of that church tower of Belaugh against the sky that gave me a passion for churches, so that every church I've been past since I've wanted to stop and look in.

The air: the Old Hundredth.* The place: Bressingham. The diocese: Norwich, which includes most of Norfolk and a little bit of Suffolk.

> What would you be, you wide East Anglian sky,
> Without church towers to recognise you by?
> What centuries of faith, in flint and stone,
> Wait in this watery landscape, all alone?
> To antiquaries, 'object of research';
> To the bored tourist, 'just another church'.
> The varied Norfolk towers could also be
> A soothing sight to mariners at sea.

This is Cley-next-the-Sea. The sea is now quite a long way off. It's a tiny place but it's got an enormous church. They must have had hopes of it being very much bigger. And look at that porch – built, I should think, about 1430. Very delicately done: almost another church in itself; and slapped on to it, very coarsely, a sundial. Time suddenly stuck into eternity.

---

* The tune (based on one in the *Geneva Psalter* of 1551) is usually used for the hymn 'All People That on Earth Do Dwell'.

Look at that, for vastness and light: light falling on carved Norfolk oak, gone silvery-grey with age. And towards the light come out the nightmare figures of marsh and forest: earth-bound creatures struggling up the bench-ends. They know they can never reach the winged celestial hosts here in the roof at Knapton.

The finest of all the woodcarving is in the neighbouring parish of Trunch. It exalts the very first sacrament: baptism by water – the first armour we put on against the assaults of hate, greed and fear on our journey back to eternity. 'Cherry Ann: your godparents make promises on your behalf and the village of Trunch bears witness.'

First steps on the journey. At Mattishall they have Sunday school on Wednesday afternoon. The 'Little People', as they call them, clutching their tambourines and triangles, come to hear the old story told anew.

Each generation makes itself heard. The past cries out to us even when we try to smother the cries. Medieval saints peer at us through godly warnings put over them by pious Elizabethans who had more use for the written word than the painted picture. We can help the past come through a hundredth of an inch at a time. Miss Pauline Plummer is revealing the secrets of the chancel screen at Ranworth and soon will show it in its medieval glory.

In the fifteenth century Norwich was famous for its painters. They delighted in herbs and flowers and living creatures. The lithe and feathered figure of the Archangel Michael is by no provincial hand. It's rather a masterpiece. The Norwich artists also painted on glass, and light came in to every Norfolk church through golden late-medieval windows.

Men hate beauty. They think it's wicked. Self-righteous church-wardens delighted in smashing it. Village boys flung stones. Storms did the rest.

Today the famous Norwich glass is nearly all jumbled fragments. A few whole windows survive.

Here's where the artists worked: the City of Norwich, down in the valley of the Wensum. It's a city of cobbled alleys and winding footpaths. It has more medieval churches within its walls than London, York and Bristol put together. Remember

Norwich. Round the corner, down the steps, over the bridge, up the hill — there's always a church. And grandest of all, St Peter Mancroft — so large that sometimes people mistake it for the Cathedral.

The city wears its Cathedral like a crown: a coronal of flying buttresses supporting the walls of glass. The Normans started it. The stone was brought over the sea from France to build and adorn the Cathedral Church of the Holy and Undivided Trinity. It draws the whole diocese towards it; and in its cloisters, made for contemplation, mothers and grandmothers, vicars and rectors from the towns and villages of the diocese of Norwich gather together for the annual festival of the Mothers' Union.

Bawdeswell greets Stratton Strawless. Potter Heigham is on terms with Little Snoring. North Creake sits beside Melton Constable. And for everyone there's the chance to meet the Bishop: Maurice Wood, Diocesan Bishop of Norwich. When not entertaining, he's Maurice Norvic, Father-in-God to the clergy.

The Bishop institutes a new rector to the living of Holt in north Norfolk. By the laying on of hands, the Bishop commits to the priest the spiritual care of the parish.

With every parish church there's a house, rectory or vicarage — usually beside the churchyard. I think you probably need money of your own to be rector of Great Snoring because the rectory house is a Tudor palace, with moulded autumn-coloured brick and elaborate chimney stacks. And the date: about 1525. It's the usual practice now, though, to sell big rectories and build labour-saving villas in their place.

At Weston Longville, in Georgian days, Parson Woodforde wrote his worldly diaries, full of good dinners. The present rector types the parish magazine. Reverend James:

> We send belated birthday greetings to Mr Walter Pardon of Weston Longville who reached the splendid age of 89 years on February 17th.
>
> Little Johnny Atherton, aged three-and-a-half years, broke his leg on February 17th. Bad luck. We hope you get well soon, Johnny.
>
> It is only a rumour but there is talk of a sponsored streak for church funds.

By whom? we wonder. Not, I think, by members of the Parochial Church Council at Letheringsett: the PCC. It's meeting this evening in the church hall, with the Rector in the chair.

If it isn't the tower, it's the transept or the North porch. And the answer is usually a fête to raise another few pounds. We can rely on the parish to rally round.

> God bless the Church of England,
> The rectory lawn that gave
> A trodden space for that bazaar
> That underpinned the nave.
>
> We must dip into our pockets,
> For our hearts are full of dread
> At the thought of all the damage
> Since the roof was stripped of lead.★

And it's always worth a try to get the key, however remote the church. In fact, the remoter the better: there's more chance of its being left unspoiled.

St Mary Belaugh, in the valley of the Wensum. Look. The pulpit. This is a perfect example of a church in a park in the time of Jane Austen. The woodwork is all of oak. Notice that altarpiece with the Creed, the Commandments and the Lord's Prayer painted on it, and here is a three-decker pulpit in full sail. This is where the parish clerk said 'Amen' at the end of the prayers and announced the name of the hymn tune or the psalm tune. Here, a gentle staircase leads to the middle deck and this is where the minister, as he was called, read the holy offices of morning and evening prayer and the lessons. And if he was in the mood, or if it was the fourth Sunday in the month or something like that, he would ascend to the top deck to preach a sermon. And from here the parson could survey

★ 'God Bless the Church of England' was an uncompleted poem that Betjeman had drafted but not published. A longer version of it, but without the second stanza above and with a differently worded second line in the first stanza, appears in *Poems in the Porch: The Radio Poems of John Betjeman*, ed. Kevin Gardner (Continuum, 2008).

his whole parish. In the big box pew there, the squire from the hall, slumbering while a fire crackled in the grate; the large farmers in the pews in front; the cottagers and lesser tenantry behind; all by country custom in their place in the church by law established.

The cottagers and lesser tenantry would have had a good long walk by field and footpath to the isolated parish church of St Margaret, Felbrigg. The squire would have had a gentle stroll: it is in the park of the big house. I wonder who fall to their knees here today?

Oh – the new cottage industry: brass-rubbing. Memorial brasses to former generations of squires of Felbrigg and their ladies. Medieval effigies that tell us nothing of the people they represent, they're so calm and bland and self-controlled. Outlined there, as large as life, Sir Simon and Lady Margaret Felbrigg: he a Garter knight and she a cousin of the Queen. It must have been the day of days, the day they took their vows.

Ringing the changes, treble bell to tenor, unites young and old. Captain of the Tower and sixty years a ringer, Billy West:

BILLY WEST: Ah, that's music in your ear, that's music in the ear. Once that gets hold of you, I suppose that's like smoking cigarettes; once that gets a hold of you that, that's a drug: you can't get rid of it. There's something about it, I don't know what it is, but you'd go anywhere for it. If there weren't somewhere where there were some bells I'd go crazy, I know I should. Bells are life to me. I mean, it never seems a Sunday to me if we don't hear the bells. That never seems Sunday if you can't hear church bells going.

BETJEMAN:
I hear a deep, sad undertone in bells –
Which calls the Middle Ages back to me.
From prime to compline, the monastic hours
Echo in bells along the windy marsh
And fade away. They leave me to the ghosts
Which seem to look from this enormous sky
Upon the ruins of a grandeur gone.

St Benet's Abbey by the River Bure:
Now but an archway and a Georgian mill –
A lone memorial of the cloistered life.

Alone? No, not alone. Serene, secure,
The sisters of All Hallows, Ditchingham,
In this brick convent, for over a century now,
Have taught and trained the young and nursed the sick
And founded rescue homes.
A homely practical community.
Their souls are fed with daily Eucharists.
You see the impress there upon the bread;
You see the impress also in their lives.
Their motto:
Semper orantes, semper laborantes.
Always at prayer, and always at their work.

An Anglican convent in East Anglia.
A place to think of when the world seems mad
With too much speed and noise.
A pleasant place to come to for retreat.
There's really not much risk of being stung.★

Just as some people are holy, so are places. They draw us to them
whether we will or not. In the misty past in the 1920s and '30s
people came to Norfolk by train, by steam: by the Great Eastern
and more locally by the Midland and Great Northern Joint. They
came on pilgrimage by train, faith-enlightened, full of hope and on
the way to Walsingham.

This is all that remains of the railway track that carried all those
pilgrims to Walsingham.

And what's become of the station? It's the Orthodox church.
The Orient come to East Anglia, to this country town, where in
1061 (forgive my mentioning dates) the Lady of the Manor saw the
Virgin Mary, Mother of God.

★ We see bee-keeping.

> Then medieval pilgrims, peasants, kings,
> In thousands thronged to England's Nazareth.

The cult has been revived in modern times; suburbanised, perhaps. The Shrine of Our Lady of Walsingham: 1930s red-brick Romanesque. But inside is the goal of all the pilgrims. And very peculiar it is.

> I wonder if you'd call it superstitious?
> Here in this warm, mysterious, holy house,
> The figure of Our Lady and Her Child;
> Or do you think that forces are around,
> Strong, frightening, loving and just out of reach
> But waiting, waiting, somewhere to be asked?
> And is that somewhere here at Walsingham?
>
> The water bubbles from the Holy Well.
> By water we were brought into the Church;
> By water we are blessed along the way.

I've seen processions like this in Sicily. You can see them in the streets of Malta, too. But it's an exotic flowering of the Church of England, here in a Norfolk garden. The Anglican Church has got a bit of everything. It's very tolerant – and that is part of its strength.

Farewell to the pilgrims; here come the tourists. Sandringham is the Queen's country estate. The parish church is used by both the villagers and the Royal Family. It seems appropriate to arrive in style. [We see Betjeman arriving at Sandringham in an old Bentley.]

Originally, says the guidebook, Sandringham Church had little or nothing to distinguish it from any village church in Norfolk. Well, at first glance it rather reminds me of the Wee Kirk o' the Heather in Hollywood: those silver panels on the pulpit, that jewel-encrusted bible. But in fact it's very Edwardian, for here worshipped King Edward VII and Queen Alexandra. The ornate furnishings, this altar of solid silver, were given by Mr Rodman Wanamaker, a very rich American admirer of our royalty.

Sandringham Church has its homely touches, too. Of all the details in this church I think this is my favourite. You can tell from the swirls and the curves who the sculptor was. He was Sir Alfred Gilbert, who designed, you'll remember, Eros in Piccadilly Circus. In Sandringham he's done the figure of St George.

> I wade my way alone, no tourists near,
> Through last year's autumn leaves
> To Booton's haunting weird Victorian church.
> Its pinnacles outlined against the sky
> Seem outsize pinnacles, copies of others elsewhere,
> But they look so big
> I fear the church will topple with their weight.
> A rich Victorian rector paid for them
> And paid for all the stained-glass windows too.
> No painful crucifixions here.
> The heavenly choir, in Victorian dress,
> Makes joyful music unto the Lord of Hosts.

Let everything that hath breath praise the Lord – but practise first in the rectory at Martham, between the Broads and the sea. (Meanwhile, in his room above, the Rector, Father Cooling, model engineer, oils his parish wheels [we see the Rector busying himself with his model trainset] – and indeed they run themselves most smoothly.) Everywhere church choirs prepare for Easter. Wymondham's* Norman Abbey is the town's parish church; and in this century Sir Ninian Comper made the East wall a lofty reredos of sculptured gold. Scale is the secret of its majesty.

Scale was Comper's secret.[†] In 1914 they let him loose in this plain old country church. He turned it into a treasure house. The golden church of Lound, Suffolk, in the diocese of Norwich. Gold on the font cover to emphasise the sacrament of Baptism – entry into the Church; gold on the screen to veil the mystery of Holy Communion at the high altar.

---

* Pronounced 'Windom'.
[†] See also 'Wellingborough', p. 208.

I knew Comper. He died a few years ago and he looked rather like that advertisement for Colonel Sanders Kentucky chicken. Little white pointed beard and he spoke in a very lah-di-dah manner: 'My wark, doncha know, in that charch . . .' And his wark in this charch is really marvellous. I think this is what a late-medieval English church probably looked like when it was new. Colour very important; saints, angels and symbolic figures everywhere. Comper was much influenced by the colour and decoration of Spanish, Sicilian and Greek churches. He didn't mind about style. Sometimes he mixed Classical with Gothic. That he called 'unity by inclusion'.

As I look through this rood screen I can see the colours of the altar hangings. Pink predominates. It's called Comper Pink, and he had it specially made in Spain. He used to buy scarlet silk and there have it bleached in the sun till it was just the shade he wanted. 'Incomperable', as people used to say.

'A church should pray of itself with its architecture,' said Comper. 'It is its own prayer and should bring you to your knees when you come in.'

But there's another way. At his ordination, every Anglican priest promises to say Morning and Evening Prayer, daily. The Vicar of Flordon has rung the bell for matins each day for the past eleven years. It doesn't matter that there's no one there. It doesn't matter when they do not come. The villagers know the parson is praying for them in their church.

> In some churches all prayer has ceased.
> St Benedict's, Norwich, is a tower alone.
> But better let it stand
> A lighthouse beckoning to a changing world.
>
> St Edmund Fishergate – a store for soles of shoes.
> Once it was working for the souls of men.
>
> Churches are what make Norwich different.
> 'A church for every Sunday of the year,'
> They used to say of it. 'A use for every church'

Is what we say today, St Lawrence here –
Spacious and filled with mitigated light.
The matchless words of the Book of Common Prayer
Once rolled along these walls.
Now young artists use it for a studio.
Better that than let the building fall.

Artists come to St Mary Coslany, too. In this church John Sell
Cotman, the Norfolk watercolour painter, was baptised, and here
Crome the artist was married. The present congregation is well
upholstered. It is all stored here for charity.

A use for every church – a thought not new.
Four hundred years ago St Helen's, Norwich,
Became a hostel and a hospital.
Men in the nave, ladies in the chancel,
The parish church in between.
This is the upper floor of the chancel, the Eagle Ward.
And here you can be cared for till you die.

And should we let the poor old churches die?
Do the stones speak? My word, of course they do.
Here in the midst of life they cry aloud:
'You've used us to build houses for your prayer;
You've left us here to die beside the road.'

Christ, son of God, come down to me and save:
How fearful and how final seems the grave.
Only through death can resurrection come;
Only from shadows can we see the light;
Only at our lowest comes the gleam:
Help us, we're all alone and full of fear.
Drowning, we stretch our hands to you for aid
And wholly unexpectedly you come:
Most tolerant and all-embracing Church.

Wide is the compass of the Church of England. The Smith's Point Lighthouse is the furthest point of the Norwich diocese, twenty-two miles out to sea. The Revd Maurice Chant, Chaplain of the Missions to Seamen in Great Yarmouth, comes aboard to meet the men, see if there are any problems and to be there just in case he's needed. He distributes the Mission's magazine and pastoral greetings.

On inland waters, Canon Blackburne, Chaplain of the Norfolk Broads, summons the floating members of his flock to Easter service.

Easter Day. Dawn over the easternmost tip of Britain: Ness Point, Lowestoft. At six o'clock in the morning, led by the band of the Salvation Army, all churches join in the first Easter service and greet the rising sun.

> Peaceful their lives are, calm and unsurprising,
> The almshouse ladies here at Castle Rising;
> And suited to the little brick-built square
> The Jacobean hats and cloaks they wear.
> See from the separate rooms in which they dwell
> Each one process. The Warden pulls the bell:
> Fingers and knees not yet too stiff to pray
> And thank the Lord for life this Easter Day.
>
> Bells of St Peter Mancroft loudly pealing
> Fill the whole city with an Easter feeling.
> 'Is risen today, is risen today,' they plead,
> Where footpath, lane and steep up-alley lead.
>
> Across the diocese from tower to tower
> The church bells exercise compelling power.
> 'Come all to church, good people,'* hear them say;
> 'Come all to church, today is Easter Day.'
> Over our Vicar we may not agree,
> He seems too High to you, too Low to me;

* From 'Bredon Hill' in *A Shropshire Lad* by A. E. Housman (1859–1936).

But still the faith of centuries is seen
In those who walk to church across the green.
The faith of centuries is in the sound
Of Easter bells that ring all Norfolk round;
And though for church we may not seem to care,
It's deeply part of us. Thank God it's there.

NORTHAMPTONSHIRE

WELLINGBOROUGH

From the Shell series *Discovering Britain with John Betjeman*
Random Film Productions Ltd
ITV, 24 February 1956
Director: Peter Woosnam-Mills

• • •

Wellingborough is a town in Northamptonshire that makes boots. You can see it was once an old place from those cottages there on the right but today it's mostly an ordinary industrial town – and then suddenly, out of the comfortable humdrum houses, you see this enormous building rising: St Mary's Church, built of the local brown Northamptonshire stone.

It's quite plain outside, but inside – there! That screen that stretches right across the church is of wood covered with gold leaf and burnished with an agate. See how it takes the morning sunlight. And those columns are orangey-brown and of local ironstone. The mouldings on them are like the Parthenon: Greek, yes – but look at the roof: it's Gothic and vaulted. All styles are blended into one here and you can spend hours in this church looking at the detail. That organ case is of burnished gold and the pipes are silver; and look at those decorations below: they're pale lilac and green, painted on a creamy white background.

A gallery crosses from the organ loft over to the great screen; and while you're looking at the details of the screen, I must tell you something about St Mary's Church, Wellingborough.

It was started in the year I was born: 1906 – and everything you see was done by British craftsmen in our own lifetime. The architect, Sir Ninian Comper, is still alive. He didn't just build the outside walls and leave it: he supervised every detail as well – colour, stained glass, carving in stone and wood, hangings and ironwork. This, his greatest work, is generally considered the finest modern church in England – and it's not just a pointless riot of colour. There's a scheme behind it all. D'you see that round thing coming into view? There's Adam and Eve; and there above, Christ on the Cross; and above that, Christ triumphant, sitting on clouds under a blue roof adorned with gold stars and angels. But the heart of the building is the altar: a lantern for the church, a place to bring you to your knees.

Wellingborough is sixty-six miles from London and sixty miles from Birmingham.

OXFORDSHIRE

GREAT COXWELL

From the Shell series *Discovering Britain with John Betjeman*
Random Film Productions Ltd
ITV, 14 October 1955
Director: Peter Woosnam-Mills

. . .

You can get to this place from London by going over the Thames into Abingdon, once the capital of Berkshire. If you're coming from Birmingham to what we're going to see, you come through the Cotswolds, as here at Alvescot. Stone walls everywhere: stone used as though it was wood – and honey-coloured stone that never looks out of place.

And then we come to the little Berkshire town of Faringdon, which really is a country town and not a suburb, with its own town hall and shops. And out on the road to Highworth we come to this almost hidden signpost – 'Great Coxwell' – and little would you know what a surprise you're in for, a little down the lane.

Into the farmyard – and there it is, this enormous medieval tithe barn. It looks like a church and it was built six hundred years ago for the monks of Beaulieu Abbey.

Have a look at the outside. You see that man going past? Well, he'll give you some idea of how enormous the barn is. The view I like best is here, from the duck pond. Just look at the height of that roof. Do you see how the tiles are small at the top and then, as we come down the roof, they get bigger until here at the eaves they're almost as big as gravestones? Those stone tiles came from a local quarry – and here is a local quarry that has just the same limestone as our barn.

Stone walls, stone roof – and inside, a cathedral but a very dark cathedral: you have to get used to the lack of light. And rising from stone pillars, oak masts fifty feet high support the roof. And just look at the beams carrying that tremendous weight of stone: not a nail anywhere; and the walls are four feet thick, taking the main weight. In the middle there are transepts; and up there, that's where the overseer used to watch the tenth part of the Abbey land brought in.

It's good to see it still used for farming today and not as some cultural museum of folk art. Really, those tractors and the Dutch barn behind them fit in with this old building just as well as did the Berkshire wagons and the flails of the medieval peasants.

Great Coxwell is about two miles west of Faringdon, Berkshire, so that makes it seventy-one from London and about sixty-five south of Birmingham.

ABINGDON

From the Shell series *Discovering Britain with John Betjeman*
Random Film Productions Ltd
ITV, 21 October 1955
Director: Peter Woosnam-Mills

• • •

For a thousand people who go to Oxford, only one goes to Abingdon seven miles away. It was once the capital of Berkshire and the beautiful street of St Helen's reminds you of its greatness. These houses on the left, though they may look modest enough in front, have long flowery gardens at the back and fine front doors like this one. (I should think it dates from George II's reign.)

When we come to the churchyard, we find round it a sort of paradise of almshouses. There are three separate buildings. These are some of the newest and they're 250 years old but I think the best of all is the oldest of all: it's this almshouse called Christ's Hospital, built five hundred years ago almost as it is now. That lantern in the middle and those paintings in the squares above the entrance were done while Shakespeare was alive and therefore they're quite new.

The part I like is this Long Gallery, where the alms-people can sit when it's raining. Their houses lead off it. It's flagged with stone and through its wooden arcading you can see Abingdon Parish Church. The lantern was put there in 1605 because it looked nice on the skyline. You can see it from underneath if you stand in the hall; and in this hall, since Queen Elizabeth's time, the governors of Christ's Hospital have met. Even the fire buckets are ancient: 1805 I think the date is, and they're made of leather.

Here you see the two men who helped to found the almshouse and who gave the money to build that bridge over the Thames at Abingdon that brought prosperity to the town. This oak table cost £4 to make in 1618. It must have been made in the room, since there's no way of getting it out without sawing it in half.

Charity doesn't mean soup and jelly: it means loving your neighbour. In the windows are the arms of people who loved their neighbours enough to give money to this hospital.

Three hundred years ago Samuel Pepys came here and put in his diary, 'So did give to the poor, which they would not take but in their money box, two-and-sixpence.' Yes, in that money box. Let us do the same.

You'll find these almshouses down by the Thames in Abingdon, and Abingdon's fifty-six miles west of London and seventy-one from Birmingham.

EDINBURGH AND OXFORD

An item within the series *Panorama*
BBC Television, 5 December 1955

• • •

[There are plans to build a car park to serve Edinburgh Castle. The plan is discussed by experts in Edinburgh and then the subject is thrown to the studio in London where the host of *Panorama*, Richard Dimbleby, passes the questioning to Malcolm Muggeridge.]

MUGGERIDGE: John, I know that this is a subject about which you've got very strong views. I know that anything in the nature of a car park is infinitely repugnant to you. What do you think about this controversy that we've just been hearing about?

BETJEMAN: Well I love Edinburgh. I think it's the most beautiful capital – and it is a capital – in Europe. And I think Princes Street . . . the building side of it is pretty dull but what makes Princes Street marvellous is that great sweep of garden, the outline up above the Old Town. And there's one good thing about that car park: it's underground. It isn't messing up the outline, which is the great thing in Edinburgh.

MUGGERIDGE: So in general you're in favour of it?

BETJEMAN: I'm in favour of an underground car park in Edinburgh.

MUGGERIDGE: An underground car park in Edinburgh?

BETJEMAN: Yes.

MUGGERIDGE: Now what about – isn't there some sort of controversy going on in Oxford of a similar order?

BETJEMAN: Oh dear boy, yes. And there's Oxford High Street [we see an old photograph of Oxford] and I don't know whether you can see it but there are some old-fashioned motor cars there and a nice cart in front of the buildings. They look all right but of course it's absolute tripe to say that cars are beautiful because they express their purpose in front of an old building.

MUGGERIDGE: Now wait, John. I know you've got . . . I know all the tricks of yours. I mean, nobody was saying that cars are beautiful. We're only dealing with a particular problem, which is parking them.

BETJEMAN: Oh yes, they're beautiful in their way but in Oxford they look absolutely hideous, and the chief thing that makes Oxford appalling now is parked cars, so anything that will get rid of parked cars is what's really wanted, and I think the controversy about the roads that's going on now is slightly putting the – oh, you know – cart before the horse. I mean, the engine behind the bonnet, or whatever the phrase is, but because Oxford is still what it was in medieval times, it's still a stone city surrounded by meadows (admittedly there's Cowley, an enormous new thing, outside it) and that really at all costs should be preserved.

MUGGERIDGE: No, but does this road – I mean *this* road – is that going to destroy . . .

BETJEMAN: That's going to go right through that.

MUGGERIDGE: Now is that necessary, do you think?

BETJEMAN: Well that's what I'm not sure about. I'm not certain that in Oxford any proper traffic census has been taken. We know there are too many cars parked but we ought really to find out more about what sort of cars come into the place, more about how many stay for a long time, all sorts of things like that: that hasn't been done; nor what size cars come into the place. And then enough car parks should be provided. That's the first thing.

MUGGERIDGE: But where, John – I mean, the point is, I quite agree with you: nobody wants to destroy anything beautiful wantonly, but something has got to be done, hasn't it, about this problem of motor traffic?

BETJEMAN: And the first thing to do is to take an adequate census. The next thing to do is to make adequate by-passes out in the outer fringe and then see whether they need these things. But don't let's ruin the green surrounds of Oxford until it's essential.

MUGGERIDGE: What would you yourself do, for instance, about the centre of Oxford, which is a frightful traffic congestion, isn't it?

BETJEMAN: Oh, I'd clear all the cars away and never allow anybody to drive anything there, except a horse and cart or go on foot. I wouldn't even have a bicycle.

MUGGERIDGE: Supposing . . . What would you do . . . what would you do with the motor cars?

BETJEMAN: Burn them up! I mean, they're a frightful nuisance in Oxford. They shouldn't be there. They ruin the place. They absolutely make it simply hideous, as they make every old town in England hideous.

MUGGERIDGE: You would destroy them all?

BETJEMAN: Yes. And what will town clerks and borough engineers do who run the country for us and run our towns for us and smash everything we like? They want to take down every old building which is irreplaceable and put a car park in its place.

MUGGERIDGE: You know what I would like to do with you, John? I would like to make you town clerk of some rather obscure borough and it would be extremely interesting to see what you did there. And at the same time it would shut you up to a certain extent on this particular mania of yours, wouldn't it.

BETJEMAN: Oh no. Well, I don't think it's a mania. I mean, I feel desperately serious about this.

MUGGERIDGE: But are you talking sense about it? That's the real point.

BETJEMAN: Well, I think that old buildings are more important than modern motor cars because modern motor cars can be replaced and can be parked somewhere; old buildings can't be replaced.

MUGGERIDGE: And therefore, if you've got to have communications, there may come a point when you have to choose between communications and an old building.

BETJEMAN: Well, supposing you had to choose between Oxford and Morris cars? Well, I know nowadays, of course, everyone will say Morris cars are much more important than those old buildings – that we live in barbarism.

MUGGERIDGE: I think it's a fallacy, John.

CHASTLETON HOUSE

From the Shell series *Discovering Britain with John Betjeman*
Random Film Productions Ltd
ITV, 2 March 1956
Director: Peter Woosnam-Mills

• • •

We're on the road from Stow-on-the-Wold to Chipping Norton. There's a signpost saying 'Chastleton House 1603'.* Turn off and we're in deepest Cotswold quiet. No poles or wires to spoil the scene. The paddock, the church, golden stone weathered by centuries of sun and rain, the gateway arch. And there it is: Chastleton House – a royalist stronghold of the Civil Wars.

In the Dining Room, you can get the feel of the place. The same family has lived here – the Joneses – since the house was built in 1603, so there are treasures of all dates laid out for you to see, and this Jacobean ceiling hangs over the Great Chamber. Marble chimney piece, Chinese lacquer cabinets and, on the wall, what is generally considered the finest panelling of its date in England.

I said the family was royalist: let's go and look at a mystery of

* Betjeman pronounces the date as 'sixteen-three'.

the house. Arthur Jones fought for Charles II at Worcester. The Roundheads followed him here. He rushed up to this room, through that secret door which was then hidden in tapestry, across this little room, and hid himself in this cupboard. The Roundheads couldn't find him. Meanwhile his wife, Mistress Jones, put a drug into their beer and when they were asleep Arthur Jones escaped.

Here he is. His portrait hangs in the Entrance Hall and all those weapons and armour you can see hanging on the walls belonged to the Jones family, which was loyal to the Stuarts and fought for the King. And on that long table is the greatest treasure in the house: it's the Bible that King Charles I used on the scaffold. It's bound in orange leather with the royal arms stamped on it in gold. What I am holding now Charles I held as he stepped out to the block in Whitehall. These pages were the last the royal martyr saw.

Loyalty to the Stuarts. Chastleton was loyal – and the sign is this Scotch fir in the garden.*

Chastleton is five miles from Chipping Norton, which is forty-six miles from Birmingham and seventy-four from London.

* The tree was planted as a late tribute to Bonnie Prince Charlie and the Jacobite cause, possibly in the early nineteenth century.

SHROPSHIRE

STOKESAY CASTLE

From the Shell series *Discovering Britain with John Betjeman*
Random Film Productions Ltd
ITV, Spring 1956 (exact date unknown)
Director: Peter Woosnam-Mills

• • •

I was lost in a side road in remotest Shropshire and in the distance I saw what looked like a castle. Yes, Stokesay Castle – rebuilt like this by John de Vernon in 1240, before he went to the Crusades. It has a moat all round and is fortified: I suppose it's fortified against the Welsh. (This half-timbered bit looks to me as though it's seventeenth century.) And from the churchyard, what a marvellous and varied outline Stokesay presents against the bare hills.

The proper entrance is through this Elizabethan gatehouse, built in an age when it was no longer necessary to fortify yourself against your neighbour. It's worth looking at this gatehouse in some detail, for its carving. On the left of the entrance is Adam; and on the right, Eve; and is that the Serpent or an elephant's trunk?

Straight ahead there, you can see the Banqueting Hall but let's go into the Solar first, with its fine seventeenth-century carved chimney piece. Here lived the lord and lady of the manor in a world of their own. They could turn from the carving and look down into this Banqueting Hall. The fire was in the middle of the floor – and this is how they kept the weather out. [We see a man close a pair of huge wooden shutters.] Only churches had glass windows in those days. I imagine that they opened those shutters in the upper lights to let the smoke out.

Let's go up the staircase, made of solid oak baulks. (Do you notice how the rail is grooved to fit the hand?) From the top of these stairs you can see the roof with its smoke-blackened timbers. The stone tiles are held on to the battens by wooden pegs.

Stokesay Castle: it's the only fortified thirteenth-century manor house in England. No one has lived in it for two hundred years, and you'll find it five miles from Ludlow and forty-five from Birmingham.

SOMERSET

CROWCOMBE

From the first programme in the series *Meeting Point: John Betjeman's ABC of Churches*
A BBC West Region Film Unit production
BBC Television, 15 May 1960
Producer: Kenneth Savidge
Director: Dennis Towler

• • •

Somerset is one of the best of English counties.* The road leads to Crowcombe, near where William Temple, the great archbishop, used to spend his summer holidays, and it's set in the Quantock Hills.

The first thing I saw was unusual: a church house of the Middle Ages. Once it was used for handing out ale on feast days; now it is used for school dinners.

When I went to Crowcombe it was a fine, cold spring morning, or just before spring, and I met the Rector at the churchyard gate. I wish you'd seen the sun on that many-coloured stone in the churchyard and on the church: pink and gold and grey and red contrasting with the dark yew and the still wintry brown grass. I plied the Rector with questions: What's this? A preaching cross or a market cross? A preaching cross, used for open-air sermons in the days before there were tombstones in the churchyard and when plays and sports went on here outside the church; and where the living danced on the grass with the dead underneath them.

The porch was obviously something extra special with a room above it. And village schools started in the porches of churches; and in the sixteenth century, when this church was built, the children

---

* This commentary follows on from that on Blisland, p. 89.

of Crowcombe must have learned their ABC under that fan-vaulted roof.

I can never resist the notices in a church porch. They tell you what the rector's like – and the Rector of Crowcombe is a good and remarkable man and full of humour. I mean, look at how he arranges the Guild of Church Cleaners and makes drawings of the different jobs they do to keep the church so beautifully; and they certainly do keep it very clean. And if that's the Rector's wife, she's much nicer looking than that.

Step back for a moment and look at the South aisle which with the porch forms a single composition. It's far grander than what you usually get in village churches. You know, I think that in the sixteenth century they must have got an architect over from Wells to design it for them, and a mason to carve the gargoyles in that wonderful pinkish stone all along underneath the parapet.

At the top of the churchyard the Rector took me up to what looked like the tomb of some eccentric Somerset man. But it wasn't anything of the sort: it was the top of the spire that was originally on the tower of the church. This is how it must have looked. And then one day in 1725, just when a service had started in the afternoon, it fell on to the roof – and nobody was killed.

But if you stand at the top of the church tower today, you can see all round you magnificent beech plantations laid out in the grand manner, which means that somewhere there must be a country house – and there is: Crowcombe Court, rebuilt in early Georgian days by an architect named Parker of Bath, for the Trollope-Bellews, a family that has lived at Crowcombe since the Conquest. They don't live there any more but in a small house in the village; and the Court has become a nursing home.

That's where the Trollope-Bellews have their special entry into the church; and that's their special panelled pew, centrally heated now, though once there must have been a fireplace.

And those diamonds up there on the roof are the funereal coats of arms – the hatchments – of their forebears; and there's the stained-glass window put in by Victorian piety. And here are more hatchments. They hung on the front of the Court when its owner was dead and they were carried into the church with his coffin and hung in the family pew. And there are the more permanent memorials in marble and brass – a beautiful one by Tyler to the rebuilder of Crowcombe Court.

The family pew is really a sort of opera box, apart from the church and looking down into it, and when you step down from this panelled pew into the church you get quite a different view and quite a different feeling.

The Rector took me round to near the font where there is an enormous chest in which he keeps the records and he showed me two old books there that contained entries, one recording the fall of the spire and another recording the designing of a new screen, to take the place of the one that had been knocked down by Thomas Parker, the man who rebuilt Crowcombe Court, and that screen is still there in the chancel.

That's a Victorian reredos at the back and here's the screen with its delicate carving, the nearest the eighteenth century could get to the Middle Ages; and those gates, so well proportioned in relation to the arch above. And of course almost the best thing in this church is a marvellous series of medieval and early-Renaissance bench-ends: a Jack-in-the-Green,* done in the new way and done in the old way; the Girt Worm;† a merman. And then look at the font. It's these details that are so worth seeing: the charming figure of St Anne teaching Our Lady; and some bishop of Bath and Wells of about 1450 holding a model of Crowcombe Church, much loved and very much alive.

* A May Day character.
† Another May Day character.

CLEVEDON

From the strand 'In the West Country with John Betjeman' in the series
    Wales and the West
TWW, 26 November 1963
Producer: Jim Douglas-Henry
Director: Jonathan Stedall

• • •

Clevedon, Somerset, a Victorian seaside town of gabled villas, wide
streets and trees, spaciously laid out by the Eltons of Clevedon
Court on their own land, a century ago. The Eltons: patrons of
art and letters, whose forebears are buried in the parish church
here, as is Arthur Hallam, Tennyson's friend of 'In Memoriam'.
Clevedon.

> There, twice a day, The Severn fills;
>   The salt sea water passes by
>   And hushes half the babbling Wye
> And makes a silence in the hills.★

'Well, it has been a cold February, hasn't it?
The holiday-makers left months ago.
The younger folk have all gone to Bristol, to business,
And at this time in the morning
It's only us old people who are left behind
In the hotel. Ah, it's nice to know
I haven't got to get up in a hurry any more
To see to someone's breakfast or to catch a train.
Nice in a way. It's nice to have my own breakfast
Brought to me in bed. They're very kind to us here.
Of course, there are quite a lot of us — all sorts —

★ From 'In Memoriam A.H.H.' by Alfred, Lord Tennyson (1809–92).

So that we can keep each other company.
Sometimes people put their wireless on too loud
And that's a nuisance. I'm in Number 11.
You needn't be afraid to come in.
And I shan't get up yet. Not now:
I've got this new number of *The Lady*.
I'm very comfortable here, really.
I've got a nice room and they allow me
To keep some of the things I used to have at home
So that it isn't quite so impersonal
As most hotel bedrooms.
Of course, I don't go down to the lounge in the early morning.
What with the whirr of the vacuum cleaner
And the smell of furniture polish
I don't feel wanted;
And people like to be left on their own after breakfast, don't
    they?
They're not exactly sociable, then.
I must say, it's a time when I like to be left alone myself.
There's such a lot to think about in the morning:
The news – it's nearly always bad.'

'I thought I ought to let you know
That I've decided to settle down here more or less
    permanently,
Or for as long as they'll have an old woman like me.
My room looks over the Severn estuary;
Some people call it the sea.
I've got that photograph of you on your wedding day by my
    bed.
I hope you're both still as happy now as you were on that day.
Of course I had rather a lot of trouble arranging my things,
But by putting a chest of drawers in front of the chimney
    piece
I've managed to get together quite a little gallery of family
    photographs.
There's you and Betty, either side of that group taken in India

Long before you were born,
I've put some of the ornaments from home on this shelf.
There's a picture of the fourth generation
And above it one of me as a little girl with my mother.
One thing about being in an hotel is that you're independent:
You can pick and choose who to talk to –
Which reminds me that I must go down to lunch:
There's someone there I said I've have a glass of sherry with
And I don't really think I ought to keep the old dear waiting
    any longer.'

'"He fell to the floor with a thud
And his brains were scattered all over the carpet."'

'With a sweet white wine like this,
I think one ought to have a dry biscuit:
It brings out the flavour a little better.'

'We could put them into a jumble sale, couldn't we?'
'Oh, don't you think they're rather too good for a jumble
    sale?'
'Well, we could sell them privately then.'
'I hardly like to do that.'

'One thing about staying alone in an hotel is that
You do manage to overhear the most extraordinary
    conversations
Just as you're dropping off after lunch.'

Clevedon in winter: too misty today to see the distant hills of
Wales, over there across the Severn estuary.

'Of course at our age we have to be very careful
At this time of year:
The steep hills are so treacherous and slippery –
A single fall and you may be in bed for months;
Still, one must take exercise: it's so important.'

'Oh, I wouldn't miss my afternoon walk for anything in the
    world,
Whatever the weather.'

Clevedon in winter: beloved by T. E. Brown:*

> There is no colour but one ashen light
>   On shore and hill and tree[†]
> The little church below the grassy height[‡]
>   Is grey as sky or sea.
>   . . . . . .
> And far below you hear the Channel sweep[§]
>   And all his waves complain,
> As Hallam's dirge through all the years must keep
>   Its monotone of pain.

Ah well, back to the hotel, and tea and chatter.

An hotel teatime: the hour of cosy confidences and wondering
about this and that.

'Five o'clock. It's hardly worth getting the evening paper, is it?
There'll be the News at six.
Ah now, shall I dress for dinner? It will be something to do
And I can have a bath and then down to the bar.'

'I always look forward to this moment of the evening.
It takes me back, you know.
I've been all over the world:
To Shepheard's at Cairo, when Cairo was Cairo,
And we were there;

---

* Betjeman's attribution is wrong. The poem 'Clevedon Church (In memoriam
H. B.)', of which what follows is an excerpt, comes from 'Grass of Parnassus' by
Andrew Lang (1844–1912). Thomas Edward Brown (1830–97) was a Manx poet who
taught at Clifton College and wrote poems in Anglo-Manx.
† Should be 'On tower and lonely tree.'
‡ Should be 'The little church upon the windy height'.
§ Should be 'And far below I hear the Channel sweep'.

Raffles Hotel in Singapore;
And I've stayed in Government houses
When we were the chief nation in the world.
I've seen Monte Carlo, Cannes, Nice –
Oh, I've done everything.
But do you know, I'm very happy here.
And it's because I'm interested in people.
I always say: "You're only as old as you feel" –
And I feel young.
There's always someone to talk to here:
Like you, for instance.*
I must say, I prefer whisky
To these synthetic cocktails they drink nowadays:
It's a good clean drink.'

Family photographs.

'This is the latest she sent.
I think it's rather a good one. Don't you?'

'Our youngest granddaughter:
Taken last summer.
Couldn't we both go there? Go out next summer?
It would be such a change.
What do you think? –
We'd be in the way?'

'Dinner will be served in the dining room from seven o'clock
    onwards.'

'No, I don't think I want any savoury tonight, thank you.'

'Well, I suppose he's good in his way,†
But I must say I preferred Jack Buchanan:

---

* The speaker is talking to the barman.
† The pop singer Joe Brown is seen here on a television set.

He was so much more gentlemanly.
How tiresome it is there isn't someone here
Who knows which knob to turn,
To stop all those lines going across the screen.★
Personally I'd rather they switched it on to something else.
I wonder if it's the BBC: you can never tell these days.
I get tired of watching all this teenage stuff.'

'There's no need to watch the television.
With a little self-discipline you can read a good book.'

Bed-time. Another long corridor and another long, long night. Do the old sleep well or badly?

From their hotel bedrooms perched high
Above the Severn sea,
Are they lulled to sleep by tide,
Filling the gap between Somerset and Wales?
Do they remember Tennyson's lines
On his friend Hallam, buried here in Clevedon churchyard?

When on my bed the moonlight falls,
    I know that in thy place of rest
    By that broad water of the west,
There comes a glory on the walls:

Thy marble bright in dark appears,
    As slowly steals a silver flame
    Along the letters of thy name,
And o'er the number of thy years.

The mystic glory swims away;
    From off my bed the moonlight dies;
    And closing eaves of wearied eyes
I sleep till dusk is dipt in gray:

★ The 'lines' are the product of recording television on film and would not have been seen by the viewer whose thoughts Betjeman is imagining.

And then I know the mist is drawn,
A lucid veil from coast to coast,
And in the dark church like a ghost
Thy tablet glimmers to the dawn.★

BATH

From the strand 'In the West Country with John Betjeman' in the series
  Wales and the West
TWW, 1 October 1962
Producer: Jim Douglas-Henry
Director: Jonathan Stedall

• • •

Bath is, I suppose, the only town in Britain whose fame, prosperity and beauty depend entirely – or almost entirely – on Georgian architecture. And the story of how that came about I'm going to tell you.

But before I do so, I must tell you that whenever I look at an old building in England (and Bath's full of beautiful old buildings), when I see a particularly beautiful one, a sort of evil voice comes into my ear of a developer coming down from London who says,[†] 'Um, ah well, Mr Benjamin, it's all very well for you to speak about old buildings: you don't have to live in them, do you?' And then he'll put forward falsely humanitarian views – you know, he'll say, 'Well, that's absurd, having a room of that capacity – cubic capacity – today: far too big,' meaning he wants to take it down and build a lot of square boxes and cells for us to live in, so as to get a fat rent out of the site.

But oddly enough, in Bath, in an age of real civilisation, it was a

★ From 'In Memoriam A. H. H.' by Alfred, Lord Tennyson.
† Betjeman speaks in a cockney voice here and throughout the programme when he is quoting the imaginary developer.

developer who started the story I'm going to tell you; and the only portrait of that developer is here in Bath – or at least it's a copy of it – of John Wood of Bath. And there he is, in a public house in Bath, on the corner of Quiet Street, where I'm standing.

John Wood arrived in Bath from London in 1727. He found a Somerset cloth town on the banks of the Avon. He was in the building trade but he'd heard there was money in the place. There was a fellow called Ralph Allen running a post office and making £12,000 a year. The Avon was to be made navigable and Bath to be turned into a port, and indeed in 1800 it was. And Bristol was linked through Bath to London by water through the Kennet and Avon Canal – and it starts here in Bath.

But what John Wood saw he didn't much like: just a typical country town clustered round an abbey. Old roofs and narrow alleys. And a voice inside me hears someone saying, 'Most unhygienic.' Yes: but wait and see what Wood dreamed he would make of Bath.

Though he was a speculative builder, he was a romantic and an architect. People came to Bath to take the water. The baths were Roman in origin and Wood decided to build a new Rome here in Britain. The Abbey there seemed dull and new; he'd design a Roman palace, such as he'd seen in Grosvenor Square.* There's his design for Queen Square, Bath. It looks like a huge country house but when you come to look closely you see a whole row of front doors along the ground-floor storey. Queen Square, Bath, must be the first terrace in the world built to look like a single house.

And this is Wood's South Parade, Bath. It was meant to look out on a Roman forum. Wood had never been to Rome but he'd seen old prints of it and he wanted to build a forum in Bath, but this dream was never realised. The houses he designed now look instead on to a car park and empty space.

But another dream was realised. Up the hill from Queen Square, John Wood was going to have a Roman colosseum from which the invalids who came to Bath would be able to watch performing animals, but when he came to build it, it was much smaller than the original one in Rome (as you can see in that comparative drawing)

---

* In London.

and it was turned inside out and made into a circle of houses – and indeed it was the first circle of houses of its kind in the world. There it is: the Circus at Bath by John Wood Sr, and finished by his son John Wood Jr in 1754. I can hear the developer's voice in my ear saying, 'It's very monotonous. I grant you that for its time the Circus was quite a daring innovation but today we've got to consider the teenagers. I mean, an enterprising corporation could have made a motorbike track here and a much-needed car park where we're standing. And there was no need to repair those houses in the old-fashioned style.' So you think.

But the Circus at Bath was copied in London and all over the world: Piccadilly Circus, Oxford Circus . . . They are the origin of the traffic roundabout.

John Wood Jr was as great a man as his father. He designed the Assembly Rooms – but come and see his most exciting achievement. High up on a sunny slope above the stuffy hollow of the city, he stretched out half his father's Circus into an ellipse and he called it the Royal Crescent, Bath: the first crescent ever built. 1767. Notice the correct oblong panes in the windows.

It set a fashion, Royal Crescent did: Buxton had one; Brighton had a humbler one. But my favourite is Lansdown Crescent, Bath, by Palmer, 1789. It's very plain. Ironwork instead of carved stone is used for decoration: notice its delicate design against the sky. 'Well, Mr Betjeman, it serves no useful purpose today. And you don't consider the cost of repainting that, I suppose: what it costs the ratepayers.' Notice the curve as Lansdown Crescent turns in an S-bend to Somerset Place. These plain crescents high above Bath were among the last to be built. I like them best of all. They depend on proportion.

But people were getting tired of living in crescents and they wanted to live in Bath permanently and have houses of their own. The Englishman's house is his castle – or in this case, on Bathwick Hill, a Greek villa, of about 1830; and next to it an Italian palace of about 1840. And if he couldn't afford that, he could at any rate have half a house in this charming semi-detached row of early-Victorian houses near Prior Park. They're very plain but they depend, again, entirely for their effect on proportion. As in those two houses there [we see a pair of semi-detached Victorian villas]: do you see how the window panes on the right give scale to the building, and on the left, where plate glass has been put in, the house looks blind and bombed?

At the end of the road, do you notice a falling-off? [We see a typical 1950s housing estate.] 'I can't say I do. I like those houses beyond. I like to see bold exterior plumbing, as on this new estate at Twerton. I mean, compare it with this Georgéan you so much admire, Mr Betjeman, in this back garden: it's very dull, this. I'm glad to see that the advertising profession at this particular place has taken the opportunity to enliven the monotony with bright notes of health-giving products showing our modern civilisation and a brightness that we so vitally need here in Bath, or you might need here in Bath – on that corner, for instance. [We see hoardings on the sides of buildings, advertising beer and cigarettes: 'Guinness: Good for You'; 'Player's: Please so Much'; 'You can't improve on the taste of Mackeson'; 'Guards: finest Virginia'; 'Kensitas' etc.] There's something really worth looking at [an advertising hoarding for Bristol cigarettes: 'Gives a man more smoking enjoyment']. As a Londoner I like to see a new building in an old setting – as here, in your new "Tech",* where the monotony of one side has been relieved very cleverly by a little projecting window. Today, building must express itself honestly and sincerely – as, for instance, in this feature, which might be termed the "vital buttocks" of the construction. As you can see, it expresses its purpose, whatever that may be, sincerely and that causes it to blend harmoniously with that Georgéan on the left there. Each age should express itself as it really feels – and you can see how this age feels about Georgéan.'

Well, I suppose you may be right. You must know what you're talking about, as you make such a lot of money as a developer, but come with me and look at a bit of development that has never finished. Camden Crescent, Bath. 1788. And if you stand by the old

---

* Bath Technical College, a rectangular slab except for an odd projection at the rear. In his poem 'The Newest Bath Guide', Betjeman referred to 'the terrible "Tech" with its pointed behind'.

buildings opposite, you can look down into the valley. 'Well, I can't say I'm surprised it wasn't a success. You've only got to look down in the valley here to see how people ought to be housed [we see a twelve-storey point block]; and you can see too that they've had amenities supplied [we see one small sapling fenced off in a tarmac play area]: Dame Nature, wildlife, sylviculture, just as in front of the Royal Crescent – the same kind of thing.'

Well if you think – and there is the Royal Crescent – that there's any similarity between this and what we've just seen, you must be stupid and also malevolent. 'There's no cause to be offensive, Mr Baychmen. I don't like the Royal Crescent and what's more, neither you nor I have to live in it. I mean, think about Bath practically: look at those balconies. They may be Georgéan or somewhere or other but then you couldn't put a kiddie's pram in them, whereas if you compare that with these new flats, well, a housewife could put her pram there. And I would emphasise to you that this is the age of the housewife. She has everything she requires. Everything must be hygienically packaged and temptingly displayed to the housewife. I look forward to the day when my company has razed Georgéan Bath to the ground and has produced plans that will astonish the world with their beauty, boldness and enterprise – I'm glad to see it has started already [we see Georgian buildings in the course of being demolished] – and also considerably to the profit of my company and at the same time benefiting the human race.'

[A four-minute conversation, on location, follows between Betjeman and his friend Oliver Messel, who helped restore the interiors of the Assembly Rooms and the Octagon. Professor Albert Richardson, whom they mention, was responsible for the architecture.]

BETJEMAN: What I like very much is the way you come out of a dim alley like that and then suddenly there's this huge Assembly Rooms in front of you – the unexpected: one of the great secrets of a successfully planned English town. Oliver, there's one question I want to ask you. Your family for years has been associated with Bath – and you have.

MESSEL: Well, the first time I came to Bath, I kind of fell in love with the place because I found it was so wonderful – to find there were so many of all these marvellous buildings that hadn't been pulled down and the way that the whole city's planned with one thought and so that all these terraces had a kind of unity to them. I've got some wonderful early guidebooks, some of the earliest guidebooks, which had illustrations of the Assembly Rooms and there were all the full descriptions of the Assembly Rooms, particularly of the Ballroom. They've still got in the library a small sample of the duck-egg blue that was the colour of the walls; and then it describes how the ceiling was interspersed with Naples yellow and how the ceiling of the Octagon was very much the same as the ceiling of the Ballroom. But after the building was destroyed . . .

BETJEMAN: Ah, you can remember it being destroyed, do you remember the – did you see it?

MESSEL: I was stationed near here in the army and so I came to see what was left of it and it was in a very bad state.

BETJEMAN: It's amazing, really, that they've managed to reconstruct it so well and so convincingly. Who was the architect for the reconstruction? Wasn't it Professor Richardson? – my old friend.

MESSEL: Yes indeed it was.

BETJEMAN: And then you did the decorative work and the plaster.

MESSEL: Yes I did. You know, one of the most difficult things was the ceiling in the Ballroom. There were records of the other ceilings. They found fragments of the Tearoom. But there was nothing left of the Ballroom.

BETJEMAN: What did you have to go on?

MESSEL: Well, fortunately, I had one of the early photographs that showed a little bit fairly clearly of the ceiling and then, having known it before, I was able to redraw it all up.

BETJEMAN: And you'll be glad to hear that in the film, when we take people into the Assembly Rooms, you'll be able to see that ceiling you've done superbly well — it really is a great triumph, as indeed is all of your work, of the plasterwork and of the Professor's reconstruction we're showing. But there's one or two rather regrettable things that I know you've had nothing to do with — I'm sure you haven't because there's been controversy in the paper about it. Those NAAFI tables and chairs: how did they come to be there? I don't know, but they must only be temporary. I suppose they hadn't got enough cash for everything. And the bar: did you do a design for a bar? — because . . .

MESSEL: Well, the Corporation asked me to do a design of a bar, which I don't, myself, really feel that the Octagon should have, but then of course I did design a bar that was accepted by the Corporation and by the National Trust, which is more like a piece of eighteenth-century furniture, like a piece of Hepplewhite furniture. But somehow at the last moment, after I'd gone away this autumn, they decided they wanted to have something else, something larger.

BETJEMAN: It has rather a British Railways look but I'm sure it's only temporary.

MESSEL: I think it's only temporary.

BETJEMAN: Well, now has come the moment — and it's a very exciting one — for going into the Assembly Rooms as they've been restored by Mr Oliver Messel, whom I've been talking to, doing the plasterwork and the colours, and Professor Richardson the constructional part — and I expect, between them, you'll be thrilled by what you'll see they've done.

Imagine yourself, then, in a sedan chair, arriving at the Assembly Rooms and to the music of Mozart, without any words, we'll make a progress through those Assembly Rooms, avoiding looking at the modern fittings, looking at the plaster and that kind of thing, through the carved room to the Tea Room, ending in the Ballroom – and after that there's a surprise, which you must wait and see. Now – ready?

[The camera now progresses through the Assembly Rooms, without commentary. They are clean and characterless, like a wedding cake, with a large, crude electric chandelier. Betjeman then points out items in the exhibition.]

Look at that ball dress: it's called Morning Glory. It was made in 1899 by Worth for the American heiress Lady Curzon (her husband was Viceroy of India at the time) and it's in the Museum of Costume, here in the Assembly Rooms.

The museum was got together by Doris Langley Moore and what's very nice about it is it's not too museum-y. There are different rooms showing the different periods and you can see things going on in them. I mean, come and look at this one. There's a house, on the outskirts of Bath, of about 1850 – a mid-Victorian interior – and 'at mah feet, a wee Scottish-dressed' English kiddie and I notice that its dad has Scottish trews too. That of course is because of Balmoral.

And now everything was growing respectable and houses were so comfortable that people didn't like to go from them. The large Assembly Rooms we were looking at weren't popular any more. Instead there was home entertainment for the middle classes: I mean that stereoscope of 1850 – well, it shows three dimensions, which we can't show on telly.

And I'm sorry the telly doesn't work by gas, either. That gaslight in 1875 shone down on the dressing table there of this young girl putting the final touches to herself before she went to a dance, from some high-up bedroom in a Bath crescent. And I expect the dance was going to be in a private house. And you can see that her poor sister – the younger sister – isn't allowed to go: she's got a migraine or she's too young and she doesn't want Mummy to go either. But Mummy's all right: there's a nice hot-water bottle there for the sister and Mummy's going to the dance and feels all right because, do you see, coming up the stairs at the back there is Martha, paid five bob a week and probably comes up fifty stone stairs carrying the hot water and she'll look after the house while the rest are at the dance and will see to the little sister.

Victorian Bath; Georgian Bath. I think really it's the eighteenth-century Georgian Bath that sticks most in your mind after you've seen Rome revived in Somerset. Take one last look, as though you were going in a carriage a hundred years ago, down the long perspective of Great Pulteney Street: eighteenth century. Today of course it's littered with motor cars instead of elegant carriages but still you have to admit that Bath, with its mellow stone and elegant perspectives, is the most beautiful Georgian city in England.

CREWKERNE

From 'Chippenham and Crewkerne'
From the strand 'In the West Country with John Betjeman' in the series
 Wales and the West
TWW, 3 September 1962
Producer: Jim Douglas-Henry
Director: Jonathan Stedall

• • •

Now for another traffic-murdered town:* Crewkerne. It's a sort of Clapham Junction of main roads in the valley of the Parrett in Somerset. Local tradesmen sometimes still think that heavy traffic brings business. It doesn't. It takes it away to larger places and makes the old streets smelly, noisy and dangerous and unfit to shop in.

I never thought of looking at Crewkerne till this visit. I'm glad I stopped. You never know.

Let's start at this yard of the chief hotel,† as visitors should, and go

---

* The first part of this two-part programme deals with Chippenham. (See p. 263).
† The George Hotel.

outside and explore Church Street, an old official street – and, ah! cloth mills! Crewkerne made sail-cloth, webbing and girths; now it makes shirts. Weaving was its trade from Somerset wool. Davis's Almshouses, 1707, built for poor weavers. That's what Crewkerne thinks of the building today. [We see the building derelict with its front gates chained and its windows smashed.] Rich weavers lived in Georgian houses – like that – and banked at a private bank, as it was then, whose owner put his crest on top of the bank.

Many a good Georgian door with fanlight above it. Much well-wrought ironwork. Crewkerne seems to have delighted in ironwork two centuries ago. Houses were plain outside but no expense and trouble spared inside. I mean, look at this staircase. The house now belongs to the local council; and as you pay your rates, I suppose, you mount these stairs and notice those well-formed triple banisters★ at every tread. Remember that staircase.

Here's a house of about 1880: windows getting smaller towards the top. Inside, a very plain staircase – Regency – depending for its effect entirely on shape and simplicity.

But Crewkerne must be older than what we have seen, and so it is if I look closely. Finely carved Tudor beams in this café. A medieval inn. And that looks Elizabethan. Crewkerne has been a prosperous weaving town since the Middle Ages: a Bradford of the South.

The likelihood is that a prosperous old weaving town like this will have a large and prosperous church, and so it has. First, those iron railings – iron so popular in Crewkerne in Georgian days – and then the medieval church, built of that golden Ham Hill stone that Somerset masons loved to carve, and a statue of St Bartholomew, to whom the church is dedicated, over the porch. A many-vista'd Somerset interior: chapel beyond chapel, chapels built by the medieval guilds of weavers and by big families like the Merefields; and this curiosity: you remember that advertisement for Monkey Brand soap, with a monkey looking at its face in a glass? I'm sure it came from this brass.

Outside the church is the old Crewkerne Grammar School,

★ Betjeman means 'balusters'.

where Hardy, Nelson's flag captain, was educated. I should think that was once the headmaster's house. And even if this isn't a rectory, it looks like one.

Remember, traffic is the enemy. Get off the main roads if you want to see a place. I went down this lane and found myself in the dentist's garden and saw his Regency house of cut stone: solid and satisfying. Look at the panes of the window in relation to the wall and the magnolia. Opposite was the manor house, with superb eighteenth-century wrought-iron gates – some of the best anywhere: about 1760, I should think – and at the top, the crest of the lords of the manor, the Merefields. I expect they built this summerhouse, also about 1760: plain without* and, like Crewkerne, rich when you look inside; it's partly a tool shed, partly a studio. What about that plasterwork! This summerhouse looked across the peaceful garden; now it hears the main road. Crewkerne – remember Chippenham! Turn out the heavy traffic while there's still time!

WESTON-SUPER-MARE

From the strand 'In the West Country with John Betjeman' in the series
   Wales and the West
TWW, 17 December 1963
Producer: Jim Douglas-Henry
Director: Jonathan Stedall

• • •

Weston-super-Mare (or, as some say, 'Weston-super-Maré'): 'Gem of the Somerset coast', 'Star of the Severn Sea', here

---

* Not so plain: single-storey with a pair of tall windows five panes high plus fanlight, either side of a canopied door, set into a stone front flanked by pilasters and topped with a white-rendered Dutch-style ornamental gable above.

we are. I've come dressed for both sorts of weather. Let's see what the guidebook has to say about it. Here we are: 'Really wet days are exceptional and sports can be enjoyed at any season.' Let's try the summer sport of looking for a lodging house.

Weston is a town of B&B, bed and breakfast: miles of bay-windowed houses, let to lodgings. Blenheim, Chatsworth, Claremont. Constant hot water. Lyndhurst, Parkhurst, Holloway. No vacancies. Imagine yourself free for the one fortnight in the year: the children are crying, Mother's tired after the long journey, Father's a bit irritable. Which shall it be? Homeleigh? Homestill? Sea View? And then: have they kept our reservations? Will they remember us from last year? Will we have to get to know new people who are stuck up or will it be the same jolly lot we had before? Never mind: we're on holiday.

Down here on the front, you can see somebody's been brave enough to have had a swim. But it looks a bit empty down here. Must be time for tea:* baked beans, sausages and tomatoes. Nearly six o'clock. Time to go in: let's try this one.

'It's nice to sit down to something you haven't cooked yourself. Makes a bit of a change from home cooking, too.'

'I wonder if I ought to have put on a coat. He seems to have done.'

'Well, we don't have to wash up afterwards, anyhow, and that's a blessing.'

'Time you kiddies went to bed. Get to sleep quickly, now. Your Dad and I want to go and look at the lights.'

Oh yes, come along and see them: they're quite a feature. And look at the sunset. That's the isle of Steep Holm over there. And that's Anchor Head. Weston – good night!

And Weston – good morning! Let me read again from the guidebook. 'Among the town's chief attractions are the miles of

* Betjeman indicates class through working-class language: 'tea' rather than 'dinner' or 'supper'.

240

sun-bathed sands, which slope gently down to the sea. Here, the grown-ups can relax happily in deckchairs while the kiddies build sand-castles.' That's a guidebook sentence well worth reading twice: 'Here, the grown-ups can relax happily in deckchairs while the kiddies build sand-castles.'* Among other juvenile joys are Weston's famous donkeys and pony carriages.

'Yes, it's the first time he's ever been on a horse.'

'Well, they aren't horses, actually, are they? They're donkeys.'

'I like to see the kiddies enjoying themselves.'

'I think the donkeys enjoy themselves just as much, don't you? I expect they remember it all the rest of the year – that's if they've got memories. You never know with animals.'

'Ah, this is better than making machine tools on the night shift at the works. Makes you feel young again, doesn't it?'

'Hurry up: it's nearly dinner-time.† We must be off and watch the floral clock: fifty thousand plants, they say – all different colours. But then, if you wait, Mr Cuckoo will come out of his chalet at half past twelve. Now, Brenda, Mum'll look at her watch and you tell me when he comes out. There! Now let's go and find Dad and get some dinner.'

'You've got to find dinner somewhere: I mean, they don't allow you back to the hotel till five o'clock and you've got to eat. It's a long time between breakfast and tea.'

'You can generally find something somewhere. It's all right as long as it doesn't rain.'

'I like something tasty myself that I can take down to the sands.'

---

* The film shows the grown-ups and the children doing the exact opposite.
† Betjeman again indicates class through language: 'dinner', not 'luncheon'.

And after dinner it's good to lie down with your feet up and get a bit of peace.

> 'Dear Doreen, we are having quite a nice time here. There's quite a nice beach. I'm learning to swim, at last, in the swimming pool here, which is quite nice. It holds 1,500 people at once. Marilyn's still afraid of the water and Carol sits and shivers. Dad spends all day on the putting course and Mum sends her love. Love, Glad.'

Well, just look beyond those dads on the putting course and come and see a bit of old Weston: I mean, look at those Regency houses there on the right; and the Georgian terrace right at the back – can you see it?

I want to show you some bits of old Weston that are here when all the holiday people are gone home. For instance, inland. There's the home farm: seventeenth century on the right, earlier on the left. St Crispin's College: mostly Victorian, 1487 foundation. And the centre of the old town has got a quality of East Anglia with the brick and the half-timber; and I'm sorry to see that at those old houses there, there's the fatal notice-board that says there's going to be a supermarket and they'll be pulled down. But you can get the real spirit of the place down by the river where there's the half-timber house blending in so very well with that manor house of local stone that I should think, from that oriel window, must be fifteenth century.* Quite a good model, isn't it? – one of the sights of Weston-super-Mare. Ah well: it's a curious thing that most of what we like to look at nowadays has to be make-believe.

---

* The camera now reveals Betjeman to be looking at a model town.

EVERCREECH TO BURNHAM-ON-SEA

Original title: 'Let's Imagine a Branch-Line Railway'
Filmed with the co-operation of British Railways (Western Region)
BBC Television, 29 March 1963
Producer and director: Brian Johnson

• • •

Evercreech Junction, Somerset. It was to be the Clapham Junction of the West, the place where one line branched away to Bath and collared the Midland trade and the main line ran to Highbridge and collared the coal from Cardiff.

That Pickwickian figure in the frightful hat is, I'm sorry to say, me talking to the stationmaster. But a stationmaster's life – that's something worth living.* And you can see why Evercreech Junction wins the prizes for flowers and tidiness. The level-crossing gates are worked from the signal box. And here comes the 12.32 from Sturminster Newton on her way to Bath, calling at Evercreech Junction – change for Glastonbury, Shapwick and stations to Highbridge! And as we say goodbye to the stationmaster, please notice that, on expenses, I'm travelling First.

Forget motor cars. Forget anxiety. And here, to the rhythm of the Somerset & Dorset Joint Railway, dream again that ambitious Victorian dream that caused this long railway still to be running through deepest, quietest, flattest, remotest, least-spoiled Somerset.

This is the line we'll be travelling on [we see a map of the Somerset & Dorset Joint Railway]. Once it was part of a grand scheme to unite Wales and the South-West and even to stretch to France. The scheme failed and the main line went along there on the right to Bath and the Midlands. And here's our own bit of line,

* See 'I Wish I Were a Stationmaster', in *Tennis Whites and Teacakes*, pp. 186–9.

reduced to a branch – and even that has lost its twigs to Wells and Bridgwater.

The Great Western was the first friend the Somerset Central ever had and it's the Somerset Central we're travelling now. It's rather a relief to be drawn by steam through this uneventful countryside and just to hear the noises we knew as children. It's the sad road to the sea. West Pennard Station, built of the local limestone. And one of the reasons why the Great Western liked this line a century ago was because it was also broad gauge, like the Great Western used to be – oh, by the way, there's Glastonbury Tor, and how nice to see it without a foreground of villas and petrol stations.*

In a second or two, you'll find we come to a broad bridge and as you look through it you can see how the track was once broad, for broad gauge.

Glastonbury Station. I suppose the promoters of the Somerset & Dorset hoped that this place was going to become a vast industrial town. As the train, when it stops, waits here for two minutes, I always like to get out and have a look. There's always something to see in a railway station. Let's have a look at the waiting room. Gas light. Solid furniture† – Georgian tradition carried on into Victorian times.

I say, I hope you're enjoying this journey as much as I am. You really see much more country, once you've got out of the railway station, from a train than ever you do from a motor car. No hoardings, no road signs, no lorries in front of you and no neurotics hooting behind you. This is Sedgemoor. Do you remember Hardy's poem 'A Trampwoman's Tragedy'? It's written to a sort of railway metre and it fits here:

> From Wynyard's Gap the livelong day
>   The livelong day,
> We beat afoot the northward way
>   We had travelled times before.
> The sun-blaze burning on our backs,
> Our shoulders sticking to our packs,
> By fosseway, fields, and turnpike tracks

---

* As one does from the road.
† We see a room with wooden dado panelling, a wooden table and wooden chairs.

> We skirted sad Sedge-Moor.
>
> . . . .
>
> For months we had padded side by side,
> >   Ay, side by side
> Through the Great Forest, Blackmoor wide,
> >   And where the Parrett ran.
> We'd face the gusts on Mendip ridge,
> Had crossed the Yeo unhelped by bridge,
> Been stung by every Marshwood midge,
> >   I and my fancy-man.*

This quiet part of Somerset has got its industries besides farming: cutting withies for basket-making, and the railway carries a lot of the peat that is cut on Sedgemoor. The villages are a long way from the station: this is the village of Shapwick – grey limestone. I suppose they hoped there'd be houses all along the road from the village to the station, two miles off. And at Eddington and Burtles they built a railway hotel by the station: I suppose they thought you'd need a rest before the walk to the village. [We see the Eddington and Burtles stationmaster opening the pair of level-crossing gates to let through a flat-bed lorry with 'WILLETT & SON: cattle · pig' painted on the side.] Go away you brute, you enemy of railways and comfortable travel. [We see a sequence of signs, warning motorists about trains.]

You know, I'm not just being nostalgic and sentimental and unpractical about railways. Railways are bound to be used again, they're not a thing of the past, and it's heartbreaking to see them left to rot, to see the fine men who served them all their lives made uncertain about their own futures and about their jobs. What's more, it's wrong in every way when we all of us know that road traffic is becoming increasingly hellish on this over-crowded island and that in ten years from now there'll be three times as much traffic on English roads as there is today. What will the West Country be like then? How will we get anywhere in summer except by railway? How will we see any country except from a train? I think it's more than likely that we'll deeply regret the branch lines we've torn up

---

* From 'A Trampwoman's Tragedy' by Thomas Hardy (1840–1928).

and the branch lines we've let go to rot. I mean, even in America they're already building new suburban railway lines.

Here's Highbridge, the end of the passenger line of the Somerset & Dorset, so I suppose I'd better get out. The old Somerset Central Railway, which later became the Somerset & Dorset Joint, started here on its long journey to the English Channel in 1852, and Highbridge is a piece of railway history. It's also a railway contrast. Come and see the older station (there it is, with a diesel hurrying through it to the west to Bridgwater and Exeter): one of Brunel's original stations, with a broad eaves and the cut stone for the door-ways and the windows.

Now cross over the bridge and come and see the slightly younger station: Highbridge of the Somerset & Dorset Joint. You see, Highbridge was the Crewe of the old Somerset & Dorset. And there is the war memorial to the Somerset & Dorset men who fell in the 1914 War, for this place was the headquarters of the Somerset & Dorset line and I suppose that's why it is that the seats are rather special cast iron. If you want to see why it's the Crewe, come and look at the works. There they are. The turntable is still used for turning engines [we see it turning an engine]: that's an old Midland engine made in Derby. It used to turn – that turntable – the blue S&D ones. The Midland owned the line when the Somerset & Dorset was given up and then the Great Western came on.

By the way, what's that? [We see an old, vandalised railway car-riage in a siding.] Oh yes! That's an old push-and-pull, branch-line, GW car, smashed by Teds★ from Highbridge. [Betjeman climbs up and gets in to look. He walks through broken glass and debris.] Where did it go from, I wonder? Between Dawlish Warren, Starcross and Exeter? Between Bourne End and Marlow? Or Castlebar, Park Halt and Ealing Broadway? Or was it on the Staines branch or the Uxbridge branch? And I wonder what City gents planned their holidays as they strap-hung and looked to these sepia photographs and wondered where to go. I can't tell you, because this car's now been smashed to bits since I was there. People hate anything well made, you know. It gives them a guilty conscience.

★ Teddy boys.

This was the Carriage Works and here they made the S&D coaches. I can just remember them. [We see Betjeman walking through an empty shed and we cut to the S&D emblem on the side of a carriage.]

And now let's go to the Loco Works. [Betjeman walks into another huge, mostly empty and apparently derelict building; we then cut to a photo of an engine.] That little tank engine was made here at Highbridge and given its royal-blue livery. This shed is still used for maintenance work. And there's a Great Western engine. The Western Region still runs the line.

Oh, let's go inside this store, if we can get in. Yes. I wonder what they kept here. [Betjeman looks through the window of a derelict service counter.] Neep oil for the lamps? Coupling rods? Or phosphor bronze? Well, it was all part of the family life of a friendly little railway, of men who lived here in Highbridge in these brick terraces in a faded Swindon, a forgotten Crewe. [We see a row of Victorian workers' housing.]

I think you ought to see the good side of the line. There's still a lot of goods traffic and that means that roads are that amount clearer. [We see engines shunting and coupling.] And if we go on a goods train, we can take a look at Pylle, which was once a station and is now a halt, and with no one to look after it. I doubt if there's a quieter, sadder sight in Somerset than Pylle when the train has left and it sinks back to silence. [We see a goods train go through Pylle and leave behind deserted tracks and station architecture, overgrown with grass.]

See the fringe of Sedgemoor from the footplate of a goods train. The line is single track and the driver hands a staff that locks the points and signals to a porter. [We see the driver hand over a curiously shaped metal rod with a large hoop at one end, shaped like a lightbulb.] Now the track behind us is secure. [We see a signalman in a signal box throw a lever.]

Do you remember I told you that the Great Western and the Somerset Central were friends a century ago, when the line we're travelling on was first built? Well, now that we're coming into Highbridge you can see an extraordinary survival of that long friendship between two railways that were formerly broad gauge:

the Great Western – there is its main line from Bristol to Exeter running through Highbridge Great Western Station – and there, right across that important main line, runs the little branch to Highbridge Wharf and Burnham-on-Sea of the Somerset & Dorset Joint. The line is used for goods only, now, and we'll follow the goods train through the town of Highbridge to its lonely end. Regardless of roads and motor traffic, we'll cross the town and come to Highbridge Wharf.

There it is: the place the Somerset & Dorset hoped to establish as an enormous port. Here were to be Welsh colliers from Cardiff and, who knows, perhaps Somerset colliers taking Somerset coal to Wales. [We see Betjeman duck under a stationary wagon]. The rattle of trains, the noise of shunting, goods trains puffing with heavy loads of coal for Somerset, Devon and Cornwall – this was to be the Barry★ of the South-West. Up here somewhere is where the colliers and cargo boats were to unload. The hope was partly realised.

[We see an overgrown industrial wasteland]. That's what it's like now.

> Highbridge Wharf: your hopes have died.
> They flow like driftwood down the tide,
> Out, out into the open sea.
> Oh, sad forgotten S&D.

But let's not be too mournful. There was still another hope for this part of the Somerset & Dorset Railway: excursionists. In 1858 the little line to Burnham was opened and the station is still there. Huge crowds were expected and it's worth looking at the station in some detail as an untouched example of early railway architecture. It's got a roof over it, like a big terminus. I couldn't get into the waiting rooms and the booking hall because they were locked but the Southern Railway, which was one of the many companies that operated this line, renamed the place Burnham-on-Sea in a hope to attract railway traffic. The line still runs, beyond the station, out to meet the sea. There was a pier at the end for steamship passengers crossing the Bristol Channel. [We see Betjeman, in a white rain-

★ Barry was one of the main ports for the South Wales coal industry.

coat, flapping his arms merrily and running along a deserted railway track.] Welsh people, after a holiday in Bournemouth, could run merrily back to Wales and vice versa. Now, all that remains is this [we see more derelict track and a car park] – and a gradient going down to the sea. [Betjeman drapes himself over a set of buffers.]

The railway bought its own paddle steamer in 1884 [we see a poster for the Burnham and Cardiff New Fast 'Sherbro' Steamer] and in 1905 the Barry Railway in Wales ran steamer excursions over here to Burnham. All gone. All gone.

Transport, more than anything, changes a place.* See how the railway changed Burnham. First the railway hotel, then boarding houses of the 1880s – Bristol style – built with railway prosperity, and Victorian hotels on the sea-front, and slap-up buildings along the sea-front of Victorian times [we see a curving stone-fronted terrace, in Victorian Classical style] and signs out to attract the motorist of today. Villas for retired folk as permanent residences in the side roads where golfers† lived in the 1920s and bungalows for our own age of the small car.

Burnham, with its shining sands, was a Georgian town before the railway came. Let's have a look at it. It's a beautiful seaside place and the air on the sands and on the pier is like wine.

Burnham-on-Sea. The Somerset & Dorset Railway brought you prosperity a century ago. Burnham-on-Sea. [We see Betjeman, still in his raincoat, walk down from the sea-front to the sand and suddenly take a playful leap over a crater of sea water that children have dug, then stumble into another – this one dry, thankfully.] In ten years' time, when the roads are so full of traffic we'll be going by train again, you'll be grateful you still have a railway to your town. Don't let Dr Beeching‡ take it away from you.

---

* For Betjeman on the same theme, see 'Northlew', p. 101.

† Betjeman says 'goffers'.

‡ In 1961 the Government offered Dr Richard Beeching a five-year secondment from ICI to become chairman of the British Railways Board and cut Britain's loss-making railway network. His recommendations led to a massive closure programme especially of little-used rural lines, the closure of some 2,000 stations and the loss of as many as 70,000 railway jobs. Although the cuts were unpopular, there was considerable political support at the time for greater investment in road-building.

WILTSHIRE

LONGLEAT*

Letter to Andrew Miller Jones,
BBC Television Department,
27 May 1949

• • •

D ear Mellor-Jones,[†]
I said I would write to you a letter about our conversation on Tuesday morning while I was dressing and after.

I have been thinking about the televising of Longleat and fear that my ideas are too abstract to be interpreted in visual terms. But you, as the expert, will know whether there is anything in them or not.

I think that the emphasis in Longleat should be on the big estate in its two aspects. (1) As a business concern. (2) As a feudal kingdom within a kingdom.

The 'business concern' part is largely one on which the Agent should be chief director. The Longleat estate, I have no doubt, has its own sawmills, architect, surveyor and offices as well as a system of farming that makes full use of the land. All this should be easy to illustrate, I should say, with the Agent talking about different sorts of farming and what pays and what does not. Possibly one may be allowed a glimpse at account books, which you could show on the screen. Then he can show you how, if an estate is as big as Longleat's is, fences may be repaired with one's own timber, and new trees planted to replace those that have been felled. He can show saw-

---

* A programme on Longleat was broadcast by the BBC on 20 June 1949 but without Betjeman's participation; he was, however, paid a consultancy fee.
† See footnote, p. 8.

mills, dairy farming, prize cattle and any other sources of income that come into the estate. You might even get his auditor or one of the clerks to say what paid and what did not pay this year. But the point is that the running of a big estate, as you probably know, is not at all the same as running a big farm. It is much more complicated, varied and, I should say, interesting.

The 'kingdom within a kingdom' part is where Lord Bath comes in, for a large estate, unlike a large industrial combine, provides a full way of life. Lord Nuffield is a devil and Lord Bath is an angel, if you are going to contrast the ways of life that these two industrialists provide. Anyhow, Lord Bath should be allowed to stress the personal-relations side of this kingdom within a kingdom. He could talk about village halls, characters on the estate, insides of cottages, cricket teams, medical advice, the parson and the village churches. All this, I should have thought, would provide ample opportunity for showing photographs and possibly having different local tenants speaking while they were being shown.

Finally, the flower of all this business activity on the Agent's part and benevolent land ownership on Lord Bath's part is the beautiful house that you are now going to enter. And you then make an architectural tour of the house. And if you are going to illustrate different members of the family, their behaviour and appearance become doubly interesting when related to the estate itself, of which your listeners will already have been made aware.

As I said, I am afraid the suggestion that I should spend a day or two on this work by June 20th comes a little too late because I am already committed with these eight West Country broadcasts about seaside towns.* I thank you so much for coming to see me and hope this reiteration of what was in my mind then will not have tried your patience. I have not written to Lord Bath but if you will send me your permission I will send him a copy of this letter.

Yours sincerely,

J. Betjeman

* See *Trains and Buttered Toast*, pp. 255–271.

251

AVEBURY

From the Shell series *Discovering Britain with John Betjeman*
Random Film Productions Ltd
ITV, 23 September 1955
Director: Peter Woosnam-Mills

• • •

On the Bath Road between Marlborough and Calne you see these things like grass mosquito bites: they're burial mounds three thousand years old. Silbury Hill here is artificial – goodness knows what it was for. It was dug by a people whose only spades were the shoulder blades of oxen.

Just near it, this ordinary Wiltshire lane leads to Avebury, where stands the biggest prehistoric temple in northern Europe.

Bronze Age people came to worship here among these stones 3,500 years ago. The whole temple is surrounded by a mound, not to defend it but to keep the spirits of the dead who are buried here from escaping from this holy place.

The stones themselves are made of 'sarsen', an outcrop that is found scattered about on these chalk downs. They weren't decorated, they were cut into two sorts of shape: tall and straight or short and square, a sort of irregular diamond. People were found buried under some of them with a beaker containing food, for the soul was expected to eat after death. No one knows what strange religious rites occurred here but there, within the outer circle, is an inner one – the holiest place of all. It was the Mecca of the Iron Age, a sort of St Peter's Rome of Europe – but for pagans.

How did they move the stones? They hadn't horses or wheels, these Beaker people. How *did* they move them? In the little museum at Avebury you can see how. They used wooden stakes and timber baulks and their ropes were probably of rawhide. They weren't savage half-apes, these Bronze Age people: they were peaceful and highly civilised. They made that beaker three thousand years ago.

Even the old cottages in the village look quite new beside these stones.

What makes Avebury so strange is its sinister atmosphere. What did they do here? Who did they worship? You probably don't know any more than I do but you'll find Avebury by going a mile off the Bath Road. It's six miles west of Marlborough and seventy-nine from London.

CROFTON PUMPING STATION

From the Shell series *Discovering Britain with John Betjeman*
Random Film Productions Ltd
ITV, 11 November 1955
Director: Peter Woosnam-Mills

• • •

Roads, canals, railways – and now roads again. Turn off the Bath Road near Hungerford: you cross the railway and come to Crofton, the engine house at the summit of the Kennet and Avon Canal, the only inland water link between Bristol and London.

That tall chimney and engine house have been there for 150 years, pumping water into the canal all that time. It's done by one of the oldest steam engines still working in the world: a Cornish beam engine. Know what a beam engine is? While you're looking at its beautiful rhythmic motion, I'll try to tell you. The beam is like the top of a pair of scales (that's the pivot in its centre) and the beam's worked up and down by a steam piston on one side, which operates a suction pump on the other. Down goes the rod on the pump side, carried down by its own weight: the steam piston draws it up again and the pump sucks up water, which is eventually spurted out into the canal.

The manager of the local electricity board told me that a few years ago, he was asked to estimate for electrical machinery to take its place but he found that electricity couldn't do the pumping as cheaply as this old beam engine, which is looked after by one man whom you see greasing the piston. James Watt built engines like this and his firm supplied engines to the canal in 1808. I don't see how anyone can look at it, whether he knows how it works or not, without being moved by its precision and beauty. Listen to the strong, satisfied noises it makes. This engine had to be built to lift the water up to the top of the canal to make up for wastage. There's the sound of the water as it surges up and ripples away, down to the canal and out into the Wiltshire silence.

The Kennet and Avon was constructed by John Rennie, the great bridge engineer, more than a century and half ago. You can see it alongside the Bath Road from Reading to Hungerford, and Crofton is, I suppose, about four miles west of Hungerford.

STOURHEAD

From the Shell series *Discovering Britain with John Betjeman*
Random Film Productions Ltd
ITV, 2 December 1955
Director: Peter Woosnam-Mills

• • •

If you come from Warminster over the Wiltshire Downs to Mere, you make for one of the most wonderful garden walks in England. Down the hill, into the valley, and here's the village of Stourton, on the borders of Dorset.

The gardens of Stourhead were made in the eighteenth century, to the orders of Henry Hoare, the rich banker. Some old fish ponds were dammed to make a lake. A path takes you round it. I'm sure this is how he meant you to see the place: moving slowly along.

Out of this little Wiltshire valley he brought Italian landscape painting to life and he did it by knowing just where to put an urn, a temple, trees and shrubs, beside the winding water. And just in order not to be too Italian, he put in an old English cottage too – a fake one for a hermit to live in and with a seat for picnics. And if the sun were too hot, here in the cool grotto he placed a statue to the nymph of the spring and another to Neptune, the god of water. This feldspar grotto is all lit by hidden daylight. See that light on the left? That's what you see if you look towards it: one more Romantic painting come to lake-reflected life.

The ever-changing walk crosses the lake by a bridge whose causeway is made of grass. Aromatic bushes scent the air and the colours change with every season. In spring, this bank before the Temple of Flora will be white with narcissi – and see how skilfully the path winds up here to the Pantheon, not showing all the front at once.

What I like doing best is to look just at detail, like this: nearer and nearer, into the great purple heart of a rhododendron; then, my eye filled with colour, to look beyond the gold azaleas to where the Temple of the Sun rises, stately, above this man-made paradise.

Stourhead isn't all that easy to find. Make for Mere in Wiltshire, which is 102 miles from London and 23 west of Salisbury.

ALDBOURNE

From the first programme in the series *Meeting Point: John Betjeman's ABC of Churches*
A BBC West Region Film Unit production
BBC Television, 15 May 1960
Producer: Kenneth Savidge
Director: Dennis Towler

• • •

I have been looking at churches as long as I can remember. I can't think why I first started but once the mania gets you, nothing can get rid of it and you go on looking and looking. I mean, now

I've reached the stage where my motor car automatically itself goes slowly past any church whatever the date and if I haven't seen it I have to get out and look.

And one thing I've discovered through looking at churches constantly is that I gradually begin to learn the history of the place where they were built. I mean, you can see it right back to the time when there was just a wood and a Saxon came along and made a clearing in it and built a wooden house for God, to the time of the stone of the Normans' building, and then to what it's like today.

And I've also discovered, through looking at churches, that I can picture what England was like then and I hope that some of the mania for churches that I've got, and that you've probably got too, will be helped by the three that we are going to see that have been chosen from the West Country. They were chosen really simply because they begin with the letters of the alphabet – A, B and C.

Aldbourne is lost in the Wiltshire Downs. Before motor cars it was very remote indeed: nibbling sheep on the chalky hills all round it, silence except for larksong and the wind in the elms – and still it is full of straw-thatched houses, a golden pocket in the green of the downs.

Under the thatch, the great barns have wooden walls; and brick and flint and cob are used for the little cottages. The streets were once cobbled and white with chalk dust and the only big thing in Aldbourne is that: the church. And the only big stone building in the village is the tower – built, I should think, by Somerset masons.

Looking at Aldbourne Church is like a detective story: there are so many clues everywhere. The first church was probably of wood and there's no trace of that left but when you go into the porch and look up, there's a bit of the Norman church built when Aldbourne was just a clearing in dense forest. And when they made the church bigger in about 1300 by adding aisles to it, they used some of the Norman mouldings from the old church. You see, in these new arches, in a lovely flinty place like this, carved building stone would be very hard to come by.

I said there was detective work. Come into the chancel where, four centuries ago, or rather more than that, John Stone was vicar and said Mass. He left a penny to every poor man who came to his burying in 1524. And that's his tomb. And he left to his parish 'a new chalice that I bought late in London' – and I think this is the chalice.

On the other side of John Stone's tomb there was a chapel for the Guild of St Mary. This had its own priest. And here he is in brass: Henry Frekylton, asking us to pray for his soul.

Those two cheerful Elizabethans are the Waldronde brothers: hereditary foresters of Aldbourne Chase and much given to hospitality. They seem to have taken over St Mary's Chapel after the Reformation and married into the Goddards, the other big family of the parish, who made their money out of wool.

Just have one look at the church as it is today and imagine it as it may have been at the time of the Reformation. A screen right across all the side chapels, no pews, but painting and coloured glass. There was a lot of thatch in Aldbourne and there still is, and they kept that eighteenth-century fire engine in the church – and it's been used in living memory.

But the glory of Aldbourne Church is yet to come: the bells. Listen to them. England, you know, is the only country where the bell is rung right the way round: down, then up and down again, and the rope rushes through the ringer's hand and he has to catch it at just the right moment or it takes all the skin off his fingers – or if he hangs on to it, it might carry him up to the roof. Right, away, all eight bells of Aldbourne [we see a group of bell-ringers starting to pull their ropes] – six of them made here in Aldbourne village, where there was a famous bell foundry; two of them have been here since the Middle Ages. That tenor bell, the deepest, has been ringing since 1516. For centuries these bells have called across the Wiltshire Downs.*

* This three-part programme continued with Blisland, p. 89.

SWINDON

From 'Northlew to Swindon'
From the strand 'In the West Country with John Betjeman' in the series
  Wales and the West
TWW, 17 September 1962
Producer: Jim Douglas-Henry
Director: Jonathan Stedall

• • •

From a place the railways cut short* to a place the railways made great. From the London and South-Western in north Devon to its rival, the Great Western at Swindon.

There they are, the Swindon works, where steam locomotives have been built for the Great Western since 1841. Between the North Star and the old Broad Gauge to 'County' class (the last to be made for the Great Western), between Daniel Gooch and Frederick Hawksworth,† there's a long list of names that are thrilling to lovers of railways. In Swindon it has always been an honour to be employed in the works – 'Inside', as it's called in the town.

People may call Swindon ugly; I've come to love it because I know so many of its people.

[We see a map of old Swindon.] That's how the railway part of the town started: with shops, church, cricket ground, public gardens. And here survives what must be the first garden city in the world, built by the Great Western for its employees in 1841 out of stone taken from the Box Tunnel. They're still called the Company's Houses, each with its bit of garden in front and behind. There was once plenty of green space round the works, which

---

* This is the continuation of the first part of this programme, about Northlew, p. 101.

† Heroes of the Swindon railway works. Sir Daniel Gooch (1816–89) was the first chief mechanical engineer and built up the town and its industry. Frederick Hawksworth (1884–1976) was the last.

were on the other side of the line. What is called New Swindon is a fascinating history of industrial England, an open book to you who have the eyes to see it; for as the town grew in prosperity and more people came, out of the flat Great Western valley, up the hill, private speculators spilled their ribbons of houses.

The richer you were, the higher you moved up the hill, until you attained an architect-designed home of your own, right at the top – I suppose in the early thirties. [We see a white house with pantiles and Crittall metal windows.]

Traffic changes everything. British Railways killed the Great Western's spirit and a new spirit of 'planning' was abroad: hygienic, high-minded, high-thinking. Twenty thousand workers from London were imported in the 1950s to Swindon for new industries. [We see a new housing estate, filmed from a low angle to emphasise the concrete ground.] You wouldn't know you were in Wiltshire; you wouldn't even know you were in Swindon. [We see the newly built Queen's Drive Methodist church.]

Nobody knows quite what is the right size for a newly planned town; nobody knows whether the new community is going to mix with the one that's already there. And they don't seem to know quite where the shops ought to be. [We see a mobile shop in a converted bus that says 'BILL'S MOBILE SHOP – GROCERIES & VEGE-TABLES' on its side.]

This place isn't a haphazard growth like New Swindon of the railway was: it's sudden and deliberate, like a bomb. [By contrast, throughout this section, we see children playing happily.] Swindon is already the biggest borough in Wiltshire and it wants to expand more but there aren't enough playing fields yet, it seems, for the children. Everything looks impersonal, though it's well meant. Is this Swindon? Is this? [We see newly built prefabricated houses, bare gardens, shabby chain-link and concrete-panel fencing.] Is it anywhere?

But here at the top of the hill is Wiltshire again: the distant downs, the smell of earth, the irregular shapes of the trees, the Wiltshire that Richard Jefferies* knew and the country way of life.

---

* Richard Jefferies (1848–87) was a Swindon-born naturalist.

We're back where this film started. [We see at a distance and then in close-up an old man with a flat cap and a pipe resting on the grass in a field, enjoying the sun and the view.] Before the railway came in the last century, before the new industries came in this century, the market town of Swindon crowned its hill. That fine Georgian house.

Traffic changes everything: first the railways, then the motor car; but it hasn't changed Old Swindon.

I don't know what progress is, but if it hadn't been for modern planners we wouldn't have had this oasis of quiet, this bit of real Wiltshire – an old country town, preserved and alive thank God, in the biggest borough in the county.

Old Swindon and Northlew: they've a lot in common.

DEVIZES

From the strand 'In the West Country with John Betjeman' in the series
  Wales and the West
TWW, 24 September 1962
Producer: Jim Douglas-Henry
Director: Jonathan Stedall

• • •

For how long has man been civilised? For thousands of years before Christ. Silbury Hill on the Wiltshire Downs: the biggest prehistoric earthwork in Europe. No one knows what it was for, when it was made and who lies under it. And what strange rites went on nearby, here at Avebury? No one knows. This was the chief temple of northern Europe three to four thousand years ago. But we do know that the Bronze Age people who worshipped here – long before Druids were thought of – were a peaceful people, highly organised and who made beautiful pottery. We know too that they shaped these stones and moved them by rolling them on logs from

a distant valley; and they probably built that ditch that surrounds
Avebury to keep the evil spirits of the dead from escaping out into
the open downland where the living people farmed.

And when the Bronze Age people looked down over the edge
of these downs four thousand years ago – notice the ridges of early
cultivation – all they saw below them was thick forest and impene-
trable swamp and where are now West Wiltshire's fresh fields and
dairy farms.

Skip two thousand years to only a thousand years ago, when the
Normans built a castle here at Devizes on the edge of Saxon Wessex
to patrol the forest. More impressive, I think, than its Victorian
mock-ancient turrets is the genuine Norman tower – there, at St
John's Church. I think a church is a very good place – and a Norman
church like this one: look at its East end – to start out on a tour of
this too-little-regarded Wiltshire assize town of Devizes.

And, by the way, always look down alleys if you want to find the
real history of a town. I mean, look at those half-timbered houses,
built before brick was used and when stone was so rare it was only
used for castles and churches. I should think that's fifteenth century
– late fifteenth.

And then notice that splendid altar tomb surrounded by railings
in the churchyard there: mid-Georgian by the look of it. Now I
wonder where he lived who lies under there. Across the road, in
that house? Probably not: he was dead before that and this house I
should think is about 1790. It's a Devizes version of the Adam style,
with Ionic capitals to the porch and ironwork balconies that remind
me of Exeter and the West Country, which isn't far off. Yes, that
street's mostly Georgian, built at a time when it was fashionable to
hide the roofs of houses behind a brick parapet: anything from 1800
and later. And there's an earlier house where the roof shows. Look
at that rainwater head: come closer.

The grand and older houses of Devizes belonging to the merchants and lawyers are in the middle of the town. Humbler ones are
on the outskirts. We might, here, be in a Wiltshire village with a
green in front of the houses and a pond and another Devizes church
reflected in it: St James's.

I hope you don't mind all this detective work I'm doing but it really makes any town interesting, especially one as old as Devizes. Look at those staddle stones, doing what they're meant to do: keeping a shed above rat level; and go down that alley and enter the marketplace: a perfect marketplace for a Wiltshire country town. Potterne, Seend, Bishop's Lavington – where have you come from, you with your produce? And did you come from Leeds? [We see a rack of girls' frocks.]

In the middle of the marketplace there's a monument and really you must listen to the awful tale recorded on it. On this spot, Ruth Pierce of Potterne in 1753 withheld some money she owed for wheat. When asked if she'd paid, she said she wished she might drop down dead if she had not. 'She rashly repeated this awful Wish: when, to the Consternation and Terror of the surrounding Multitude, She instantly fell down and expired, having the Money concealed in her Hand.' Think of that and walk into the covered market. There's no need for me to talk here: just look around.

Ah, a Wiltshire cheese.

All right, go on reading: we won't disturb you.

That's the old Town Hall, which they used to sell cheese under when the ground floor was open to the street. And there's the new Town Hall at the end of the street, built by Baldwin of Bath in 1808 and with a splendid Assembly Room on the first floor. The Assize Courts, 1835. Devizes Assizes: a county town. And down the road that's where the Wiltshire Constabulary hang out. And here's the barracks – Victorian of course, and very military looking: once headquarters of the Wiltshire Regiment and now the Territorial Army. Oh, and I forgot this: the Bear Hotel in the marketplace: a relic of coaching days. Look at that ironwork. About 1800, I should think. And then follow along to the older part. Sir Thomas Lawrence, the portrait painter, was born here; his father was the inn-keeper. (I like that great fat lettering across the front.) And next to the Bear, there's the Corn Exchange, 1858, with the arms of Devizes on the top: a Norman castle to remind you it's an old borough.

And now prepare for the unexpected. Devizes hides one of the great engineering triumphs of the world: the Kennet and Avon Canal, built 1794–1810. Twenty-nine locks descend here from the chalk downs into the cheese valley. It was made partly to protect England against France and to ensure an inland route existed from Bristol to London in case the French seized the English Channel.

The railways destroyed the canal trade and ignored Devizes and chose Swindon instead. Look at it now. England's most wonderful waterway, forgotten and neglected. Do you remember Avebury? How long has man been civilised?

CHIPPENHAM

From 'Chippenham and Crewkerne'
From the strand 'In the West Country with John Betjeman' in the series
   Wales and the West
TWW, 3 September 1962
Producer: Jim Douglas-Henry
Director: Jonathan Stedall

• • •

Modern motor traffic is no friend to an old town. Take Chippenham, here. The road from London to Bath and Bristol thunders through it. At the top of the marketplace there's the Bear Hotel, once the town house of a local landowner. There's just time, before we're run over, to look at the carved bear. And near it there's the Yelde Hall with the borough arms: medieval. It looks rather a museum piece now – islanded in a sea of traffic. Can you hear me?

Do you remember the Bear? That's the view from it today and here's the same view in about 1880. These are the sounds you would have heard as you'd looked down the high street to the distant farms with their rich cheese and corn among the Wiltshire elms. [We hear muted conversation and horses' hooves and no other noise.] There's the town bridge over the Avon as it was till four years ago – modern traffic takes its toll – and here it is today. Do you really think it's an improvement? There's a fine Georgian house that once stood in the High Street – modern traffic takes its toll – and there's the site today [we see a 1930s building housing F. W. Woolworth & Co. Ltd].

When Brunel brought the Great Western main line through Chippenham, he designed this bridge as a grand triumphal entry to the town; British Railways see fit to deface it with hoardings.

Modern traffic hates the pedestrian: it stinks, it shouts, it kills. I wonder what it's going to do to that bit of Tudor Chippenham in the High Street. [We see a three-roofed half-timbered building with a sign saying 'FREEHOLD SOLD'.] I hardly need to ask.

Modern traffic is driving even the Borough Council out of these Georgian store houses it occupies in the middle of the town. That's going.

Modern traffic is draining Chippenham dry. [We see a sign on the exterior of 'Salway and Son: Funeral Directors' that now says 'THIS BUSINESS HAS BEEN TRANSFERRED TO'.] This is the death of what was once River Street. The old houses have been destroyed to make a car park. I dare say the rest will go.

I'm not a mad preservationist but I hate to see the heart of an old town left to go to ruin. No one wants slums preserved but thousands of old cottages, condemned and dead, could so easily be repaired and enlarged and made habitable. I dare say these could.

Modern traffic hit Chippenham so hard, you wouldn't know this was left behind. The Wiltshire Avon. Dead quiet. All the best things in England are hidden. Look at this range of old houses with gardens sloping down to the river bank. A beautiful old house in its own little park within yards only of the noise of the noisy Market Place with an eighteenth-century view and Monckton House beyond, wisely saved from 'development' by the borough.

When the Avon was more used for traffic than it is now – oh, by the way, watch out for that tall Adam-style house appearing on the left between the trees. When the Avon was more used than it is now, this was the common slip by which the people of Chippenham walked up into what once used to be their High Street, now called St Mary Street and, I think, one of the prettiest streets in England. (There's that Adam-style house I told you about.)

And now step up on to the churchyard wall and look across to those houses whose gardens we saw just now: timber, brick, stone. Timber on the right, seventeenth century; bricks and stone, eighteenth century. It's worth a closer look: it used to be the surgeon's home. Then the Rectory: stone. And beyond it, a cottage such as you see in a Wiltshire village – a Wiltshire village lane.

And so back to the High Street, at the end there, and the heavy traffic that has nearly killed but not quite killed Chippenham.

MALMESBURY

For the strand 'In the West Country with John Betjeman' in the series
   Wales and the West
TWW, 10 December 1963
Producer: Jim Douglas-Henry
Director: Jonathan Stedall

• • •

Here in the upper room in the porch of Malmesbury Abbey, far away in the north of Wiltshire, are some illuminated manuscripts drawn by monks in the fifteenth century. Flowers and leaves and fruit: I dare say they couldn't draw very accurately but they liked the small flowers, the unregarded weeds we throw out of the garden. They liked them for their shape and colour. And almost everything we're going to see in this visit to Malmesbury is what has been here for centuries and will, please God, be here long after we're dead and buried. Ordinary things: flowers and trees and streams, here in the Wiltshire meadows, among small elmy hills in what's considered 'good hunting country'.

First, just soak in the atmosphere of the place.

William Morris, the Victorian poet, craftsman and socialist, dreamed of just such a setting as Malmesbury has when he described medieval London in the opening lines of his poem 'The Earthly Paradise':

> Forget six counties overhung with smoke,
> Forget the snorting steam and piston stroke,
> Forget the spreading of the hideous town;
> Think rather of the pack-horse on the down,
> And dream of London, small and white and clean,
> The clear Thames bordered by its gardens green.

Small and white and clean: that's what Malmesbury still is. You could throw a stone from the town down into the country where we're standing here. I don't think words are needed in a place like this: the birds are enough.

Small rivers run round three sides of the town. Malmesbury is a city set on a hill and these rivers that surround it are the beginnings of the Wiltshire Avon, which flows on to Bath and Bristol and out into the estuary of the Severn. No concrete paddling ponds for the 'kiddies'. No litter baskets. No neat municipal flower beds. Real country, sluices, mill ponds, mill leets and clear streams. Real country laps right up to the three reedy shores of this limestone town.

You wouldn't know, driving through Malmesbury in a motor car, what a sacred and peculiar place it is; you wouldn't know what gives it an atmosphere you can almost touch and see – but this is what does it, this is what makes Malmesbury different: it was one of the chief places of pilgrimage in the Middle Ages. Its huge Benedictine abbey was a centre of learning of European fame. And I know you haven't seen the Abbey yet but you will. There's a sense of expectancy here: so near, as though we ourselves were pilgrims from the past.

The Abbey was the shrine of Aldhelm, the Saxon saint and, later, Bishop of Sherbourne; and in Malmesbury lived King Athelstan, Alfred's grandson, the first king of all England: he had a palace here a thousand years ago and was buried in the Abbey. William of Malmesbury, the most famous medieval historian, was a monk here; and in the Abbey there were relics of the True Cross and a fragment of the Crown of Thorns.

The Abbey had sixteen chapels, a West tower and a central spire higher than that of Salisbury Cathedral.

What made people go on pilgrimages in the Middle Ages – by

boat up the river, on foot along causeways and on pack-horses through mirey lanes? Partly it was their form of holiday, like our expeditions to the Costa Brava; partly it was to find God. They thought of Christ very much as God-made-man, who had walked on Earth. Just as in his lifetime in Palestine people struggled to get near him through the crowds, if only to touch the hem of his garment, so they plodded along to Malmesbury in their pattens and clogs to see the relics of his Cross and thorny Crown and to be near the shrines of his saints and kings. Possibly they came along this very path by Daniel's Well on their way to the city set on a hill; and as they crossed the last river and reached the outskirts, they looked up and saw the end of their journey. There it is, on its hill.

Even today it's very much as it was then, for Malmesbury has stayed the same size, growing neither much bigger nor smaller. The arched gateways by which you used to enter it by road have disappeared but it's still surrounded by a skirt of old cottages whose gardens go down to the river. You can get the sense of enclosure by walking along one of these cottage gardens before you start to climb up to the Abbey. It's much best done on foot, like this: treat this cottage, for instance, as though it were the city wall – and let's go through it.

You can think yourselves back into the past. Here we are, entering the famous city, and now we'll start the climb to the distant sound of the Abbey bells, past limestone walls stuffed with toadflax and topped with valerian and wallflower. Up and up and up, between the gardens and the houses, all the time getting nearer to the end of the pilgrimage, and as you reach the summit of the hill you can stop and look back and see how Malmesbury is surrounded by open country and small streams – unique in southern England.

That's the view from the doctor's garden, and his house is in the middle of the town.

By the way, the spire that you'll see coming into view above the cow parsley there isn't the Abbey: it belongs to one of the parish churches.

Of course, Malmesbury is a market town too and has its own old corporation and court and ancient charters and market cross and inns like this where farmers closed their bargains with a drink. And there's the market cross at the end of the high street – and beyond it, the Abbey. Vast, isn't it? – like something in northern France. Vast, isn't it? Yes. Vast, wasn't it? – for all that's left now of the mighty Abbey is the nave, the South aisle and the South porch; and this South porch, the finest Norman porch in England, must have seemed like the gate of heaven to pilgrims after their journey over the downs and then through the forests and undrained land.

Look at the carving. Twelfth century. Late Norman. Done when England was an island belonging to the dukes of Normandy and Europe was known as Christendom; and over the inner door there's a carving of Christ in glory; and there's the nave of the Abbey as you first see it. That's Brother Elmer, a Malmesbury monk who tried to fly nine hundred years ago: he fixed wings to his hands and feet, jumped off a high tower, flew for a furlong and then fell to the ground, breaking both his legs. William of Malmesbury tells the story and it was William who must have seen those hounds and owls carved on the arches of the nave. And really, if you don't look east inside the Abbey, where it's all shorn off, but look upwards instead and then turn west, you can get an idea of the former grandeur. Look at the slender tracery of the great West window.

But here at the East end, ruins. Here's where the great central tower was, standing on those arches and supporting a spire higher – to say it again – than that of Salisbury Cathedral; and beyond the crossing, the choir and chapels. This was the mighty beacon to pilgrims and students from all England and Europe. What faith was theirs who built such an abbey.

Malmesbury: a city set on a hill, which cannot be hid.★

★ Cf. Matthew 5:14, from the Sermon on the Mount: 'Ye are the light of the world. A city that is set on a hill cannot be hid.'

MARLBOROUGH

From the strand 'In the West Country with John Betjeman' in the series
   Wales and the West
TWW, 3 December 1963
Producer: Jim Douglas-Henry
Director: Jonathan Stedall

•   •   •

Oh crisp and cold, this Wiltshire winter's sun.
At Marlborough Grammar School the work is done.
Home to tea, by walls of brick and flint;
This boy strolls slowly, that one starts to sprint.

Teatime and Marlborough, youth's most magic hour.
The clock strikes four from grey St Mary's tower.
Strong, bold and old – portentous and profound –
O'er gabled roofs that bell has echoed round
For centuries, with its releasing sound.

For centuries, too, these alleys have run down
To the broad High Street of the red-tiled town.
There in the traffic roar the schoolboy stops,
Safe in the calm of colonnaded shops.

Teatime and Marlborough. Lucky seemed to me
Those boys and gels who could go home to tea:
To carpets on the floor, to sister, brother,
Fire, pictures, books, enough to eat, and mother.

But what of us? – the boys of Marlborough College:
Five years we boarded here, imbibing knowledge;
Five years we shivered in exiguous shorts;
Five years we ran to changing rooms from sports.

Serenely flowed the Kennet, till it froze;
Peaceful the place looked in the winter snows.
But was it peaceful? Well do I recall
The sudden impact of the hockey ball,
The running in from games, the hearty shout:
'Speed up, Betjeman: mind what you're about!'
And then the dread, when to my house I got,
Whether the shower water would still be hot.
Oh blessed heat! – reviving frozen limbs,
Where in the steam we chanted songs and hymns.

Shades of my prison house:* they come to view
Just as they were in 1922:
The stone-flagged passages, the iron bars,
The dressing gowns, the faggings, hats and scars.
As they come back, the memory comes to me
Of my enormous appetite for tea –
A meal I now decidedly detest
But which in those days always seemed the best.
Of course the college teas were just a joke;
You only ate them when quite stony broke.
The boys who had to queue for tea in hall
Had spent their pocket money: that was all.

The dining hall we're looking at is new.
I wonder if it smells of Irish stew
In the same way the old one used to do.
I wonder if they call the butter 'marg',
I wonder if they grumble and enlarge
On how the tea is made from stewed-up socks
And how the cakes are harder than the rocks.
I wonder if they talk of art and song –
'Hurry up, Huggins: pass the marg along' –
Or hotly argue, blame or praise or grouse

---

* A reference to 'Shades of the prison-house begin to close / Upon the growing Boy'
in 'Intimations of Immortality' by William Wordsworth (1770–1850).

About some match and who will be cock house.
Dear boys, I leave you to your luscious fare.
Teatime and Marlborough: let us look elsewhere
While you are eating merrily in there.

Cross from the school's new dining hall and see
Those still with pocket money having tea
In a strange quarter known as Upper School –
Run, it is said, by democratic rule.
Ah, how a schoolboy, when the kettle sings,
Lives in a world as rich as is a king's.
How sweet are tastes to him, how deep his dreams,
How hopeful and how possible his schemes.
Though he can mix what turns old stomachs sick
And bite through slices thicker than a brick
And live surrounded by such smells and sights
As would give older people sleepless nights,
Though he seems reckless, worldly, dashing, free★ –
Still he is not what he pretends to be.

Let's join some seniors in the study team:
'Brewing' we called it. Though it's like a slum,
It's round the gas we hear the gossip come.
It's round the gas and with the jam and toast
We hear the rumours that delight us most.
'You don't say? Ooh, good heavens! He'll be sacked!'
'They say the doctor caught him in the act,
Forging his health certificate.' 'So, he couldn't have.
It's just the doctor's word against his own.'
'Well – if you think so, good!'
This is all right: better than College food.
Those study teas: the gossip I have known
Since first a Marlborough study was my own.
The stories, jokes and laughter that we shared;
First gettings-on with those for whom we cared.

★ We see a girlie pin-up on the wall of the boys' study.

271

After the noisy life we'd known before
We liked the quieter studies all the more.
We liked the taste of food we'd cooked ourselves.
We liked to look around and see the shelves
With our own things, and view our decoration:
Symbols of laughter of our own creation.

Parents with boys at boarding school, remember
That dreadful void from autumn to December.
A ten-bob note, even a postal order
For something less, restores the stomach's order.★
You need not eat the things they choose to eat;
You merely need to make them feel replete.
You need to recollect the ravenous craving
For most peculiar dishes. Though you're slaving
To keep them there at school, a timely quid
Will make them love you more than once they did.
Recall the hunger that a schoolboy feels
Nor boggle at the strangeness of his meals.

Whose is the Bentley in the High Street there?
Perhaps a rich-ish parent: don't let's stare.
But in the lounge room of the Castle and Ball
My own embarrassments I well recall:
My terror lest my family said some word
That others, listening, might think absurd.
I talked in quiet tones: we tried to be
Nonchalant, silent, very ordinary.
Football, the test match – anything would do
That others round us wouldn't listen to,
Terrified lest an enemy murmured 'That's
His sister over there: the one with plaits.'

★ We see a boy buying sweets in a sweet shop.

And in the Polly Tearooms, Marlborough boys
And Marlborough parents make a gentle noise
Consuming cakes and eatables by dozens:
Brothers, sisters, uncles, aunts and cousins.
'Tongs for the scones? My dear, how quite delightful.'
'Not too much butter, for my figure's frightful.'
And in the sweet relaxingness of tea
The strain dies down and all is harmony.

Marlborough and teatime. Now we have in view
The traffic that is ever passing through.
Another world from our accustomed groove,
A travelling world that's always on the move.
Coach-load on coach-load pours into the town,
Stops half an hour but never settles down
To more than just one plateful of the best –
Then on to Bath and Bristol and the West
Or back to London's syndicated food,
Synthetic life and hurried, angry mood.
A lonelier world of strangers, sadder far
Than those more stable Marlborough teatimes are.
Time to digest a sausage; time to fly:
So Marlborough sees the other world go by.
Here in the sound of grey St Mary's bells
Cakes, kettles, coaches, schoolboys – fare you well.

YORKSHIRE

PATRINGTON

From the Shell series *Discovering Britain with John Betjeman*
Random Film Productions Ltd
ITV, 16 March 1956
Director: Peter Woosnam-Mills

• • •

The Humber widens to meet the cold North Sea. Here in the village of Paull we are east of Hull, on its long nose called Holderness – a flat land of wide skies where ships ride down the rippling Humber and church towers sail over the vast flat landscape. Some of the grandest churches in Britain – great silvery stone galleons like this at Hedon – are to be found in Holderness. Hedon's the smallest borough in England but its church is big enough to be a cathedral. And if Hedon is a galleon, then the smaller village churches, like this at Ottringham, are fishing smacks to sail across the open plough.

But the far-off village of Patrington has the finest church of all, 'the Queen of Holderness'. Most old English churches show the gradual growth of centuries – bits added here and there as people had the money to build them. But Patrington is all of a piece, the product of a genius who designed this lovely spire nearly two hundred feet high, with its graceful coronal of arches, its sculptured waterspouts and mouldings, all made of a silvery stone, weathered now by six centuries of wind and rain.

This great church wasn't the work of a village builder. It was probably built by Robert of Patrington, who was master mason of York Minster about six hundred years ago. The archbishops of York were lords of the manor here and they often visited the place to breathe the fresh sea breeze. And the church isn't so very different from what it was in their day. You must imagine it then with six glittering altars, coloured wooden screens between them, no

274

pews and probably umber-coloured paintings on the walls done by people with faces rather like those the master mason caused to be carved on different parts of the church.

A few years ago a living architect, Harold Gibbons, designed this gold and coloured reredos above the high altar.

Patrington! The Queen of Holderness: built to the glory of God, still used to the glory of God, the richest village flower in the garden of the Middle Ages.

It is sixteen miles east of Hull, and Hull is ninety-three miles from Manchester.

BURTON AGNES

From the Shell series *Discovering Britain with John Betjeman*
Random Film Productions Ltd
ITV, 30 March 1956
Director: Peter Woosnam-Mills

• • •

The East Riding of Yorkshire. The chalky part of it near the sea, and we're on the road from Bridlington to Driffield. Great garden walls of rose-red brick mean a big house somewhere near. And there through its gatehouse you can see it: Burton Agnes, an Elizabethan manor house, looking very much as it must have done in Shakespeare's time when it was built, 350 years ago.

There's been a house here since the Norman Conquest. There's the owner crossing the grass with his retriever. He is Marcus Wickham-Boynton, whose family has lived here for three centuries; and they married a family that had lived here three centuries before that – six hundred years.

The Great Hall is Jacobean at its richest and most exuberant. Look at this fireplace with an alabaster frieze above it done by sculptors pleased to be free at last from carving monuments in churches.

The foolish virgins rioting here have kicked over their lamps but the wise ones are spinning.

The great oak staircase, broad and slippery, with double newel posts, soars up the whole height of the house. Some of the bedrooms are haunted. The screaming skull is one of the ghosts at Burton Agnes. I do not know whether this room is haunted. I brought you in to see the ceiling. The hangings of this Queen Anne bed are blue silk and at the top they look as though the silk is carved.

And beyond it, Jacobean again, this marvellous spreading pattern of honeysuckle on the ceiling. See how the winding stem of the plant loops over a leaf.

And here's the Long Gallery at the top of the house. People always say, 'Oh, you couldn't do anything like this today. There aren't the craftsmen about.' Well, this ceiling was made in 1951 by craftsmen from Leeds. They copied it from an old print. There's the goat, the crest of the Boyntons.

Burton Agnes has the best of everything, in paintings, tapestries and furniture: the best of every date. It is not a museum full of period rooms, it is a home that has grown with the centuries. It is lived in and it is loved, and that is its appeal.

Burton Agnes is six miles from Bridlington and thirty-five miles east of York.

WAKEFIELD

From the Shell series *Discovering Britain with John Betjeman*
Random Film Productions Ltd
ITV, Spring 1956 (exact date unknown)
Director: Peter Woosnam-Mills

• • •

We're on the road to Wakefield, a cathedral city and the capital of the West Riding of Yorkshire. It's an ancient cloth place, though it's now full of modern industry, but you can turn off the main roads and still find a Georgian square like this one, where once the clack of the shuttle never broke on the ear of the stately citizen.

But I love present-day Wakefield for its friendly Yorkshire people. They're like their houses: unpretentious and a bit grim on the outside but warm and kind within. Windows are clean, doorsteps are white, linoleum is polished. Behind coffee-coloured curtains, enormous high teas are eaten in front of warm coal fires.

Outward splendour is reserved for public occasions. Here in Wood Street is one of the finest ranges of public buildings in the North: Victorian Town Hall, then the Georgian Courthouse with Greek porch.

And there at the top, the home of West Riding government: the County Council offices, which control a greater population and revenue than some European countries. It was built in 1896 and I don't see why something has to be very old before you're allowed to admire it. As I walk about this place, I like to think of myself as the newly elected councillor for some West Riding town where rows of gloomy houses are crushed among factories and coal tips. What a contrast! Elegant ladies painted on the walls. And then, as I walk, awe-stricken, into the Ante-Room, I can look round at historical scenes done in plaster. They'll while away the time in case nobody is going to speak to me because I'm a new boy. And finally I'm ready to sit down in this Committee Room.

And now let me ask you to look at the electric light fittings. Better than those awful things like pig troughs that make the tea look like custard, aren't they? Trouble has been taken over the switch boxes. This isn't pomposity: it's delight in craftsmanship.

Look at the Council Chamber. A great council deserves such a worthy setting. (That letter 'M' over the seat is of inlaid ivory.) I know nothing about the architects, Gibson and Russell, but you can see for yourselves, they did a fine job.

Wakefield is nine miles from Leeds and thirty-eight from Manchester.

PERIPHERY

GLAMORGAN, WALES

CASTEL COCH

From the Shell series *Discovering Britain with John Betjeman*
Random Film Productions Ltd
ITV, Spring 1956 (exact date unknown)
Director: Peter Woosnam-Mills

• • •

You see those turrets? They were Castel Coch. One of the cheering things about these grim mining valleys of South Wales is that you can suddenly find yourself in deep country and in a place like this. Castel Coch means 'Red Castle' in English. Oh yes, the guidebook says it's thirteenth century and certainly those outside walls are. But look at this: the drawbridge works and so does the portcullis. It's the thirteenth century come to life.

In the castle yard there are no human beings about, only the dog and the cat to kill the wolf and the rat. We're in a medieval dream. To quote a local bard:*

> 'Tis grim without but rich within.
> See sitting there three Fates who spin
> All everlastingly in stone
> The thread of life: child, maiden, crone
> With shears in hand to cut the thread.

This amazing place was reconstructed in Victorian times for Lord Bute, who owned it. He and his architect William Burges were mad on the Middle Ages and nowhere in the British Isles is there

---

* Not in fact a 'local bard' but Betjeman himself. He quotes here an extract from his poem 'Castel Coch', which he repeated in full in the second of his three-part television series *Steam and Stained Glass* in April 1962.

so complete a recreation of what an old castle was like. It's not just a copy: it's a Victorian work of art.

Burges knew all about the Middle Ages and he loved animals, birds and flowers and insects; so he covered the inside walls of these state rooms with pictures of the wildlife of the Welsh woods and hills outside – and a few jokes too. Like most architects of those days, William Burges designed all the furniture as well. (Here's the bed that was used by Lady Bute. It's painted in red and gold with crystal knobs.) And he designed every single detail, down to the taps on the wash-stand and to the fishes swimming round in the basin.

The dungeons of the ancient castle remain, dark and damp, to remind us that the Middle Ages were not all that glittering fairy tale we've been looking at here.

Castel Coch is six miles north-east of Cardiff.

CHANNEL ISLANDS

ST BRELADE'S CHURCH, JERSEY*

Letter to Ken Savidge
3 March 1963

• • •

Dear Ken,
My typewriter has bust so I am writing this outline treatment very large in the hope that you will be able to read it clearly.

Jersey is part of the Duchy of Normandy of which England was once but another Channel isle. When England became a separate nation with the break-up of Christendom and France became another separate nation, Jersey went on with the Norman French language and was still part of the diocese of Coutances, whose cathedral is still visible from Mount Orgeuil, though in 1499 Henry VII put it under the Bishop of Winchester, but that made little difference.

We are right to put Jersey under J, for although it is divided into twelve parishes, they are not like our parishes. The Duke of Normandy, not the Lord Chancellor, has the patronage of the livings. They are civil as well as ecclesiastical units and run their own voluntary police; the churches are also forts and arsenals as well as places of worship.

The Normans did not like the new 'France', whether it was royalist or atheist republican, and so Jersey became a place for refugees from 'France'. First came the Huguenots, expelled by French Roman Catholic kings before our own Reformation. As they spoke the same language as the Jerseymen, their Calvinist religion ousted Roman Catholicism on the island completely and

---

* 'St Brelade's Church, Jersey' was followed by 'Kingston' (Dorset) and 'Launcells' in the fourth programme (J, K, L) in the BBC series *Meeting Point: John Betjeman's ABC of Churches* on 28 July 1963.

as there was no episcopal direction from England the wonder is that the old churches even became Anglican at all after their two centuries (roughly the late sixteenth to late eighteenth centuries) of Calvinistic worship, with ministers who did not believe in episcopacy or sacraments in the rectories. The list of rectors on a board in St Brelade's shows this, though it is not visually interesting, though the seating arrangement in St Martin's Church which we saw with the Dean is a more interesting visual sign and would not exist in an English church.

Something – and I think it must have been Jersey's loyalty to the Duke of Normandy at the time of the French Revolution – must have made the ducal appointments to livings of Anglicans the cause of the slow change-over from Calvinism to the Church of England from 1825, the first time since the Reformation that a Bishop of Winchester actually visited the island. Anyhow, it is C. of E. now, though only three Jerseymen (Tabb at St Brelade's, Norman and one other whose name escapes me) are rectors: the rest, including the Dean, are English. Garbett, when Bishop of Winchester, was the first English bishop to take a keen interest in the church on the island. Today the Bishop of Southampton takes a keen interest but not his diocesan. Obviously the Dean ought to have power of confirmation and be a bishop instead of having annual confirmations by a visiting English bishop.

Whether I will be able to say any of all this as we pan round 360 degrees, nearly, in St Brelade's Bay, remains to be seen but obviously the main point of our film must be to show the great difference between Jersey churches and English ones, historically and architecturally.

In order to give visual point to our theme, your tricky camera arrangements will be external ones – to show the relation of the Fishermen's Chapel to the church and them both to the Refuge Path, or whatever it is called, by which anyone who has made his confession to the Rector and received absolution from the Rector for his crime can walk with the Rector out of the church, down the sanctuary path steps and into a boat and go scot-free to wherever he likes, provided he never sets foot in Jersey again. This is still Jersey law and was last exercised in St Brelade's in 1800.

Now for the visual treatment to give point to our story of the difference between Jersey and England.

Titles are over and a Le Capelain* view or views of the Jersey coast.

Dissolve to St Brelade's Bay with or without me on it, standing at low or half tide so that we can pan round from Point Le Fret or La Cotte Point and the rocks, pan round till we come to the first clearly distinguishable Moderne hotel into which we might zoom, which would give one a chance to describe modern *rentier* non-churchgoing income-tax-escaping exiles from England. Then show the concrete wall erected by the Germans which contains the bones of Russian prisoners flogged to death by the Nazis or starved to death by them, thus venting their sadism on the Russians instead of the Jerseymen, whom they merely starved. When we are nearly at the end of this long pan, we see the abrupt change from the German concrete sea wall to the wall of pink Jersey granite taken off the beach that traps the sea away from the church. Move closer to this granite and then up to the East ends of the Fishermen's Chapel and church and, if possible, the sanctuary path steps.

It is important to show the way the Fishermen's Chapel and the chancel of the parish church are next to one another and that a round tower (like those in Ireland and at St Malo) is built into the parish church, showing how these two buildings, the chancel and the Fishermen's Chapel, which are sixth century in origin, were cells of Celtic saints originally, who brought Christianity to Jersey from Cornwall.

Pan round from the round tower and South transept of the Fishermen's Chapel to the entrance of the latter, which I might be seen entering.

General view of the Fishermen's Chapel looking east inside.

Details of wall paintings – whichever you think look best.

Cut to a view of the South wall of the parish church nave and pan to look at the weird granite fleur-de-lis of France over the hoodmould of one of the windows. See the West door of the porch and

* John Le Capelain (1812–48), a Jersey landscape painter.

show the alms box with a French inscription in the outside wall (these are outside all Jersey parish churches and [the inscription says that] the money in them is given to the 'deserving poor', not to rotters). Open the door and haul out a cannon (the Rector has one) which was stored in the porch (as in all Jersey churches) and show a cannonball or two (the Rector has some) which were found fired into the walls of the church. We thus show the churches were also fortresses against the French.

Show the interior of the church from the West end and here fit in a few captions* of interiors of Jersey churches that have retained their plaster – for example, St Peter's, St Martin's or St Helier's – and in St Martin's we might close in on a caption of the North aisle showing westward-facing seats, as seen from the South aisle, with the pulpit in foreground and I can explain the Calvinist interlude; then look up at a plaster vaulted ceiling and I explain how these roofs were made of crushed seashells boiled in water and then pounded over the stones so as to form a lime.

Dissolve to the stripped roof of the inside of St Brelade's and zoom into a limpet (there are hundreds there) still showing, which must have been on the stone since 1611, when the roof was raised and replastered.

Continue to track down the nave, looking into the North aisle as we do so: first the granite ashlar columns, then when we're through the screen catch a glimpse of the Lady Chapel and pan round to the stone altar.

Show a caption of the stone altar slab with its fine consecration crosses.

Then turn west and see me going through the screen and turning south to meet the Rector, who stops in the vestry and shows me his eighteenth-century Dutch† bureau there. He shows the secret drawer where he concealed his wireless during the German occupation.

We then go out, the Rector in cassock (or vested? – he has linen vestments), down the churchyard to the sanctuary path while he

* See note on p. 159.
† Corrected in the script to 'Belgian'.

explains (or I explain – better he, probably) how criminals could escape that way scot-free, and we look down the steps to where a boat is waiting in the bay below. We turn and walk towards the camera.

Cut to the interior of the Fishermen's Chapel with the East window open and the Rector at the stone altar there saying the Lord's Prayer in Norman Jersey patois in front of the altar:

> Nôtre Père, qui es au Cieux, Ton nom soit santifié, Ton règne vienne, Ta volonté soit faite sur la terre comme au ciel. Donne-nous nôtre pain quotidien. Pardonne-nous nos péchés, comme aussi nous pardonnons à ceux qui nous ont offensés. Et ne nous indius point dans la tentation, mas délivre du maliu. Car à Toi appartient la règne, la paissance et la gloire à jamais. Amen.

We pass the crucifix and get nearer and nearer to the open window until in the end we are looking out from it into St Brelade's Bay, where we may well see the boat rowing away that had been at the sanctuary steps to take away the criminal (me?).

No one can say this is the ordinary church film we do, and I think it will take about twenty minutes, don't you? I do hope it will be technically possible, for it is a most strange and interesting story.

Please let me have exact dates of recording at Kingston and Minstead. I only have the dates for the recce and have muddled the other recording dates.

Yours ever,
John B.

ISLE OF MAN

ELLAN VANNIN

Original title: 'Look, Stranger – Ellan Vannin'
BBC2 Television, 10 December 1970
Editor: Noel Channon
Executive producer: Bridget Winter

• • •

Ellan Vannin – it's Manx for 'Isle of Man'. And this is Laxey Station on the electric tramway from Douglas to Ramsay. Laxey: junction for the Snaefell Mountain Railway, built in 1895. Three-foot-six-inch gauge; rolling stock by Milnes of Birkenhead (1895 too). As strong as ever: livery red and scarlet. All woodwork teak. Gradient: one in twelve. We climb to a height above two thousand feet, to the top of Snaefell, the highest mountain in Man. The line runs for the Manx season, which is from Whitsun to the second week in September.

It's autumn now and the short holiday season is over. The island is almost empty except for the Manx themselves. Some of them have gone for a holiday, so as to get a rest after the catering they've had to do. And the autumn colours have been amazing this year. The silence, emptiness even, of having this little tram to ourselves makes you feel that you're in another land. You are indeed. The Isle of Man holds a legend that whenever a British monarch comes to the Isle of Man, the island is shrouded in mist. I'm certainly not a monarch but I can see there's some mist ahead of us now.

It's a journey up to heaven. Can't make out whether we're going to come out in sunlight or cloud. I should think more probably cloud.

It's lonely up here: haunted, misty and strange. The only visitors on Snaefell's mountain top are sheep. And if there weren't any mist, you could see from here, where I'm standing, four kingdoms

– England, Scotland, Wales and Ireland – from this, the fifth: the ancient kingdom of Man. And below us, my goodness, the variety there is: those gigantic cliffs, sandy plains and dunes, tropical glens, moors and mountains and lakes, all in one country – all here.

The sea gets everywhere. You smell it in the wind; you hear it on the shore. You can never get more than two or three miles away from it. It thunders on the wild west coast, especially when sou'westers blow at gale force.

After seas and storms, how reliable and safe must have seemed this introduction to the 1870: the Isle of Man steam railways. Various companies they were, at first. West to Peel, south to Castletown and Port Erin, inland to the Foxdale lead mines, the long way round by the north-west coast to Ramsay.

Over level crossings, over brown streams full of trout and salmon, through ferny cuttings, always, always ending near the sea. Thanks to the enthusiasm of the locals and visitors, this paradise of narrow-gauge steam trains is coming to life again.

The isolation, the ancientness, the changing light of hills and valleys in this Celtic Scandinavian kingdom. Time does not matter. Lanes are made for looking and listening. And here in the north of the island, where bad weather is held back by the England hills, the land is green and fertile and palm trees grow in Celtic-looking farm lands.

Cregneash village in the lonely and exposed southern end of Man is kept by the Manx government as a folk museum. Look how the thatch is held down against the storm by ropes secured to projecting bits of stone, and half a boat serves as a cottage porch.

Oh Ellan Vannin, ancient kingdom of Man: I like to wander down your late-September lanes when dew-hung cobwebs glisten in the gorse and blackberries shine, waiting to be picked. Oh Ellan Vannin. This lane leads back to before you were a kingdom, before the Celts set foot on you or Norsemen brought their longships.

The usual drystone walls you see in the island – and over there a very familiar sight, alas: a ruined farmhouse. Tiny little farms they were. And now probably the successors of the people who lived there are in a hot little bungalow in Douglas.

I saw the ghost of a dog. I heard the ghost of a bark here among the red fuchsias.

A path leads through the field of roots. Far over there I can see the sea through the mist, and a bit of a farm – and here, in a strange waiting silence, the end of this walk. Standing stones: Neolithic. Chieftains were buried there, Stone Age chieftains, about 2000 BC. This, you'll see, is the forecourt and four thousand years ago the bodies of pagan chieftains were carried, dead, through here – and they, of course, were smaller people than I am – and they were laid in this chambered cairn. This way on, human bodies were found; and one of them here. You see, one of the cairns has got its original top to it – and for some extraordinary reason, over there, on that mound, they used fire. Here where the chieftains lay, the bodies were unburnt: so what they used the fire for, goodness only knows. But you can see here bits of slate. All these bits of slate are marked with a colour where they have been burnt.

The whole of this area where we're standing was covered over with earth and stones, and it has been long known in the island as Castal-yn-Ard, which means to say 'Castle on the Height'.

Probably this was a burial place too, this four-tiered tin-walled hill in the heart of the island. On 5 July, Midsummer Day by the old calendar, and when the sun is at its highest, the whole island waits. Shops are shut. Flags are out from remote farms in the sheedings (as the counties are called in Man). People come to watch the procession – from St John's Church to Tynwald Mound.

It is a parliamentary assembly that goes back a thousand years. The King of Man today is the British monarch; the Lieutenant Governor is the monarch's representative. He sits on top of the mound; the Judge or Deemster follows. The Bishop can speak in the Manx Parliament but not in ours. The Legislative Council is the House of Lords over there; the House of Keys is the House of Commons. This is where the people of Man hear the new laws proclaimed in Manx and English.

Tynwald is Scandinavian, but look there: Man's equivalent of Iona – St Patrick's Isle. It's Celtic. St Patrick landed here in the fifth century on his way to convert the Irish. That round tower on the left is Irish, tenth century I should think, and there on the right they built a cathedral, in the thirteenth century, out of the glorious red sandstone that is found near Peel in the west of Man. It is dedicated to St Joan. The island has also had its more modern saints: for instance, in the eighteenth century High Churchman Bishop Thomas Wilson rebuilt old churches and founded new ones like this at Old Ballaugh. It's in a sort of Manx Baroque.

I like the way those gateposts lean drunkenly apart. In fact, home-made pinnacles like these are a feature of Manx churches – here at Dalby on the west coast or there at Kirk Bradden, the old parish church at Douglas. Under that obelisk dated 1805, on the left, one of the Murray family is buried. The Murrays, who were Dukes of Atholl, inherited Man from the Stanleys, who were Earls of Derby and who held it in the Middle Ages and lived at Castle Rushen. The most complete medieval castle in Europe is Castle Rushen: inner and outer defences and all. From here the island was governed.

Castletown, the town, stands round the castle and harbour. It is the old capital of the Manx kingdom. In new snug houses with long gardens at the back lived merchants and sea captains, safe from wind and weather when Government was conducted from the castle. And as the narrow lanes open into the Market Square you can feel that the town is the capital of a small country.

That column is to Lieutenant Governor Smelt, who died in 1832. The Georgian Gothic church behind it has box pews inside, with a good view of the sea from some of the windows. The Dukes of Atholl must have thought Castletown too small for they built themselves a castle further up the coast in 1801 at Douglas. There it is: Castle Mona – now an hotel.

Had Douglas not grown enormous in Victorian times, the island would have been ruined but it was in 1863 that Governor Lord Loch encouraged the big industrial cities of the north to make Douglas their holiday playground. Douglas became the capital. There it is – the Naples of the north, with its romantic sham ruin on a rock, the tower of refuge, Douglas.

With its lights and horse traps and casinos, you wouldn't think that within about half a mile of that casino there was this, a sort of private Hyde Park in the middle of Douglas. In fact the island abounds in handsome country houses. Some were built by eighteenth-century rakes who fled from Ireland or England to Man to escape their creditors. (Not this house: the nunnery. It was built in the 1820s by a local landowner, in the popular castle style, on the site of a Celtic monastery. It stands in an English landscaped park.) Some of these houses, of course, were glorified farms, approached down magnificent avenues of beech, ash or sycamore, like this at Ballacurrie in the lush north of the island. Others are neat Georgian houses, built at the heads of glens, where hydrangeas bloom enormous and trees are taller still.

Much capital was invested in minerals and mines in the island in the first half of the last century. In 1854 a Manx engineer, Robert Casement, designed this enormous wheel at Laxey to pump the water out of the lead and copper mines.

Every glen had its watermill, originally for grinding corn. The mines are worked out but the beauty remains.

Chronology of Programmes

Longleat	BBC	20 June 1949
Avebury	ITV	23 September 1955
Great Coxwell	ITV	14 October 1955
Abingdon	ITV	21 October 1955
Eastleach Turville	ITV	28 October 1955
Bradwell juxta Mare	ITV	4 November 1955
Crofton Pumping Station	ITV	11 November 1955
Stisted Mill	ITV	18 November 1955
West Wycombe	ITV	25 November 1955
Stourhead	ITV	2 December 1955
Oxford	BBC	5 December 1955
Wellingborough	ITV	24 February 1956
Chastleton House	ITV	2 March 1956
Patrington	ITV	16 March 1956
Clifton Suspension Bridge	ITV	23 March 1956
Burton Agnes, Driffield	ITV	30 March 1956
Adlington Hall	ITV	Spring, 1956
Bolsover Castle	ITV	Spring, 1956
Castel Coch, Glamorgan	ITV	Spring, 1956
Fairfield, Romney Marsh	ITV	Spring, 1956
Fairford	ITV	Spring, 1956
Haddon Hall	ITV	Spring, 1956
Halli'th'wood	ITV	Spring, 1956
Hardwick Hall	ITV	Spring, 1956
Heaton Hall	ITV	Spring, 1956
Kedleston Hall	ITV	Spring, 1956
Meresworth Castle	ITV	Spring, 1956
Stokesay Castle	ITV	Spring, 1956
Wakefield	ITV	Spring, 1956
A Poet in London	BBC	1 March 1959
Beauty in Trust	BBC	4 August 1959

London's Exhibition Sites	BBC	28 February 1960
Aldbourne	BBC	15 May 1960
Blisland	BBC	15 May 1960
Crowcombe	BBC	15 May 1960
The Weald of Kent	BBC	26 June 1960
Kings Lynn to Hunstanton	BBC (East Anglia Region)	17 April 1961
Sidmouth	ITV (TWW)	27 August 1962
Chippenham	ITV (TWW)	3 September 1962
Crewkerne	ITV (TWW)	3 September 1962
Sherborne	ITV (TWW)	10 September 1962
Northlew	ITV (TWW)	17 September 1962
Swindon	ITV (TWW)	17 September 1962
Devizes	ITV (TWW)	24 September 1962
Bath	ITV (TWW)	1 October 1962
Evercreech to Burnham-on-Sea	BBC	29 March 1963
St Brelade's, Jersey	BBC	28 July 1963
Clevedon	ITV (TWW)	26 November 1963
Marlborough	ITV (TWW)	3 December 1963
Malmesbury	ITV (TWW)	10 December 1963
Weston-super-Mare	ITV (TWW)	17 December 1963
Diss	BBC (East Anglia Region)	25 March 1964
Minstead	BBC	5 April 1964
Milton Abbey	BBC1 (West Region)	3 March 1965
Winchester Cathedral	BBC1	18 December 1966
Canterbury	ITV (Rediffusion)	25 December 1967
Marble Arch to the Edgware Road	BBC1	31 January 1968
The Englishman's Home	BBC2	5 April 1969
Seaside Resorts in the South and South-West	BBC2	25 December 1969
Ellan Vannin (Isle of Man)	BBC2	10 December 1970
A Land for all Seasons	BBC2	18 April 1971
London on Sunday	BBC 1	10 December 1972
The Home Counties on Sunday	BBC 1	17 December 1972
Metro-land	BBC 2	26 February 1973
A Passion for Churches	BBC 2	7 December 1974

Index

Berkeley Castle, Gloucestershire, 18, 45

'Beside the Seaside' (JB; poem), 73n

Betjeman, Sir John: book reviewing, 9, 15; character and personality, 1; contractual disagreements with BBC, 15–16, 20, 23–4; decline in quality of poetry, 26–7; Poet Laureateship, 27; radio broadcasts, 9, 14; supports Labour Party, 7; TV film-making for BBC, 12–14; as TV performer, 2–3, 8–9; visiting professorship at Cincinnati, 18; wartime film-making, 6–7

Betjeman, Paul, 24

Betjeman's London (TV series), 14n

Birkenhead, Frederick Winston Furneaux Smith, 2nd Earl of, 172n

Blackburne, Canon, 206

Blackwater, river, 114

Blaise Hamley, near Bristol, 51

Blenheim Palace, Oxfordshire, 48

Blickling Hall, Norfolk, 41

Blisland, Cornwall, 89–90

Bloomfield, Robert: 'The Farmer's Boy' (poem), 55n

Blunden, Edmund, 134, 136

Bodmin Moor, 89

Bolsover Castle, Derbyshire, 91–2

Bolton, Lancashire, 146–7

Bosham, Sussex: church, 76

Boulting Brothers, 7

Bournemouth, 65

Bradwell Juxta Mare, Essex, 114–15

Brains Trust, The (radio programme), 20

Bramley, Frank, 68n

Brandelhow, Lake District, 41

Bray, Billy, 103

Brecks, Norfolk, 188

Bressingham, Norfolk, 196

Brett, Lionel, 19–20

Brighton, Sussex, 50, 75; Royal Crescent, 231

Britten, Benjamin, 4n

Bronze Age, 252, 260–1

Brooke, Rupert: 'Grantchester' (poem), 151n

Brown, Joe, 227n

Brown, Lancelot ('Capability'), 48, 109

Brown, Thomas Edward, 226 & n

Brunel, Isambard Kingdom, 67, 83–4, 246, 264

Brunenburgh, Battle of (934), 108

Buchanan, Jack, 226

Bunbury, Cheshire: St Boniface church, 18

Burges, William, 281–2

Burlington, Richard Boyle, 3rd Earl of, 49

Burney, Fanny (Mme d'Arblay), 62

Burnham-on-Sea, Somerset, 249

Burton Agnes, Yorkshire, 275–6

'Business Girls' (JB; poem), 150–1

Bute, John Patrick Crichton Stuart, 3rd Marquess of, 281

Butlin's holiday camps, 70

Buxton, Derbyshire, 231

Campbell, Colen, 133, 138

Campbell, J. M., 56n

Canterbury, 140–5; Cathedral, 27, 141, 143–5; King's School, 143, 145; St Alphege church, 143, 145

Cardiff Castle, 14n

Carstairs, John Paddy, 7

Casement, Robert, 292

Castel Coch, Glamorgan, 281–2

Castle Ashby, Northamptonshire, 18

Catherine of Aragon, Queen of Henry VIII, 109

Cavendish, Charles, 91

Chambers, Sir William, 111